D1202162

EVIL REVISITED

EVIL REVISITED

Responses and Reconsiderations

DAVID RAY GRIFFIN

STATE UNIVERSITY OF NEW YORK PRESS

Published by
State University of New York Press, Albany

For information, address State University of New York
Press, State University Plaza, Albany, N.Y., 12246

Production by E. Moore
Marketing by Dana E. Yanulavich

Library of Congress Cataloging-in-Publication Data

Griffin, David Ray, 1939–
     Evil revisited : responses and reconsiderations / David Ray
Griffin.
         p.   cm.
     Includes index.
     ISBN 0–7914–0612–1 (hard : alk paper). — ISBN 0–7914–0613–X (pbk.
: alk. paper)
     1. Theodicy.   2. Process theology.   3. Process philosophy.
4. Griffin, David Ray, 1939–   God, power, and evil.   I. Title.
BT160.G736   1991
231′.8—dc20   90–39206
                                                                      CIP

10   9   8   7   6   5   4   3   2   1

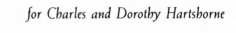

for Charles and Dorothy Hartshorne

And to Thee is nothing whatsoever evil.
                    —St. Augustine, *Confessions*

All discord, harmony not understood;
All partial evil, universal good;
And, in spite of pride, in erring reason's spite;
One truth is clear, Whatever is, is right.
                    —Alexander Pope, *Essay on Man*

The worst of unqualified omnipotence is that it is accompanied by responsibility for every detail of every happening.
                    —Alfred North Whitehead, *Adventures of Ideas*

Thus "brute power" is an indirect relation, never a direct one.
But it is none the less practically efficacious, for good or ill,
and has to be reckoned with. The one thing we need not and ought not to do is—to worship it!
                    —Charles Hartshorne, *The Divine Relativity*

If it turns out that there is a God, I don't think he's evil—I think the worst you could say of him is that basically he's an underachiever.
                    —Woody Allen, the movie *Love and Death*

CONTENTS

PREFACE

This book consists largely of responses to critiques of my book *God, Power, and Evil: A Process Theodicy*. While it is assumed that many readers will have read that earlier book, this new book is self-contained. The first half of chapter 1 contains a summary of my basic position, including criticisms of traditional solutions to the problem of evil. And the responses to the various critiques do not presuppose that readers are familiar with those critiques.

All the material in this book is published here for the first time. Chapter 8 is based on "Actuality, Possibility, and Theodicy: A Response to Nelson Pike," *Process Studies* 12/3 (Fall 1982), 168–79; my response to Pike has, however, been almost totally rewritten for this book.

I am thankful to Michael Corey, Nancy Frankenberry, and Clark Williamson for valuable help given, and especially to Robert Neville, whose critique of an earlier version of this book led to its almost complete reorganization. His evaluation cost me a lot of time, but resulted in a much better book.

Most of all I am grateful to the various persons to whom I here respond—David and Randall Basinger, Stephen Davis, Nancy Frankenberry, Peter Hare, Philip Hefner, John Hick, John Knasas, Nelson Pike, Alvin Plantinga, and Bruce Reichenbach—for their serious attention to my work. (John Roth and Frederick Sontag have also written critiques, to which I have responded elsewhere [see n. 6 of the Introduction]).

Because writing a shorter review can almost be as much work, and because it is usually a thankless task, I want to take this opportunity also to thank publicly those many persons who wrote reviews—at least the ones of whom I know: Delwin Brown, Ross Bush, Lewis S. Ford, Kenneth Hamilton, Arthur F. Holmes, Paul Knitter, Lyman T. Lundeen, George Earle Owen, Kent Harold Richards, Jerry K. Robbins, Mary Lederer Roby, H. Martin

Rumscheidt, Thomas A. Shannon, Barry L. Whitney, Warren McWilliams, and John H. Wright, S.J.

I am grateful to President Richard C. Cain and the trustees of the School of Theology at Claremont for their support, including a research leave when this book was completed; to John Cobb and Nancy Howell for making it possible for me to be away from the Center for Process Studies for a period; and to Marcia Doss and her staff in the faculty office for the typing of the manuscript. I am grateful to William Eastman of SUNY Press not only for publishing this book but also for his role in making it better than it would have been; and to Elizabeth Moore for her competence in guiding it through the production process.

I dedicate this book to Charles and Dorothy Hartshorne. My first immersion in process theism came through the writings of Charles; his formulations of many concepts and issues have become almost second nature to me. And besides everything else to be said about Dorothy, without her Charles would not be Charles—not the Charles we know, who has done and written all that he has. Their life together, with its intrinsic richness and its equally rich contributions to the lives of others, stands as a model of goodness in a human world too filled with evil.

My most immediate and heartful gratitude on a daily basis is to Ann, my own efficient, supportive, and delightful companion. If there were no other, her life would be sufficient evidence of the reality of God.

INTRODUCTION

Not many years ago, process theology's solution to the problem of evil was virtually ignored. In the years since the first publication in 1976 of my book *God, Power, and Evil: A Process Theodicy,*[1] the discussion of process theodicy has increased considerably.[2] For example, in John Hick's 400-page *Evil and the God of Love,* which had been published in 1966, the process theism based upon the philosophies of Alfred North Whitehead and Charles Hartshorne was referred to in only one sentence—and erroneously at that.[3] In 1983, by contrast, in the third edition of Hick's *Philosophy of Religion,* process theodicy is treated at length and called one of the "three main Christian responses to the problem of evil."[4]

Some of the increased discussion of this option is contained in a number of lengthy critiques my book was fortunate enough to receive,[5] many of them from well-known philosophers of religion who have themselves written major treatises on the problem of evil. Much of the present book consists of responses to various criticisms and counter-suggestions offered by them.[6] The nature of these criticisms and counter-suggestions can be seen at a glance in the table of contents.

Besides "responses," the other word in the subtitle is "reconsiderations." The reconsiderations are of two types: points that I have seen the need to reformulate, and issues on which I have changed my mind. The new formulations are scattered throughout the book, given in response to helpful criticisms, especially in chapters 3, 6, and 7. The changes in formulation have to do primarily with the fact that I did not always keep in mind the distinction between traditional all-determining theism and traditional free-will theism. Some of my statements about traditional theism apply only to the former version of it.

The changes of mind are summarized in the last two sections of chapter 1, and are also reflected throughout the book. These involve, on the one hand, a stronger doctrine of evil—a dimension of evil that I call "the demonic"—and, on the other hand, a more robust doctrine of divine power and, therefore, a stronger basis for hope. The main change since writing *God, Power, and Evil* can, in fact, be summarized as the realization that a fully adequate theodicy requires an eschatology.[7] That I did not think so while writing that earlier book is symbolized by the relegation of the question of life after death to an appendix.

Although I do not thematize the notion in the present book, I have in the intervening years come to speak of "postmodern theology,"[8] which for me means primarily a postmodern form of process theology. The development of a more hopeful eschatology is an important part of this new emphasis. I have come to believe, for one thing, that the polarization between "liberal" and "conservative" (including "evangelical") theologies most fundamentally concerns hope and therefore eschatology. Conservatives, seeing the hopeless conclusions of modern liberal theologians, often assume that the liberal method is at the root of these conclusions and must therefore be resisted. In my view, however, the problem is not the liberal method, by which I mean the method that makes reason and experience—with their criteria of self-consistency and adequacy to the facts—crucial for determining truth. The problem has instead been the distinctively *modern* assumptions with which modern liberal theologians have begun. If these are rejected in favor of postmodern starting points, the liberal method can lead to conclusions that provide a realistic basis for hope. These conclusions can be had, therefore, without the desperate attempt to hold onto belief in supernatural interventions in general and inerrant inspiration in particular. In this way, the strong polarization of recent times could be overcome.

Because the term "postmodern" is such an embattled term, and is used in such a confusing variety of ways—some of which conflict with what I have just said about reason and experience—I should comment upon my use of it. In many circles, the term denotes a deconstructive, relativistic attitude, in which there are no generally acceptable criteria of truth, and in which, accordingly, the attempt to construct a more adequate worldview is passé. I speak, by contrast, of a constructive or reconstructive postmodernism, in which a central effort is to do just that: construct a worldview more adequate than those of the past. And I make crucial, as already indicated, the standard rational-empirical criteria: self-consistency and adequacy to the facts of experience. A worldview proves itself worthy of belief, I hold, if and only if it meets these criteria at least as well as other available options.

The criterion chiefly at issue is adequacy to the facts of experience. Relativistic postmodernism maintains that there are no facts that are simply *given* to experience, that all facts are socially or personally *constructed*. There are, accordingly, no "facts of experience" that are universal, that are common to all persons, and that could therefore serve as neutral criteria in terms of which to evaluate the adequacy of alternative worldviews. I maintain with Whitehead, by contrast, that such universal facts do exist. I call them "hard-core commonsense notions." These are notions that are universally presupposed in practice, even if they are not consciously present in experience, and even if they are verbally denied. They are to be clearly distinguished from most notions that pass for "common sense" colloquially understood, such as the notion that the earth is flat, or that molecules have no feelings. These culturally conditioned ideas—which I call "soft-core commonsense notions"—are not universally shared by all human beings of all times and places, and they can be denied without contradicting one's own practice. Not so with hard-core commonsense ideas, such as causality (every event is influenced by other events, and in turn influences other events), freedom (our behavior is not wholly determined by causal factors beyond ourselves but is partially self-determining), and a real world (other things, as real as my present experience, exist beyond that experience). One can see from the behavior of all persons that these ideas are always presupposed in practice. Also, the attempt to deny one of these ideas would implicitly presuppose the idea—for example, if I tried to cause persons to give up belief in causality, or if I tried to convince other people to become solipsists.

One of the hard-core commonsense notions, I claim, is the reality of genuine evil, by which I mean evil that would retain its evilness when viewed from an all-inclusive perspective. To believe in genuine evil is to believe that some things happen that, all things considered, should not have happened: the world would have been better if some alternative possibility had happened instead. If this belief is a hard-core commonsense idea, being presupposed in practice by all persons, including those who verbally deny it, then no theodicy that denies the reality of genuine evil can be adequate to the facts of experience.[9]

Because I also consider the perfect goodness of God and the importance of self-consistency not to be negotiable, the only possible way to solve the problem of evil is to modify the traditional doctrine of divine power. That modification lies at the heart of a process theodicy.

It is important to emphasize, however, that this revision in the understanding of divine power is not carried out simply to solve the problem of evil. The solution that is thereby provided is clearly one of the most important fruits of the revision. But this revisioning of divine power has many other bases and advantages as well. Our understanding of divine power should be adequate not only to the problem of evil but to *all* relevant facts of experience. It should be adequate, for example, to the various facts that count against occasional supernatural interventions into the world. Some of these facts are: the evolutionary origin of our world; the diversity of the religions;[10] the evidence against the inerrant inspiration of the scriptures; and the recognition that events traditionally interpreted as supernatural "miracles" can better be understood as examples of the paranormal or psi events studied by parapsychologists. These facts provide some of the bases for revising the traditional understanding of divine power.

The nonsupernaturalist understanding of divine power also has several advantages besides the solution it allows to the problem of evil. For example, it allows theism to be compatible with the widespread assumption of the scientific community that the normal causal processes are not occasionally suspended. It makes clear, in this time of global crisis, that we cannot count on a supernatural divine intervention to save us from our foolish ways, but that reversing the present destructive practices of modern society is solely our responsibility. (This point does not deny that God is presently inspiring us to overcome the crisis; it says only that God cannot unilaterally overcome the crisis, and cannot even unilaterally guarantee that we will do so; how we respond to the lure of the Holy Spirit is up to us.) This denial that God exercises unilateral, controlling power is also important in another way in relation to the crisis engendered by nuclear weapons. That crisis was brought on in part, I am convinced, by a human desire to imitate deity combined with the traditional notion of divine omnipotence, especially an omnipotence that will be used at the end of history to bring about the ultimate victory of good over evil. A new view, one that sees divine power as noncoercive, noncontrolling, and nonviolent, and therefore as a persuasive, enabling, evocative power, will help us overcome our penchant for weapons of mass destruction.[11]

The modification of the traditional doctrine of divine power suggested by process theology is, therefore, not carried out simply to solve the problem of evil. Rather, it is an essential part of an overall worldview seen as having many bases and advantages. But to say this is not to belittle the problem of evil. After all is said and done, the most important thing in the world is the quality of life enjoyed by individual beings. A crucial aspect of this quality of life for *human* beings—finally the crucial aspect because we human beings are most distinctively *religious* beings—is whether we regard the world as essentially good, and as rooted in a divine, holy power. The problem of evil is the chief obstacle to this religious vision of the world and thereby ourselves. There is, hence, ultimately no theoretical problem more important than the problem of evil.

In one sense, the nature of the solution accepted does not matter as long as *some* solution is found (or presupposed). Life can then be seen as meaningful. But in another sense the question of what solution is accepted is extremely important. To give some examples: solving the problem by denying the reality of evil can lead to an indifferent quietism, or to nuclear and ecological brinkmanship. Solving the problem by denying the importance of rational consistency in this matter means affirming God by rejecting one of the divinely inspired values, a fact that makes this solution inherently unstable. Any solution that is inadequate to the facts of life will also be unstable; such a position taught to children by their parents or church may lead them to atheism later, when the position is found unable to withstand exposure to the often brutal realities of this world. A position that retains belief in a divine reality only by saying that this divine reality is partly evil can lead us willy-nilly, by virtue of the human tendency for the *imitatio dei*, to seek harmony with the divine reality through violently destructive behavior—a prospect especially dangerous in this age of weapons of mass destruction.

In *God, Power, and Evil*, I presented the one approach to the problem of evil that I find convincing in itself, adequate in relation to a wide variety of other issues, and helpful on other grounds. In the present book, I respond to the various lengthy critiques I received. In this response, I defend much of what I had suggested earlier; I improve the formulation of some of the technical points, with thanks to several of my critics; and I indicate the ways in which I now find the position of that earlier book not adequate, at least not fully so, and how I now propose to enlarge it.

Some of the new ideas in this book are neither reformulations nor changes of mind, but are instead presuppositions that were omitted from *God, Power, and Evil*. The reason for their omission can be partly explained in terms of the way the final chapter of that book came about. In the manuscript originally submitted, four chapters were devoted to developing the process theodicy. The editor at the Westminster Press said that the manuscript was too long, that the section on process theodicy was the part that should be reduced, and that it should be reduced to one chapter of about the same length as the others. Being a young, still rather inexperienced author, I acceded to his requirements.

One of the results of this reduction was that several key ideas presupposed throughout the discussion were inadvertently never mentioned, or mentioned too briefly to be noticed by most readers. My past self surely did not consciously allow them to be omitted. Rather, these ideas were probably so deeply presupposed, especially after I had been working so intensely with that material, that I did not notice their absence from the final form of the text. I recall being surprised more than once by a reviewer's misunderstanding about a point that I knew I had made crystal clear, only to discover later that that clarity was present only in the original, longer manuscript. In any case, many of my attempts in the present book to straighten out misunderstandings might have been unnecessary if the original manuscript had been published, or if my past self had been more careful in making reductions—and perhaps less willing to agree to such drastic reductions.

One confusion that appears more than once in critiques is the equation of *efficient causation* with *coercion* and of *final causation* with *persuasion*. I originally had an entire section entitled "Persuasive Efficient Causation," in which I showed at some length that God for Whitehead exerts efficient causation upon each actual occasion in providing an initial aim.

Another important discussion deleted concerned the various meanings of "coercion" and the various ways in which the distinction between persuasion and coercion can therefore be understood. In that deleted discussion I pointed out that coercion in the *relative* sense occurs in persuasive efficient causation, which is efficient causation in the primary sense, and that coercion in the *absolute* sense occurs only in efficient causation in a secondary, derivative sense.

That contrast was clarified further by distinguishing between "becoming" and "locomotion" as two types of motion or change. In *persuasive* efficient causation, the change or motion induced is the *internal becoming of an individual*, which is always partially determined by the individual itself; coercion upon an individual can, accordingly, only be *relative* coercion. In *coercive* efficient causation, meaning coercion in the *absolute* sense, the change involves the *locomotion of an aggregational society* of individuals.

This discussion showed why there is such a thing as absolute coercion in a universe comprised exclusively of partially self-determining individuals, and why God, nevertheless, being an individual, cannot exert coercion in this absolute sense. *We* can exert coercion in the absolute sense by virtue of our bodies, which respond so sensitively to our persuasion. By means of our bodies, we can then (indirectly) exert coercion on other bodies, which are likewise aggregates of individuals. But there is no divine body between God and finite beings. God's causal relations are therefore always direct, individual-to-individual relations; God has no "hands" that could serve as coercive instrumentalities. Given the centrality of this point, and the number of persons who have asked me why God's causation must be exclusively persuasive, it is hard for me now to understand why I allowed this discussion to be omitted from the final version of that book. The discussion of the mind-body relation would, for example, have probably precluded the confusions found in Nelson Pike's critique (see chapter 7), in which moving one's arm, which in my scheme is a primary example of (persuasive) efficient causation (of the mind or soul upon its body), is treated as an example of self-determination.

These omitted ideas had also been formulated, although much more briefly, in a paper I had written in 1973 in response to a critique of process philosophy's solution to the problem of evil by Peter Hare and Edward Madden. Some of the ideas in this response were contained in my brief response to Madden and Hare in *God, Power, and Evil,* but most of them were not, and the essay itself was never published. Although including the essay in this book results in some repetition, I enclose it here as an appendix, for several reasons. First, it makes quite different points in response to Madden and Hare than do the responses to their article that have previously been published.[12] Second, it makes several points that are not otherwise made in this book. Third, it constitutes a belated acknowledgment to Madden and Hare for their important role in the discussion and development of process theodicy. Fourth, the early critiques by Madden and Hare to which this essay responds are still being cited by critics of process theism—as illustrated in chapter 9 herein.

Chapter 1

THE DIVINE AND THE DEMONIC IN A HOLOCAUST UNIVERSE: A SUMMARY WITH RECONSIDERATIONS

In this chapter, I first provide a summary of my reasons for rejecting the traditional theodicies, with special attention to the traditional free-will theodicy, which is the most popular theodicy today. Then I summarize the process theodicy I have developed in earlier writings, most fully in *God, Power, and Evil*. Finally, the sections "The Demonic" and "Meaning and Hope" contain a summary of the ways in which my thinking on the topic has developed and even changed in the intervening years.

The subject of this chapter is the relation between belief in God and the fact of evil, especially those overwhelming evils that seem to be mass outbreaks of demonic power and that we call "holocausts." There are many events to which this term can be justly applied, but here I use it for events of widespread destruction caused by human agency, especially those to which it is most often applied: the Nazi destruction of European Jews and other "undesirables," and the possible destruction of most or all of the human race, and perhaps even most earthly life, by nuclear weapons or more gradual ecocide.

I focus on the question: does belief in God imply that such holocausts cannot occur? In other words, does the fact that the Nazi holocaust occurred invalidate belief in God? And if a nuclear holocaust does occur, should that be taken as the final proof, for those who might survive for a short period, that there is no God?

A. THE GENERIC IDEA OF GOD

To deal with this question it is necessary to have some definite meaning of the word "God" in mind. Besides the fact that there are countless notions of deity, there are several levels of generality and specificity in the various definitions of deity. There are very general, wholly formal definitions, such as "God is that greater than which nothing can be thought," and "God is that which is alone worthy of worship." At the other end of the spectrum there are highly specific definitions, such as "God is an omniscient, omnipotent, immutable, all-good supreme being who created the world *ex nihilo* and de-termines or at least could determine all its events." A person who holds this specific definition might consider it the only acceptable content for the purely formal definitions mentioned above. But some who accept the purely formal definitions reject this highly specific one.

A major reason for this rejection is that the reality of a God so defined seems to be contradicted by the evils of the world, especially the most over-whelming ones. They therefore hold that, while the Nazi holocaust invali-dates belief in God in *that* sense, there is some other possible way to fill out the formal notion of "that which is worthy of worship" that would not be contradicted by the world's evils. For example, they could hold to omni-science and perfect goodness, while rejecting omnipotence and creation *ex nihilo*. Or they could hold to omniscience, omnipotence, and creation *ex nihilo* while rejecting perfect goodness. These possibilities show that, between the most general and the most specific definitions of God, there are other levels of generality. For the purposes of this discussion, I shall deal with the meaning of "God" at four levels. The first two levels are so general that the more neutral term "deity" is used instead of the more specific term "God."

At the first level, I accept the purely formal definition that deity refers to "that greater than which nothing can be thought and that which is alone worthy of worship."

At the second level, which adds some substantive content while re-maining highly generic, deity refers to "the supreme power of the universe, the power that is nonderivative and ultimately most effective." I use the ex-pression "the Holy Power" to refer to this definition of that which is worthy of worship. This definition seems to apply to everything that has in fact evoked human worship in the various traditions. Insofar as other things have seemingly evoked worship, they have done so by being regarded as embodi-ments or representatives of this supreme, nonderivative power.

My third level of definition jumps over other possible levels of increasing specificity to a definition that contains much of the quite specific content that is usually present, at least implicitly, in cultures whose idea of deity comes mainly from the biblically based religions of Judaism, Christianity, and Islam. This definition contains features that would be widely agreed upon in these cultures, by believers and nonbelievers alike, as essential to the idea of God. I refer to this level of definition as "the generic idea of God." There are seven major features of this generic idea of God, the first two being the more general definitions already mentioned. In parentheses, I shall indicate which of those moves, often made to save "belief in God" in the face of the problem of evil (or other problems), are ruled out if the features of this generic definition are accepted as essential to the meaning of "God." According to this generic definition, God is:

1. Alone worthy of worship, ultimate concern, unconditional commitment. (This feature rules out giving the name "God" to anything imperfect, to any object to which we think human beings should *not* commit their lives without reservation.)
2. The Holy Power; the nonderivative, supreme, most effective power. (This feature rules out defining God as a cluster of [nonefficacious] ideals,[1] as a derivative power that emerged only at some point in the evolutionary process, or as a power ultimately less effective than some other power.)
3. The purposive creator of our world. (This feature rules out defining God as "being itself," "power itself," "energy itself," "creative interchange," or anything else devoid of aim.)[2]
4. Perfectly good. (This feature rules out thinking of God as having wholly or partially evil purposes or impulses, or as being morally neutral or indifferent, in terms of our best judgment as to what it would be for a creator to be "good.")[3]
5. The source of norms, at least *moral* norms distinguishing good from evil, especially right from wrong uses of power by human beings. (This feature rules out as God any ultimate creative power that cannot embody norms and that would sanction the principle that "might makes right," because to declare power to be its own norm is to say that there are no norms for its use.)[4]
6. The ultimate guarantee for the meaningfulness of human life. (This feature supports the widespread intuition that atheism ultimately implies nihilism. It rules out any definition of God that provides no basis for an affirmation of the ultimate meaningfulness of human life.)[5]
7. The trustworthy ground for hope in the ultimate victory of good over evil. (This feature follows from the second and fourth features, and rules out definitions that do not see God as a power for good in history now or

in the future, and also those doctrines that regard this providential power as too impotent ultimately to overcome the power of evil.)

These seven features are widely taken to be essential to the meaning of "God" by persons in our culture, both theists and atheists, so that we cannot take seriously any "solutions" to the problem of evil that seem to deny one or more of these features. The question is, then, Does the reality of evil in general, and of holocausts in particular, make belief in God in this sense incredible?

Many would answer yes. For example, Richard Rubenstein argues that, *After Auschwitz*, no Jew, and really no one, should believe in the biblical God of history.[6] He can still affirm a Holy Power. But he cannot understand it in terms of any of the other features (3 through 7) of the biblically based notion of God. Auschwitz empirically disproves, he holds, that the Holy Power of the universe is good in any moral sense of the term, and therefore that there is any transhuman source of norms, especially of any norms that are effective enough to provide for a victory of good over evil and therefore to guarantee the meaningfulness of human life.[7] Other thinkers say that, although belief in God does not rule out evil, even an evil as great as that of the Nazi holocaust, it does rule out the possibility of total annihilation. For example, some persons would consider such an event the ultimate victory of evil over good; it would therefore show that there had never been a trustworthy ground for hope in the ultimate victory of good over evil. Some persons go so far as to say that the annihilation of human life would destroy all meaning whatsoever.[8] This annihilation would obviously prove, accordingly, that there is no ultimate guarantee of the meaningfulness of human life (the sixth feature) and thereby no God. Some persons in fact hold that the very possibility that a nuclear annihilation could occur—which they see no reason in history to deny—already disproves the existence of God for these reasons. Surely, they say, or at least feel, a world in which such an eventuality is even a possibility cannot be grounded in a supreme power that is "perfectly good" by any meaning we could give to this notion. The ultimate power of the universe must at best be indifferent, at worst demonic (which is a denial of the fourth feature).

All these views have one point in common, which I reject. The point at issue here involves two ways of further specifying the second feature of the generic definition, which is that "God" by definition refers to the Holy Power—the supreme power in the universe, the power that is finally most effective. This further specification brings us to the fourth level of the definition. The two ways of specifying how to understand the Holy Power give us a contrast between two fourth-level definitions of God, which I will here call "traditional theism" and "process theism." The contrast involves two ideas of the relation between God and the aboriginal power of the universe, and consequently a contrast between two kinds of power attributed to God.

According to traditional (or classical) theism, all of the aboriginal power of the universe essentially belongs to God. Monotheism essentially means monism. There is no power that essentially and aboriginally belongs to any other being (dualism) or beings (pluralism). If any other beings seem to have power of their own, this is either an illusion or is due to the fact that God has voluntarily given power to them. Their power is either merely apparent or it is derivative; it is not both genuine and inherent. God's power in relation to the world is therefore *unilateral* power. God *can* unilaterally determine what will happen, if God chooses to do so. There are two major versions of this traditional theism.

B. TRADITIONAL ALL-DETERMINING THEISM

The first version of traditional theism can be called "all-determining theism." It is found in the theologies of Augustine, Thomas, Calvin, Luther, and Barth. God in fact totally determines every event, including all human decisions and actions, and therefore all "sinful" acts. But how, then, do we explain evil, especially those forms we call "demonic?" Traditional Christian theism spoke of Satan as God's cosmic opponent. Behind the imagery allowed for popular consumption, however, the ultimate monism of traditional monotheism had to hold that Satan was a mere creature of God. To say otherwise would have been disallowable dualism. Satan was a creature who had fallen away, but this fall itself had been unilaterally engineered by God. To say otherwise would have been to imply that there was some power in the universe not totally under God's control.

Not to allow any uncontrollable power, however, seems to make all the talk about sin meaningless, if "sin" means going against the divine will. Theologians gave a verbal solution to this problem by distinguishing between two "wills" in God (in spite of their insistence otherwise on the divine simplicity). When we sin, we violate the "revealed" or "commanding" will of God. But monism was protected by adding that our sinful activity was itself caused by the "hidden" or "secret" will of God. Does this addition mean that God causes evil? Yes, in one sense. God was said to do all sorts of things that cannot seem other than evil to us, given our limited perspective. These things were attributed by some theologians to God's "left hand." Was this not admitting that the demonic was within the Godhead, that Satan is nothing but a mythological projection of the "shadow-side" of God?

That would seem to be the conclusion—except for one fact. These traditional theists finally denied that there *is* any genuine evil in the universe.

From a less limited standpoint than we now have, we will sometime come to realize that all things—including even the holocausts and other things that seemed most demonic at the time—were for the best. Partial evil, universal good; whatever is, is right. The realization that this traditional view of God implied that Auschwitz must finally be regarded as good is what led Rubenstein to renounce theism. Many others are horrified today by the realization that many fundamentalist Christians believe that a nuclear holocaust would not be genuinely evil, from a God's-eye view. The conclusion is logical. If God is the sole power in reality and perfectly good, there is no evil. Then let us quit bemoaning the last holocaust and trying to prevent a future one.

One way out of this conclusion is to deny that our various theological propositions have to be logically consistent. We can admit that the doctrine that God is all-good and the sole power *should* (logically) mean that there is no freedom and therefore no possibility of genuine evil in the world, while nevertheless holding that freedom and evil are genuine. We do this by denying that theology must abide by the basic principle of rationality, the law of noncontradiction. We can thereby say all these things: the demonic happens; God is the sole power; yet God is not demonic.[9]

But this desperate solution implies special pleading, allowing inconsistency (or even celebrating it as a virtue) in our own tradition while using the presence of inconsistencies in rival doctrines (Marxism, Hinduism, capitalism, scientism, materialism, dualism, flat-earthism, astrology) to argue against their credibility. The only way to hold without inconsistency that self-contradictions within one's own theology do not prove its falsity would be to allow all other theologies to claim equal exemption from the law of noncontradiction. But of course when one has claimed the right to violate the law of noncontradiction in one case, there is no reason not to be inconsistent in this matter. One can simply say that inconsistencies in all other traditions show that they are false, but that inconsistencies in one's own theology do not count against its truth.

C. TRADITIONAL FREE-WILL THEISM

Not being able to countenance either of these desperate attempts to salvage belief in God in a holocaust world—denying either the reality of genuine evil or the idea that theology must conform to logic—some theologians holding the traditional view on divine power have taken another approach, hinted at earlier. They suggest that, although God *essentially* has all the power in the universe, God has *voluntarily* delegated power to creatures. The "creatures" in question *could* be all of them, down to subatomic elements; but usually the creatures thought to have some freedom are limited to animals, and in fact primarily to *human* beings (at least on this planet). Freedom in this form of traditional theism is understood to mean that free acts are not totally determined by God. "Compatibilism" is rejected: genuine human freedom is not, contrary to Thomas Aquinas, compatible with complete divine determinism. This move provides the basics for a "free-will defense" of God in the face of the world's evils, including its holocausts.

This traditional free-will theism is the second of the two major versions of classical or traditional theism. It offers the hypothesis that reliable laws of nature and genuine human freedom *vis-à-vis* God, which are seldom if ever interrupted, are necessary aspects of God's overall purpose for the creation, which is a good purpose (perhaps the "best conceivable" one). This purpose is to encourage the formation of beings who freely develop moral-spiritual character. Given this perspective, the occurrence of natural and moral evil is said not to contradict God's goodness and power. God *could*, of course, interrupt the laws of nature to alter the otherwise inevitable spatiotemporal features of physical things (bullets, bombs, cancerous cells) or the decisions of free subjects that would otherwise lead to massive suffering. God could have prevented Auschwitz, Hiroshima, Wounded Knee, and the current mass starvation in the world. But to have done this to avoid momentary pain and suffering would actually have hindered the realization of the long-term purpose, the development of moral and spiritual qualities through free decisions. This is the case not only because this purpose requires genuine freedom and regular laws of cause and consequence, but also because pain and suffering are essential conditions to the realization of many of the most important moral and spiritual qualities. Without suffering, for example, there cannot be courageous endurance of suffering. Although some forms of suffering seem counterproductive to this purpose, because they seem to defeat rather than to stimulate the process of soul-making, it is often precisely the most horrendous evils, those that seem least capable of being understood as contributing to any moral-spiritual purpose, that evoke the deepest compassion in others.[10] They are thus not counterproductive after all.

Although this position can be presented in an initially plausible manner, it can be seen, upon closer examination, to have severe shortcomings. To see these, we need to consider a little more fully the basic hypothesis. According to traditional theism, we recall, all power essentially belongs to God. There are no other entities with inherent power whose cooperation God must have in determining the details of the world, at least up to the point where free beings are created. And the basic structure of the world (in contrast with its concrete details or events at the level where free beings are involved) is unilaterally determined by God. This being the case, there could not be any basic principles, other than purely logical ones, to which the structure of the world would have to conform. Not only those principles normally called the "laws of nature," but also those more general principles often thought to be "metaphysical" or "ontological" because applicable to being *qua* being, would be products of the divine decision. There would therefore be no necessity that a world develop gradually through a long, evolutionary process; that it have such things as earthquakes, hurricanes, and droughts; that its living cells have the capacity to become cancerous; that physical things be composed of elements that could be fashioned into weapons capable of destroying a planet; that living organisms be susceptible to pain, especially to any pain-producing mechanism that could not be voluntarily turned off when it was no longer serving a useful warning purpose. Because God essentially has all the power, so that creatures have power only insofar as God has freely delegated some to them, all of these and similar "laws" were (by hypothesis) imposed on the world from without, by God's unilateral action. When all this is kept in mind, several questions arise that make the free-will defense of God's goodness questionable. I will raise ten.

The first question is already implicit in the previous paragraph: Is it plausible, granting that virtue often presupposes suffering, that *every* basic structural aspect of the world can be justified as necessary to the promotion of creatures with moral and spiritual qualities? As some critics have focused the question: Can a carcinogenic and holocaust universe be the unilateral product of a perfectly good God? By hypothesis, the universe could have been in most respects similar to ours without having the capacity to produce cancerous cells or nuclear weapons. Does not the assumption that these capacities contribute to the overall good strain credulity? It may not constitute an outright refutation of this free-will defense, but it at least prevents us from saying unambivalently, "Yes, things are as they should be!," even if we have accepted the basic principles of the theodicy.

The second problem is that much of the suffering in the world produces not virtue but its opposite. Poverty and hunger, especially because they are unequally distributed, often lead to crime and war rather than to industry and cooperation. A lack of material necessities often leads to preoccupation with material things rather than to a spiritual outlook. Debilitating illness often leads to despair and bitterness rather than to hope. Much suffering seems so pointless that it leads to atheism rather than to faith. The way of the world is often so cruel that it leads human beings to curse the universe and its creator rather than to love them. And so on. If the creator set up the world to produce virtuous beings, the plan seems to have backfired on a massive scale, suggesting incompetence.

At this point, the traditional free-will theist usually agrees that some evil is so horrendous, that it is so unequally distributed, and that it produces saints so seldom, that the critic's position would be sound if life in this world were alone taken into account. Accordingly, the traditional free-will defense, to be convincing, must include as an essential component the doctrine that human life continues on beyond bodily death. We can believe that in this future life, all injustices will be righted, and that it will become evident that all the sufferings were worth undergoing. Kant's vision of a realm in which virtue and happiness are coincident will be realized. Without this belief, the traditional free-will theist admits, the kind of world we have could not be regarded as the unilateral creation of a perfectly good power. This conclusion will follow all the more if a nuclear holocaust results in agonizing illness and finally death for billions of human beings. This feature of the traditional free-will theodicy—that it makes belief in life after death an *essential* element of the theodicy as a whole—has to be regarded as a fatal weakness by those who do not believe in life after death, and as at least a serious weakness by those who think the idea doubtful.

A third problem involves the importance of freedom *vis-à-vis* God, which I call "theological freedom." Part of the initial plausibility of the free-will defense derives from the consent that we give almost unthinkingly to the importance of having genuine freedom. We know how precious social and political freedoms are. We do not want to be subjected to a totalitarian form of government. We do not want to be put in prison, especially without due process. We do not want any violations of our freedoms of speech, of the press, of assembly, of religion, of suffrage, and so on. By not having them, Native Americans, African Americans, and to some extent women in this country have experienced how important these freedoms are for many of the activities we find most valuable. We recognize that freedom has its costs, that countries in which citizens have large degrees of social, political, and economic freedom have to risk putting up with certain forms of evil that more totalitarian governments can suppress. But we would be unwilling to make the trade. When a theodicy justifies all the forms of evil in the world as inevitable corollaries of genuine freedom, we are therefore predisposed to nod in agreement.

A closer look, however, shows us that there is no connection between these forms of freedom and the theological freedom *vis-à-vis* God around which the traditional free-will defense revolves. Social, political, and economic freedoms do not require theological freedom. In fact, one could easily argue that it is theological freedom that leads to restrictions upon those other forms of freedom, because these restrictions usually result from human sin, which means activity that goes against the will of God. If human beings had no freedom to go against God's will, they would enjoy far more social, political, and economic freedom than they now do, on every part of the planet.

In this light, we have to ask if it was justifiable for God to give us genuine theological freedom. We cannot (within this theological position) base an affirmative answer on the principle that freedom in relation to God is part and parcel of all the values unique to human beings. An omnipotent God, by hypothesis, could have created beings who were like us in all respects except for having no genuine freedom *vis-à-vis* God. Such beings could have enjoyed all the forms of value we enjoy, such as great music (both the creating and the listening), great art, great food and drink, great love and sex, the joy of a job well done, parenting, friendship, and sports. And all of these could have been enjoyed without the ambiguity that infects so much of them in our present existence, due to fear, hate, greed, and other manifestations and effects of sin. The world could indeed have been a paradise.

In response, it could be argued by the traditional free-will theist that theological freedom is necessary for the most important kind of enjoyment: unless we are genuinely free, we could not enjoy the feeling that we have freely avoided sin, that we have freely developed moral and spiritual virtues. The answer to this claim is that, by hypothesis, God could have made it so that we *thought* we were genuinely free, even though we were not. (According to the all-determining theism of Augustine, Thomas, Luther, and Calvin, that was indeed the case.) Only God would know that we were not really free. The only one who would lose any genuine value would therefore be God; that is, God would not enjoy the value of knowing that those of us who developed moral character and spiritual virtue, especially the virtue of faith in and love for God, did so freely. God would know that our virtues were not authentic. The only one who really benefits from the presence of creaturely freedom *vis-à-vis* God is, accordingly, God. Can we unambivalently praise the goodness of a creator who unilaterally created a carcinogenic and holocaust world instead of a paradise if that creator is the only one who benefits from this choice?

In response, the traditional free-will theodicist can point out that it would be deceptive of God to give us the illusion of being free when we really were not, and that this deceptiveness would count against God's perfect goodness. But this response leaves a difficult question: Which of these two pictures of God is less morally reprehensible—a God who created an earthly paradise but deceived its self-conscious inhabitants about their true status, or a God who freely and unilaterally made all the forms of evil in our world possible solely for the value that would thereby accrue to God? Once the question is thus posed, many, I suspect, would find neither being worthy of worship and thereby worthy of the name "God."

In response to the claim that, on their premises, this world could have been a paradise, traditional free-will theists reply that God indeed could have made the world into a "hedonistic paradise," but that this was not the type of "best possible world" that God wanted. God wanted it instead to be a "vale of soul-making." This hypothesis creates a fourth problem, which is that this theodicy requires an excessive belittling of the importance of enjoyment and suffering in comparison with virtue and vice. Besides the pejorative term "hedonistic" to describe a pain-free and sin-free world (the kind of world toward which God is by hypothesis leading us!), we read statements such as the following from advocates of this point of view: "sin is the chief intrinsic evil, in comparison with which the intrinsic disvalue of pain is of minor importance, just as sanctification is of supreme worth and pleasure a trifle."[11]

Many of us can indeed agree that the more active and creative values, which include the development of moral and spiritual virtues, are ultimately more important than the more passive or receptive forms of enjoyment: character is more important than enjoyment, sin is worse than suffering. But the degree to which the traditional free-will defenders are forced to go in making the sin-virtue spectrum virtually all-important, and the enjoyment-suffering spectrum virtually irrelevant, seems excessive. They are forced into this extreme position by their basic premise. Because God, by hypothesis, built the capacity for so much suffering into the world deliberately, for the sole purpose of stimulating moral and spiritual virtues, the theologian must conclude that the question of suffering is very trivial in comparison with the question of virtue.

A fifth problem with this position is moral: it could promote callousness. It could be used to belittle the importance of liberating persons from conditions producing suffering. If God does not think suffering is a serious evil, and if God in fact deliberately creates conditions producing suffering in order to stimulate moral and spiritual qualities, such as patience in adversity, persons could easily conclude that they should not join efforts to liberate the world from suffering, lest they undermine God's purpose!

A sixth problem involves animal pain. The traditional free-will defense orients everything around the conditions necessary for human (or at least humanlike) beings to develop moral and spiritual qualities. How, then, can one justify the vast amount of pain in all those animals that do not have the capacity for moral and spiritual virtues? This failure of the traditional free-will theodicy is staggering: the pain and suffering of only one species in millions has been explained! Although some animal pain provides an opportunity for compassionate feelings and actions on the part of humans, this cannot plausibly be said of most animal pain—especially because animals had been suffering pain for hundreds of millions of years prior to the appearance of human beings. It also cannot be claimed within this framework that pain is somehow necessary as a warning signal; divine unilateral omnipotence could easily have devised some painless warning device. It cannot even be claimed (within this framework) that nature needed carnivores—creatures who prey on other creatures with the capacity for pain. William Blake's question stands: If the same creator who made the lamb also made the tiger, with its "fearful symmetry," can this creator be called wholly good?

A seventh problem with the traditional free-will theodicy involves the evolutionary process itself. If God's only purpose involves humanlike creatures, why would God have used a method to create our world that took billions of years to bring forth such creatures? By hypothesis, there were no constraints under which God operated. God did not create the present order out of a chaos of self-moving things that could only gradually be subjected to more and more complex forms of order. If God created our world out of chaos (a "formless void," as Genesis 1:1 suggests), say traditional theists, this chaos itself was created out of absolute nothingness. It therefore (contrary to Plato) had no inherent principles to confront God with any kind of "necessity." This is the theory. But when combined with the modern view that creation has involved a long evolutionary process, the resulting picture is that God devoted over 99.9 percent of the history of creation thus far to that which was mere preparation for the only part of it having any intrinsic value. By joining a premodern view of God's power, which was developed when it could be assumed that the world in its present form was created all at once, or in only six days, together with a modern, post-Darwinian view of the developmental history of our planet, this theodicy rests upon a quite implausible doctrine of creation.

An eighth problem with the traditional free-will theodicy is probably the central problem that it creates for most persons. Its basic hypothesis, it will be recalled, is that none of the power in the world, including the human power of self-determination, is inherent to the world; it was all delegated freely by God. God voluntarily relinquished omni-control. God could at any time, therefore, overrule the world's course momentarily, whether the internal decisions of human beings or the spatiotemporal characteristics of physical things, such as atoms, cells, bullets, bombs, human limbs, rain clouds, and earthquake faults. God could thereby intervene to prevent all individual acts of rape, murder, kidnapping, child molestation, and so on, and all mass sufferings, whether due to drought, earthquake, or human agency and technology. Most of us would be appalled by a Superman who had the power unilaterally to prevent such things but stood by idly on the grounds that it was best, all things considered, never to violate human freedom or to interrupt the laws of nature, even occasionally. But the traditional God is said to have just that kind of power and yet to refuse to use it, on those grounds. There are, to be sure, relevant differences between an imagined Superman and such an imagined God that weaken the force of the analogy. But after all the qualifications are made, and after all the reasons are rehearsed as to why it is good for God not to interrupt, it is hard to still the thought, when confronted with a concrete case of horrendous evil: "In *this* case God should have done something!" And that thought soon leads to another: "If there *is* a God." And then to another: "If there is, I will not *worship* such a being." Which is in effect to say: "There *is* no God—no reality worthy or worship."

A ninth problem is implicit in the very notion of a traditional free-will theodicy. In most such theodicies, freedom, in the sense of the power of self-determination vis-à-vis God, is said to be a divinely bestowed superadditive to the actuality of those beings that have it. Freedom in this sense is also thought to be given by God only to a portion of the actualities comprising the world. In most cases it is effectively limited to human beings (and to other spiritual beings, such as angels, if such are believed in). The free-will defense or theodicy therefore provides no explanation for all the "natural evils" in the world, defined as evils resulting from (nonhuman) nature—unless, of course, all such evils are said to be caused by a Satanic figure of cosmic proportions. For those who find this Satanic suggestion implausible, and also believe that plausible explanations are needed, the tendency is to suggest that all so-called natural evils might be only apparently evil. But this suggestion is equally implausible.

A tenth problem is an extension of the ninth: there is a tendency among traditional free-will theists finally to deny, after all is said and done, that *any* genuine evil occurs. The reason for this tendency is that, if God is truly omnipotent in the traditional sense as well as perfectly good and wise, God would surely have set things up so that everything works together for good. If anything really, genuinely, unredeemably evil were to happen, such theists often seem to think, it would be a smear on God's power, goodness, or wisdom. Accordingly, the answers to the earlier problems—why God allows theological freedom, why God does not intervene (at least more often), why animal pain occurs, why suffering and enjoyment are trivial in comparison with sin and virtue, and so on—move strongly in the direction of denying that any genuine evil occurs. But then this theodicy becomes as implausible as that of all-determining theism, because it denies a belief that we all presuppose in practice (even if we deny it verbally). We all—as I suggested in the Introduction—reveal by our emotions, attitudes, and actions that we believe that not everything that happens is for the best. We cannot reconcile God and evil by denying evil.

I do not pretend that these ten considerations constitute a knockdown, drag-out demonstration that the traditional free-will theodicy is impossible for any rational, sensitive person to hold. There are always counter-arguments that can be offered; questions concerning the relative importance of competing values do not lend themselves to demonstrable settlement; and the appeal to "mystery" can always be made—after all, no position can be expected to give a complete answer to every possible objection. My argument has only been that, whatever initial plausibility this theodicy has, its unsatisfactoriness becomes more and more evident as it is probed. In any case, many thoughtful persons have decided that, while it is an improvement over the all-determining version of the traditional theodicy, it does not provide a satisfactory solution.

If, therefore, the generic idea of God entailed the kind of unilateral omnipotence ascribed to God by traditional theism, the case for belief in God in a holocaust universe would seem to many of us to be shaky in the extreme. And indeed, much of the atheism in the world has been based just on this assumption.

It is important to note that those contemporary theologians who are saying that God is partly evil do so after already having presupposed the gift of freedom to human beings (see note 3). Even given the free-will defense, they find it necessary to locate the demonic within God. But by our generic definition of God, the creator cannot then be called "God," because it belongs to the definition that God be perfectly good. It seems, therefore, that unless we are willing to violate the law of noncontradiction, a monistic universe can have no God.

D. PROCESS THEISM

Would it be possible to reject the equation of monotheism and monism? This approach is taken by a number of nontraditional theisms, most explicitly and fully by *process theism*, which has been worked out by thinkers belonging to the movement known as process philosophy and theology, with Alfred North Whitehead and Charles Hartshorne as its two major originators. Process theism distinguishes between God and the aboriginal power of the universe, which it calls *creativity*. Creativity is not a thing, or a being. It is simply the ultimate activity that all concrete actualities embody. Like Aristotle's "material cause," it cannot exist apart from concrete beings that embody it. Unlike Aristotle's material cause, however, it is not passivity, but activity; and it is embodied by *all* concrete beings, including God (and any "angels" there might be).[12]

Whitehead's *creativity* is primordial power. Like Berdyaev's *Ungrund*, it could be called "uncreated freedom." This term, however, would characterize only one of its two aspects. Creativity is the twofold power of an individual (1) to create or determine itself on the basis of creative influences received from others and then (2) to be a creative influence on the self-creation or self-determination of subsequent individuals. The first aspect of this twofold power is the power of *e pluribus unum*—the power to make a unity out of a multiplicity. Creativity in this phase answers to Berdyaev's reference to it as uncreated freedom. The second phase answers to the notion of efficient causation, meaning the influence of one being or event upon another. Creativity in this second phase is not self-creation but creative influence upon future beings or events.

According to this view, the ultimate reality of the universe is an incessant twofold process: the many become one, and then this one is part of a new "many" that exerts creative influence upon still newer creative unifications. This view means that reality necessarily has a multiplicity of beings. Creativity must be *embodied*, and it must be embodied *by a multiplicity*, because the very nature of creativity involves incessant oscillation between the one and the many.

This view of reality does not fit traditional categories. It is not a dualism between God and another being of cosmic proportions, because creativity is not a being. It is not monism, because creativity is essentially embodied by nondivine individuals as well as by God. And it is not simply pluralism, because God's embodiment of creativity is categorically different from that of all other beings in some respects. God is the only primordial, omnipresent, all-inclusive embodiment of creativity. And God is the only one who characterizes creativity with perfect love. This love is twofold: God's active outgoing, creative love, and God's receptive, responsive, sympathetic, compassionate love.

It *is* pluralism, nevertheless, in the sense that there has always been and always will be a plurality of individuals. Our world was created not out of *absolute nothingness*—as if God alone existed once upon a time, or "before time"—but out of a chaos of finite events. This chaos can be called *relative nothingness* (to use Berdyaev's term), in that there were no enduring things, even such primitive enduring things as electrons or quarks. This relative nothingness did not preexist God's creative activity, but was itself the product of prior divine activity. There was no beginning. The chaos from which our world began can be considered the final state of a previous world. Creation is the gradual bringing of order out of chaos.

Because power is essentially shared, God's power cannot be thought to be unilateral power. If all creatures essentially have some power to determine themselves and to influence other things, God cannot unilaterally determine any state of affairs. God's power needs to be reconceived as *evocative* power. By perpetually offering attractive alternatives to creatures' habits, God has gradually brought forth those increasingly complex forms of order that we call atoms, molecules, macromolecules, procaryotic cells, organelles, eucaryotic cells, plants, animals, animals with central nervous systems, animals with conscious souls, and animals with self-conscious souls. God cannot unilaterally determine anything. But by taking the long view, we can see the power of the creator, who works only by evoking responses in creatures, to be finally the most effective power in reality.

This view can also be called dualistic, or better, semidualistic. We can distinguish between God's embodiment of creativity, which is primordial, all-inclusive, and characterized by perfect love, and the embodiment of creativity in the plurality of creatures. Although creativity has always been embodied by some creatures or others, no particular creature exists eternally.

And all finite beings have local rather than all-inclusive perspectives, and often respond to their fellows with indifference or hate rather than with perfect love. Creativity as embodied by God is thereby essentially different in important respects from creativity as embodied in creatures. And the creativity of creatures cannot be unilaterally controlled or canceled out by God. In this sense we can speak of a cosmic semidualism.

It is on this basis that process theology responds to the problem of evil. The existence of evil does not contradict the belief that the supreme power of the universe is perfectly good, because this supreme power is not the sole power. Creaturely freedom and causation are exerted not only by human beings, but by all individuals, down to the most primitive. Even so-called natural evils can be attributed to some extent to creaturely decisions. Because God has no monopoly on power, God's power is the creative power to evoke or persuade; it is not the unilateral power to stop, to constrain, to destroy. The reason God does not intervene in nature or human affairs to prevent some of the worst evils is not that God is evil or indifferent, or that to do so would run counter to God's policy; it is simply that God's power is of a different kind.

It can be objected, however, that if God is to be understood by analogy with us, God should have coercive as well as persuasive power. *We* have the power to control, at least within limits. We can twist arms; we can tackle or shoot a would-be murderer or rapist; we can make a shield to deflect bullets; we can use bombs to stop tanks, and rockets to stop bombers; we can put would-be perpetrators of holocausts in prison or execute them. In other words, besides the evocative, persuasive power we have in relation to other souls, we have coercive, controlling power to use on other bodies when persuasion fails. If we finite creatures have both kinds of power, why does not the creator of heaven and earth?

The answer is implicit in the essential difference between a finite, localized creature and the omnipresent, universal creator. We exercise our evocative, persuasive power not only in relation to other souls, but also in relation to those billions of centers of power constituting our bodies. This power becomes quite reliable, at least in relation to some parts of our bodies, due to structures that have been built up over billions of years of evolution, and through practice. Our power in relation to our bodies is not the power of unilateral control. This is obvious with regard to all those functions of our bodies labeled "involuntary." We have learned, to be sure, that we *can* exert more influence upon them than previously thought, but it is far from total control. Even in relation to our voluntary nervous system, we do not have total control, as becomes clear when there is lack of cooperation due to disease, alcohol, or prolonged nonuse. But to the extent that we do acquire rather strong influence over certain parts of our bodies, through which we can determine the spatial movements of our bodies quite well, it becomes an instrument through which we can exert unilateral, controlling power upon other bodies, whether animate or inanimate. It is especially through our hands that we have developed so much controlling power in relation to the world and each other's bodies, both directly, and indirectly through the instruments our hands have fashioned. The importance of hands for this kind of power is reflected etymologically in the word "manipulate," which, like "manually," refers to work done with the hands and which can be used synonymously with "control" and "coerce."

It is important to see that this controlling or manipulative power, which we have by virtue of our bodies, is a secondary, indirect form of efficient causation. Efficient causation in the direct, primary sense, which is the influence of an individual on one or more other individuals, is always persuasive causation. It influences but does not totally determine. The individuals upon whom it is exerted must make a partially self-determining response to it. The only efficient causation I as an individual (as a soul) can directly exert is persuasive. I can exert controlling or coercive efficient causation only indirectly, by means of my body, insofar as its response conforms to my persuasion upon it. Controlling or coercive causation is always produced indirectly, by means of instrumentalities. It can be exerted only by things (such as hands and billiard balls) that themselves cannot initiate activity, things that are devoid of the power of self-determination. Things that *can* initiate activity (souls, cells, and other true individuals) cannot directly exert controlling causation. They can do so only indirectly, by virtue of a body.

But God has no body, at least in this sense. We can say that the world as a whole is God's body, but there is no divine body between God (as the soul of the world) and our bodies, and this is the essential point. God has no independent body distinct from the world, which could be used to exert controlling, constraining power *on* the world. God's power in relation to us is necessarily analogous to that of one soul directly upon another, without bodily mediation, or to the direct influence of our souls upon the cellular members of our bodies. God's power is thereby necessarily evocative, persuasive, attracting power. God refrains from using controlling power upon us not voluntarily, by renouncing that kind of power, but because that kind of power cannot possibly characterize the supreme center of power of the universe as a whole.

Seen in this light, the traditional doctrine of divine power has been implicitly self-contradictory. On the one hand, the traditional theologians denied that God has a body; this denial was central to the insistence that God was "simple," not composite. On the other hand, they attributed to God the *kind of power* that can only be attributed to an agent who has a body distinct from the beings upon which the agent's power is exercised. Process theology agrees with the poem, "God has no hands but our hands." God therefore cannot manipulate. The traditional theology implicitly attributed hands to God, by assigning manipulative, unilateral power to God. And if God has hands, God must have a *left* hand (this being the metaphor used for God's causation of all those things that cannot but seem evil to us).

By denying that God has hands, meaning unilateral, controlling power, process theology can consistently say that the supreme creative power of the universe is good without denying the genuineness of evil. Because power is necessarily shared, multilateral power, so that God's purposes always require the cooperation of creatures for their realization, the possibility of genuine evil is necessary. Because it is always possible that creatures will respond positively to God's proposals, doing the best that is possible in that situation, the existence of genuine evil is not necessary (defining "genuine evil" as any occurrence that is less good than something else that could have occurred in that situation). But because God cannot guarantee this positive response in any given event, the *possibility* of evil is necessary.

Once this is clear, the question can still arise: Why is *so much* evil necessary? Why must there be the possibility of cancer, of decisions that seem to run totally counter to anything we can imagine a good creator willing, and of the degree of power that can make decisions so destructive— destructive to the point of genocide, even omnicide? In particular, why do human beings have that dual power (1) to act totally counter to the good of their own kind and the whole biosphere, and thereby (2) to threaten the very viability of their own race and of the biosphere itself—a dual power that has led many to liken the human race in the twentieth century to a cancerous growth? How can process theology justify belief in God in a holocaust universe?

E. ETERNAL PRINCIPLES OF VALUE AND POWER

The answer I have suggested to this question is based on the notion that there are some necessary principles to which any world in the making would have to conform. These principles can be regarded as belonging to the essence of the eternal reality, which is a multiplicity of nondivine events with a divine center. If there has eternally been a realm of finite events, as well as a series of divine events, it makes sense to think of a set of eternal principles in terms of which finite events interact with each other and their divine center. The crucial implication of this doctrine of creation out of chaos or relative nothingness, in contrast to the traditional doctrine of creation out of *absolute* nothingness, is that these principles should not be thought to be arbitrary. They are eternal, not the result of a voluntary decision. They could therefore (by hypothesis) not have been otherwise. That is what is meant by calling them "necessary."

Among these principles is, by hypothesis, a set of correlative variables: (1) capacity for intrinsic good, (2) capacity for intrinsic evil, (3) capacity for instrumental good, (4) capacity for instrumental evil, (5) internal power, and (6) external power. There are really only four variables. The fifth is finally identical with the first two combined, and the sixth with the third and fourth combined. But discussing them as six variables helps to bring out the main point.

The two parts to the argument involve (1) showing that these variables do in fact always rise correlatively with each other, and then (2) suggesting that this *empirical* fact about our world is a *necessary* principle that would have to obtain in any world.

An adequate argument for the universality of the correlations in our world cannot be given here; a few illustrations must suffice. That the capacities for intrinsic good and intrinsic evil are correlated is obvious: we do not suppose that inorganic entities enjoy much value; neither do we worry about their pains. Only in those forms of life to which we attribute a significant capacity for suffering do we suppose there to occur a significant level of enjoyment. Only those creatures that have the capacity for enjoying the higher forms of value sometimes find their experience so miserable that they commit suicide.

This dual capacity for intrinsic good and intrinsic evil is, I said, identical with internal power. This is the power of self-determination, or self-creation. This is freedom in its most fundamental sense, the freedom to transcend to some extent the causal power of the past (including the immediate environment) in order to decide what one's reality in that moment will be. This freedom does not mean the power to be uninfluenced by the past. Greater freedom means, rather, a greater range of alternative ways to incorporate these influences. We assume that this internal power rises proportionately with the capacity for intrinsic value: we assume that mosquitoes have more freedom than amoebae, birds more than mosquitoes, apes more than squirrels, humans more than apes. The great human capacity not to be determined by environmental influences includes the capacity not to conform highly to the influences coming from the central power of the universe, the soul of the world, God. God's decision to lure the creative process on past the higher apes entailed bringing forth creatures who could sin—who could respond with a loud and deliberate *no* to the lure to live in harmony with the ecosphere out of which they emerged. God may not play dice, but God does take risks.

The riskiness of the cosmic adventure in which we are involved becomes even clearer when we recall that this increase in internal power entails a correlative increase in external power—the power to influence others, including the entire future. The evolutionary ascent from simpler to higher forms of existence brings forth entities with more and more power to affect others—for good or ill. This is a point for which lengthy discussion would be required, because in this reductionistic and nuclear age we have come to think of the most primitive entities, the subatomic particles, as having the most power to affect the environment.

I can here only mention three ingredients for an argument to the contrary. First, the power unleashed in a nuclear explosion is not based on any extraordinary power of the subatomic entities in themselves, but on the extraordinarily strong relations in which they exist within the nucleus, the so-called strong force. Free-floating protons and neutrons have no capacity to produce explosive effects. Second, the power of a nuclear explosion results from a chain reaction involving *billions* of subatomic particles; each particle involved is responsible only for a tiny fraction of the explosive power. Third, the destructive power of a nuclear explosion on the environment is due to the fact that that environment is composed primarily, quantitatively speaking, of other subatomic particles, which are susceptible to the influences of those involved in the chain reaction. These three points taken together suggest that individual subatomic entities are not more powerful than higher entities (molecules, macromolecules, cells, psyches); they only *seem* to be more powerful because there are so overwhelmingly many more of them. Much more powerful is the mind that can make a nuclear bomb (or the Mind that can make a star).

Assuming that that argument can be made, we can see otherwise that the correlation holds, as long as the power of one individual of a higher type is compared with the power of one individual of a lower type, not with that of billions. An animal has more power to change its environment than does a plant, although each may have the same number of cells; the higher animals have more external power than lower ones; human beings have changed the face of the earth more drastically in the past ten thousand years than all the other species combined did in the previous ten million years. We are the only ones with the power to understand and manipulate matter so as to unleash the otherwise dormant destructive power in the nucleus of the atom.

Each increase in external power is an increase in the capacity for instrumental good and evil. The most fundamental type of causal influence is the passing on of values one has enjoyed to others, as grist for their mills. In one moment I experience certain values as I appropriate influences from the environment and make my self-determining response to them. In the next moment these values, which were intrinsic values for me, became instrumental values for my bodily parts and (partly) through them for the world beyond. Insofar as the values I experience are harmonious, I will tend to be a good influence upon my body and the surrounding world; insofar as they are not, I will tend to make my body ill and be a destructive influence upon the things and persons around me. Likewise, my bodily cells realize intrinsic values in each moment, however lowly these values be in comparison with our enjoyment of Mozart or friendship. These cellular values, especially those in the brain, then become instrumental values for me. They can be such as to put me in agony or ecstasy.

Although a cell may seem a rather modest creature when compared with a human being, it is infinitely rich and complex compared with an atom. Atoms realize so few values, and accordingly have so little value to contribute beyond themselves, that animal experience could not be based directly upon a cluster of them. It was necessary to have the molecules, the macromolecules, the organelles, the eucaryotic cells, and finally the central nervous system composed of cells before any high-level animal experience was possible. By generalizing this principle, we can see why it was necessary that our present world be created through a long, evolutionary process. Even if, as anthropocentrists assume, we were the only creatures with significant intrinsic value, who alone could bring delight to our creator, it would not have been possible for beings such as us to have been created at the beginning of our world. The step-by-step process was necessary. This idea is central to the notion that the creator's power is evocative power, not unilateral determination. Only when an order of beings with adequate instrumental value is stabilized (say, molecules) can God possibly evoke into existence a higher order of beings (say, macromolecules). That new level, which has greater instrumental value, provides the necessary condition for the creator to evoke yet a higher order of existence (organelles, then eucaryotic cells, then multicelled plants and animals).

Each new level of existence has more creative good to contribute, but likewise more capacity to inflict destructive evil upon its environment. The increase in external power is simultaneously an opportunity and a risk. The creation of human beings meant a quantum leap in external power to be used for good or ill. When we contemplate the potential effects of combining this leap in external power with the great leap forward in internal power that made sin possible, we can imagine that the cosmic decision to go ahead with us was not a ho-hum matter.

This ends the summary of the first step of the argument, which is to show that the six variables do in fact rise proportionately. The second step is simply to postulate that this *empirical* correlation is a *necessary* one. There could not, by hypothesis, be a world in which these correlations did not hold. These correlations are therefore beyond divine decision.

But is it not audacious to claim that the creator had no other choice, to claim that the correlations that empirically hold among those six variables in our world are necessary principles that would hold in all possible worlds? Yes, this is an audacious hypothesis. But it is less audacious than the contrary hypothesis, which is generally accepted by traditional theists and traditional atheists alike. This is the more audacious hypothesis that the correlations holding in our world would *not* necessarily hold in some other world, so that there could be high intrinsic good with little capacity for intrinsic evil, or with little freedom to deviate from the divine will. Why more audacious? Because we know empirically that a world such as our own is possible. But we have *no experiential knowledge whatsoever that a world in which these correlations do not hold is possible.* To imply that it is possible, as many atheists do, by claiming that a creator, to be worthy of worship, should have created such a world, is to engage in groundless speculation. The speculation in the process theodicy offered here is the less fanciful one of supposing that certain aspects of our world are the way they are because they could not have been otherwise. (Because that language can be used to support the *status quo* with regard to all sorts of things that could well have been otherwise, I stress that I am positing necessity only for the most general structures of our world, not for the more specific structures, let alone any concrete events. Beyond the most general structures, contingency reigns.)

The premise of my argument is that God's purpose in gradually creating a world out of a relative chaos is to bring about centers of power with the capacity for realizing more and more intrinsic good (the first variable). The creator's aim is for creatures who find existence good, and increasingly so, which means creatures who can actualize more and more of those forms of value that are inherently good.

The point of the argument is that the realization of this aim is necessarily a risky business. Because one variable cannot be increased without simultaneously increasing all the others, creatures with greater capacity for intrinsic good necessarily have more internal and external power, therefore more capacity to be more evil both intrinsically and instrumentally. We can therefore regard the creator's purpose as unambiguously good, even though the resulting world is not. Because of the "law of the variables," the good cannot be realized without the risk of the bad, the better without the risk of the worse, the best without the risk of the worst. There is an old insight: *pessima corruptio optima*—the worst is the corruption of the best. A process theodicy says that this insight reflects a necessary principle inherent in the nature of things: not even God can have the best of all possible worlds without the danger of its being corrupted into the worst. In our time, this principle means that a world with beings that can compose and enjoy the music of Mozart, articulate and to some extent live in terms of the ideals of compassion and active love for all sentient beings, and penetrate to the fundamental laws of energy, is also a world in which suicide, genocide, and omnicide are possible. We could impugn the creator's wisdom or goodness in bringing forth such a world only if we could seriously say that it would be better if there were no humanlike beings at all.

A notion that is implicit in this argument, but that I had not previously made explicit, is the possibility of demonic power as an emergent product of the creative process.

F. THE DEMONIC

The religious imagination, not only in Christianity but in many other religious traditions, has thought in terms of a cosmic power for evil in deadly combat with the good God. Traditional Christian theism could not do justice to this intuition, but process theism can.

The "demonic" should be thought of as that which intensely opposes the Divine Creativity of the universe. Divine Creativity is creativity characterized by Perfect Creative Love and Perfect Responsive Love. This view provides a way of understanding the divine as trinitarian that does not at all compromise the unity of the divine subject. The creativity of the universe, conceived in abstraction, is neutral as between truth and falsehood, beauty and ugliness, good and evil. The false, the ugly, and the evil embody neutral creativity as fully as do the true, the beautiful, and the good. But creativity is in fact not neutral, and never has been. It is primordially characterized by both Responsive and Creative Love, the latter of which gives it a bias toward truth, beauty, and goodness. (God is thus the source of norms, thereby exemplifying the fifth feature of the generic idea of God.) None of the three dimensions—Divine Creativity, Creative Love, and Responsive Love—is derivative from the others; all are equally primordial. Each of these three dimensions of God is as essential to God's divinity as the others. God is necessarily creative and necessarily good: God's Creativity cannot be exercised other than as Creative and Responsive Love.

The reason why God is necessarily good is complex, but the basic idea can be briefly stated.[13] The perfect goodness of God follows from the divine omniscience. God's knowledge should not be conceived by analogy with sensory perception, which is a very indirect way of knowing. (In vision, for example, the information is transmitted by means of myriad photonic events and then millions of neuron firings in the optic nerve.) Nor should it be thought of as abstract, inferential knowledge, which has been called "knowledge about." If we think of God as the all-pervasive soul of the universe, we should think of God's knowledge of the world by analogy with our knowledge of our bodily members, which is "knowledge by acquaintance" of the most direct sort. In this kind of knowledge, knowledge is always sympathy, or compassion, meaning a knowledge that directly feels the feeling of the other. We naturally love our own bodies, in the sense of being naturally sympathetic with them. In terms of this analogy, we can see why God, as the all-inclusive soul of the universe immediately present to every part, naturally loves all creatures impartially, being incapable of feeling hatred or indifference to any of them. God's creative impulses into the world therefore naturally seek the health of the whole and of each of the parts. Divine Creativity always takes the form of Responsive and then Creative Love.

But in us it is quite otherwise. Even in us, to be sure, creativity is not completely neutral. Because we receive a creative impulse from God, we receive a bias toward truth, beauty, and goodness. Also, the creativity we receive from the past world had been affected by this divine bias. But we have our own creativity, with which we can either conform to or diverge from that bias. And the past world (which includes our own past self) in its day had its own creativity with which it could diverge from the divinely inspired bias. And the world has been going on for a long time. Long traditions or trajectories of antidivine biases have been established—kingdoms of the lie, of ugliness, of violence. We find ourselves born into such traditions. They have already molded our characters before we know another way. We feel, however dimly, the call to truth, beauty, and goodness, and we have the creativity inherent in us with which we could respond to this prevenient grace. But the habits of the world are hard to break. And what is more: rather than using our creativity to break free and imitate the Creative and Responsive Love of the Divine Creativity, we often use it to move in the opposite direction, to increase our hate and indifference.

The demonic is creativity insofar as it diverges strongly from the Divine Creative aims in a way that is violently destructive, and with hate or indifference rather than responsive love. So understood, the demonic is not merely a creature; it is a manifestation of a primordial power. And it is in real and deadly opposition to the creator. In another sense, however, it *is* a creature. It could not emerge until there were creatures with sufficient internal power to go strongly against the will of the creator, and with sufficient external power to be violently destructive. On our planet the demonic was only latent in worldly creativity until the appearance of human beings. The idea that the demonic is a creature of God is thus supported. Prior to God's creation of human beings, there was no demonic power at work on our planet.

It is because of the demonic that there have been holocausts, and that there may sooner or later be a holocaust to end all holocausts.

But why would God provide the conditions for the emergence of the demonic? Because it is inherent in the nature of reality that creatures with the capacity for the creation and enjoyment of the highest values must also have the capacity for the greatest destruction. To be capable of the conscious pursuit of truth, beauty, and goodness is to be capable of the demonic.

From the perspective of the "law of the variables," there is a simple answer to all those why-didn't-God questions: "Why didn't God create us with more capacity for enjoyment and less for suffering?" "Why didn't God give us more creative power and less destructive power?" Or the favorite in philosophy-of-religion circles: "Why didn't God create 'rational saints,' meaning beings like us in every way except guaranteed never to sin?" The answer in each case, I suggest, is that it would have been impossible. God could no more do those things than create a round square.

Accordingly, rather than those choices, the only choice we can imagine the creator facing was that between a world such as ours and a world with far less opportunity for good as well as for evil, a world, say, in which the highest creatures would be at the level of dolphins and chimpanzees, or—to avoid pain altogether—a world without life. Accordingly, from this perspective, one can say that this genocidal and potentially omnicidal holocaust world, with its demonic power, disproves the existence of a perfectly good creator only if one believes that such a being of perfect goodness and wisdom would have forsworn humanlike beings altogether, in order to avoid the risks. As long as we do not believe that, this theodicy succeeds in reconciling the generic idea of God with all the evils of this world, actual and potential, including the possibility of sudden total annihilation through nuclear holocaust.

Or at least it does when one more fairly distinctive aspect of process theology is added: this is the idea that God is not only the primordial and constant lure to creative advance, but also the universal sharer of all that results. This is implied by saying that God is Responsive Love as well as Creative Love. God delights in the enjoyments of creatures, but also shares all the pains, being literally sympathetic, compassionate. Process theology therefore takes seriously the Christian intuition that the crucified Christ symbolizes the suffering love at the heart of the universe, a notion that much traditional theism, with its doctrine of divine impassibility, could not affirm. The relevance to the present topic is that God never lures the creation to take risks that God does not share. Without this doctrine of divine co-suffering, we would have the image of God's egging our planet on from outside, perhaps for excitement in an otherwise too-tame cosmos, but without sharing the risk. From that standpoint, if the excitement leads to genocide, or even nuclear omnicide, it would have even less effect on God than the suffering of the belligerents in a cockfight has on the spectators. But in process theology, God is not an outside spectator who could view the creatures' agonies with apathy or even sadistic pleasure; God is the participating soul of the whole who shares all its feelings. God is in fact the only being who experiences all the evil as well as all the good. The risks into which our creator has led us are risks even more for her than they are for us. With this addition, we can affirm the goodness of our creator even less ambivalently.

G. MEANING AND HOPE

At this point it would be natural to object that this theodicy, in saving the purposiveness and perfect goodness of the world's creator, and thus the third and fourth features of the generic idea of God, has given up the sixth and seventh features: that God is the ultimate guarantee of the meaningfulness of human life and the trustworthy ground for hope in the ultimate victory of good over evil. These are further points on which I move beyond my previous theodicy.

The threat of meaninglessness in the face of the inevitability of death is probably the most distinctively human evil. We share with all or at least most other forms of life the capacity for pain, and with at least the other higher animals distress and loneliness due to the loss of loved ones and also the problem of boredom. But we are probably virtually unique in consciously anticipating our own death, and in facing the question as to whether the goodness of all the intrinsic value we have experienced is ultimately undermined by this anticipation. We can, of course, console ourselves with the sense that our lives have meaning because of the contribution we make to future generations. But we can also anticipate, besides our individual death, the death of all life on earth. The threat of annihilation through nuclear war or more gradual ecological deterioration renders that once remote problem immediate. It is said that the death of the human race would be the death of meaning itself, because it is alone the expectation of the continuation of civilization that finally undergirds our sense of meaning. That annihilation would also, it is widely thought, mean that evil was triumphant over good.

Not only does this double threat—of meaninglessness and the ultimate triumph of evil—suggest that there is no ultimate ground for meaning and hope, and therefore no reality worthy of the name "God"; it also raises in new form the question of the goodness of the creator, which we had presumably settled earlier. If there is no assured ground of meaning and hope in the face of inevitable death, how can we call good the creative power that brought forth creatures with the capacity for consciously anticipating their own death and that of the world as a whole? Better to have rested content with those innocent creatures who can enjoy their frolic in the sun untroubled by existential anxiety.

Process theologians have usually dealt with the question of ultimate meaning solely by further appeal to the Responsive Love of God, technically called God's "consequent nature." If God appreciatively preserves all that we have been, there is a ground for the ultimate meaning of our lives that nothing, not even nuclear holocaust—let alone moth, rust, and thieves—can take away.

This affirmation of ultimate meaning may seem pale in comparison with traditional pictures of the resurrection of the dead, the glorious arrival of the kingdom of God, and everlasting felicity. But it is quite bold in the face of the completely nihilistic pictures of the world that have become increasingly dominant in the last century. It provides at least minimally sufficient support for the requirement that any reality worthy of the name "God" provide an ultimate ground for meaning.

With regard to hope for the ultimate triumph of good over evil, process theologians have generally spoken with less confidence, but they have not been entirely mute. It can be suggested, on the one hand, that the consequent nature of God answers this question as well as that of ultimate meaning. Good is ultimately victorious in the sense that all value is preserved in the face of the eventual destruction and decay of all worldly structures, so that value and meaning, not destruction and meaninglessness, have the last word. With regard to the historical process, on the other hand, the Creative Love of God (somewhat inadequately signified by Whitehead as God's "primordial nature")[14] provides a ground for hope, if not assurance. Because of God as the source of novelty in the world, unforeseen and unforeseeable possibilities may arise that will render obsolete all the recent predictions of doom based upon projections of current trends. It has happened before and it may happen again, even in this "age of atrocity" and of ecological and nuclear nightmares. For example, God may successfully call us into a postmodern age, in which the economism, materialism, nationalism, competitiveness, militarism, and anthropocentric domination of nature that have characterized the modern age will be transcended. The much longer reign of patriarchy and androcentrism may even be overcome. With modern and postmodern technologies in the hands of postmodern persons and institutions with holistic visions, concerned primarily about the welfare of the planet and its sentient beings as a whole, a world with a much greater balance of good over evil—a relative paradise— could be fashioned. We cannot say that such a development will necessarily, or even probably, occur. But because of the creative, providential love of God, which time and time again has brought forth unexpected transformations, we can have a not wholly unrealistic hope that it will.

These affirmations are not, however, fully adequate. In the light of the world's manifold and often demonic evils and of our anticipation of death, both individual and global, these affirmations are not sufficient to allow many of the most sensitive souls to give an unambiguous yes to the process that has brought us forth, and therefore to the Holy Spirit that has inspired it.

The doctrine of the consequent nature of God by itself seems inadequate to the longing for meaning in three respects. First, most persons' desire for immortality seems not to be satisfied by the idea that they will be objectively immortal in God—unfadingly cherished in the divine experience. They desire more life, more experience, of their own. One can say, in reply, that this desire reflects an immature egoism, that true religious maturity involves the willingness to surrender our own egos, our own finite individualities, and to be satisfied knowing that we have made an everlasting contribution to the divine experience, which is alone appropriately thought to be everlasting. But that is just the point: most of us are not that mature. Most persons do not in the course of their earthly lives achieve that type of selfless sainthood. The process that brings us forth and nurtures us seems to instill a desire for life in most humans that is far from satisfied in the course of seventy some years— not to mention the high percentage of those who die at a far younger age. And this desire seems to be universal (even if not unanimous), not merely induced by contingent features of particular cultures. If that is the case, and yet if there is no continuing life beyond bodily death, cannot the universe be considered somewhat Manichean for instilling a desire that it will not fulfill?

This question becomes pressing for theodicy insofar as the conviction that this desire will not be fulfilled leads persons to feel that their lives are not sufficiently meaningful, and that this lack of sufficient meaning undermines the value of the biological pleasures, which other creatures enjoy less reflectively, and even the uniquely human joys of life. This consideration can add a new twist to the question of whether God was justified in bringing forth supersimian creatures, given our capacity to be so intensely aware of our own mortality. We may still answer yes, but this affirmation is made ambiguous if the universe is thought to have instilled in us a passion that is necessarily to be thwarted.

The doctrine of our objective immortality in God, when taken apart from any belief in life after death, seems inadequate as an answer to the question of the ultimate meaning of our lives for a second reason. According to this doctrine, our lives have ultimate meaning because of the contribution we make to the everlasting experience of God. But not all persons can, near the ends of their lives, hear this doctrine as good news. Whether for lack of opportunity, initiative, or some combination thereof, they have not made a contribution to the universe with which they can be content. The message that their lives, just as they were, with all their emotions and decisions, will be retained everlastingly as their permanent legacy would surely be heard as more a threat than a promise. It is, in fact, probably a small minority of the human race that can find significant meaning, especially meaning of a positive sort, in the doctrine that the permanent significance of their lives consists in the contribution to God that they have made during this life. This is the sense in which I agree with John Hick's charge that process theology, apart from a doctrine of a continuing life beyond the present one, is elitist (see chapter 9). Only with such a doctrine would it be possible to believe that everyone, not just a fortunate minority, could finally make a contribution with which they could be sufficiently pleased to find the doctrine of objective immortality in God a satisfactory answer to the need for ultimate meaning. (Life after death, incidentally, does not necessarily imply literal *immortality*. It might continue only as long as a desire remained to have more experience and to make more contributions.)

A third inadequacy of the doctrine of objective immortality by itself for the question of meaning is related to the fact, just intimated, that even in the framework of this doctrine we find much of our meaning not in the direct contribution of our experiences to the divine experience but in our indirect contribution to God by means of our contribution to other creatures, especially other human beings. The importance of these contributions can come to seem relatively minimal if we believe that the lives of fellow human beings end at death. Consider parents, for example, who have completely devoted themselves to their child-raising responsibilities for many years, working long hours at back-breaking jobs and trying to instill moral, aesthetic, and religious principles in their children, but whose children are then all suddenly killed before they have had a chance to fulfill most of their potentialities. Can these parents find sufficient meaning for their own lives in the doctrine of objective immortality if they believe that death completely ended all those young lives in the making? Will they not find much more comfort in the doctrine if they believe that those young souls, which had thus far not so much lived as been prepared to live, would have a chance to reap the fruits of all that preparation and then to make meaningful contributions to still others? In general, most of us will find our contributions to God *via* our contributions to others much more meaningful if we believe that those others are on a journey that continues past the present life.

The issue of life after death is at least equally important for the question of the ultimate victory of good over evil, especially that uniquely human form of evil we call the demonic. Demonic power wins its battles against divine power by seduction, intimidation, and destruction. Through seduction it develops those attitudes, emotions, beliefs, and habits that incline us to use coercive power violently with hate or indifference. It brings persons within the orbit where violence and the things it can attain are the seemingly natural way of life. Through their instrumentality the demonic then intimidates and destroys others' lives—and also seduces others into the use of violence. The cycle of violence is thereby perpetuated; in fact it is usually intensified, so that we should speak of the *spiral* of violence. If this life is all, then we must in a real sense say that the demonic is often victorious over the divine.

Most have been seduced into using or at least supporting the use of violence through fear, hate, indifference, greed, and other violence-sanctioning emotions. And certainly many persons—an unprecedented number in this century—have had their lives prematurely ended through violence or at least lived under the intimidation of violence.

Can we hope that the divine power will ever be victorious over the demonic, so that humans will come to be characterized by the fruits of the divine spirit, which is the spirit of peace? I have suggested above that such a hope would not be wholly unrealistic, even apart from any belief in a continuing journey with God after biological death. But it seems difficult for this hope to be held by realistic persons with more confidence than doubt. And, even to the degree that we can hold it, we cannot expect the victory of the divine over the demonic to be very complete. We can at best realistically hope that the present balance will be considerably shifted.

But within the context of belief in life after death, these restraints on realistic hope can be loosened indefinitely. The attractive, persuasive power of truth, beauty, and goodness is a subtle, usually slow-working power. But when it wins its victories, they tend to be permanent. Once a person has really tried living in terms of these fruits of the divine spirit, they are found to be intrinsically satisfying, much more so in the long run than the satisfactions gained from an allegiance to the values of the demonic, which can more quickly captivate a life. If this is true, then it would follow that the longer a soul exists, the more likely it will be to overcome subjugation to the demonic through allegiance to the divine power and its values. If we believe that our present life is simply a small portion of a much longer journey, then it becomes more realistic to hope with considerable confidence for the gradual victory of good over evil through the continuation of the same type of process that has been going on for the past several billion years.

The point made earlier would still remain valid: every increase in the capacity for good is also an increase in the possibilities for evil; but possibility does not mean necessity. Given all that the divine evocative power has done in four and a half billion years on this planet, and with our species in 50,000 years or so, we have a basis for hope that, given another comparable period, it could transfigure you and me. We could come to find nothing more attractive than truth, beauty, and goodness. We could come to worship the Holy Power with all our hearts, minds, and souls, and thereby to emulate it. We would therefore revere all the fellow creatures of this Holy Power, overcoming our hate and indifference, and eschewing violence. Good would have triumphed over evil, not by destroying the evil ones, but by transforming them.

This belief itself will, incidentally, increase the chances for a victory of the divine over the demonic even within what we normally think of as "history." Belief in life after death will give us courage to resist the intimidating power of the demonic. This belief, by making us less materialistic, will make us less devoted to those things that violence can be used to acquire or protect. Belief that others are on a long, sacred journey will make us less inclined to use violence against them. And the belief that the divine power will ultimately be victorious over the demonic will make us more committed to practice those virtues, and to envisage and institutionalize those structures, that will bring about more pacific relations here and now. One reason is that this belief will increase our conviction that the persuasive, evocative power of love is truly the ultimate power of the universe, the power with which we want to be in harmony.

There might also be an interconnection between hope for the history of our planet and actual life after death (as distinct from *belief* in it). It is possible, as many of those who believe in reincarnation hold, that at least part of our continuing journey would in some mysterious way involve subsequent lives on this planet. In this way, any sanctification that occurs in that continuing journey with God could have salutary effects on the future of the human race. There are too many problems with this notion to lift it up as more than a possibility. But I mention it as a contrasting example to the way in which most modern thinking about the ultimate balance of good and evil may have assumed a far too restricted framework.

If it be granted that belief in life after death could significantly affect our thinking about ultimate meaning and the ultimate victory of good over evil, the next question is whether we have good reason to accept this belief. Without repeating what I have written on this topic elsewhere,[15] I will mention two major points. First, although most process philosophers and theologians have not stressed this point, Whiteheadian-Hartshornean process philosophy does allow for the possibility of the continuation of experience after bodily death. And it does so without any violation of the notion that divine power works exclusively through persuasive, evocative influence. If God at some time evoked from human souls the capacity to survive apart from the physical body through which they were formed, this would have been simply one more example of the divine introduction of novel capacities within the created order. In any case, neither requiring life after death nor ruling it out *a priori*, this philosophy, as Whitehead pointed out, leaves the issue to be settled by empirical evidence.

Second, when I finally did look seriously at the empirical evidence some years ago (just the year after I had written my contribution for Stephen Davis' book *Encountering Evil*), I found it to be, both qualitatively and quantitatively, surprisingly impressive. It does not, by any means, dispel all possible doubts. But, looking at it with a philosophical framework that allows for the possibility of life after death and for the kind of evidence (parapsychological) that can count in its favor, I eventually came to conclude that the reasons for believing in some form of life after death are stronger than those for doubting it. All the relevant evidence, both positive and negative, seems more naturally explained in terms of the hypothesis that human life (at least sometimes) continues past bodily death than in terms of the hypothesis that it does not. I recognize that this suggestion, even as a possibility, will strike most persons in the academy today as somewhere between quaint and bizarre, but I cannot defend this suggestion here (beyond referring to the essay cited in note 15).

Although I have changed my mind on this issue, I do maintain the same stance I took in my earlier writings on theodicy, that belief in a continuing life, if included, should be an optional element, not necessary for the entire theodicy. And I still believe that process theology, apart from this belief, provides an adequate theodicy, especially in comparison with the other available options.

But I also believe, even more strongly than before, that the addition of this element can make this theodicy much more adequate, increasing greatly our enthusiasm for the adventure in which we are participants and our devotion to the divine power behind and in that adventure. This addition, in particular, can greatly strengthen process theology's fulfillment of the sixth and seventh features of the generic idea of God, concerned with meaning and hope. It can thereby also strengthen its fulfillment of the second feature, which is that this God is truly the Holy Power of the universe—the supreme, most effective power, with which we naturally want to be in harmony.[16]

Chapter 2

THE TASK OF PHILOSOPHICAL THEOLOGY IN THE FACE OF EVIL

Having summarized in the previous chapter my theodicy, including my criticism of some other dominant approaches, I respond in this and the following chapters to various critiques my earlier presentations evoked. The fact that these critiques were based on my earlier presentations, especially *God, Power, and Evil*, is doubly significant. On the one hand, many concepts and issues are discussed in the remaining chapters that were not treated in the summary statement in chapter 1. On the other hand, the position to which the critics were responding did not contain the ideas in the final two sections of chapter 1; in some cases those ideas provide the basis for me simply to say that I now agree with the criticisms. On most questions, however, I still defend the position articulated in *God, Power, and Evil*. In these remaining chapters, I hope to show that it is more adequate than some critics thought. In several cases, I seek to do this by using criticisms and suggestions of the critics to improve the articulation of this position.

The first issue to discuss is the task of the philosophical theologian in the face of the problem of evil. Two dimensions of this issue are treated. The first is whether the philosophical theologian needs to present a *theodicy*, meaning a plausible explanation of the world's evil, assuming the existence of God. The alternative position, defended most prominently by Alvin Plantinga, is that it suffices to present a *defense*, in which one merely shows that no logical contradiction is necessarily involved in holding the propositions that evil exists and that a perfectly good and powerful God exists. The second topic involves the relation between this formal issue of the task of philosophical theology and the substantive issue of the conception of divine power. I suggest that even those traditional theists who recognize the need for a theodicy, not simply a defense, tend to rest content with a relatively defensive theodicy because their idea of divine omnipotence allows them to believe this idea to have been revealed.

A. DEFENSE OR THEODICY? A RESPONSE
TO ALVIN PLANTINGA

Alvin Plantinga, I should say at the outset, did not write a critique of my position as such. Rather, he was drawn into a discussion of some features of my position through an article by David and Randall Basinger entitled "Divine Omnipotence: Plantinga vs. Griffin,"[1] to which he replied.[2] In their article the Basingers took for the most part the side of Plantinga, defending him against my contention that he holds a form of "I omnipotence." (This notion, which is discussed in chapter 3, refers to the traditional doctrine of omnipotence, which I claim to be Incoherent—unless it is held as part of an Idealistic worldview in which the creatures of the world are not actual in relation to God.) But the Basingers criticize Plantinga on one point. They believe the philosophical theologian needs to respond to the problem of evil by providing a theodicy, not simply a defense. Plantinga responds by clarifying and defending the idea of a defense.

"The Free Will Defense," says Plantinga, "is not a theodicy, and it is not an attempt to explain the existence of evil; it is a *defense*."[3] It is a defense against the charge that the proposition p, "God is omnipotent, omniscient, and wholly good," is logically inconsistent with the proposition q, "there is evil." To defeat this charge, Plantinga says, one needs a proposition r that is consistent with p and that, together with p, entails q. The way a defense differs from a theodicy is made clear by Plantinga's account of the conditions r need not meet in order to do the job:

> Clearly it need be neither true, nor probable, nor plausible, nor believed by most theists, nor anything else of that sort. . . . The fact that a particular proffered r is implausible, or not congenial to "modern man," or a poor explanation of q, or whatever, is utterly beside the point.[4]

In the light of this conviction, Plantinga takes issue with the following statement of mine, which the Basingers had quoted with approval:

Of course, one *can* extend the free-will defense to the subhuman realm, without positing any inherent power of self-determination to its entities, by pointing to the irrefutable possibility that all evils in this realm are due to Satan and his cohorts. But such a suggestion only returns us to the previous point about the general illumination that theism needs to provide to render itself plausible in our day.[5]

In relation to this passage, the Basingers said that Plantinga "has adopted a defensive, seemingly ad hoc manner of preserving the consistency of his position." In response, Plantinga says: "I fear the Basingers perpetuate a confusion Griffin perpetrates about defenses."[6]

Plantinga here seems to interpret disagreement with his project as confusion about it. The Basingers are not confused about the difference between their project and Plantinga's; they simply disagree with the adequacy of his approach. After saying that Plantinga is "only attempting to defend the consistency of belief both in God and moral evil," they say of their own theodicy that it "is not simply defensive."[7] In my own case, I had discussed at some length the approach represented by Plantinga and several others. Pointing out that their position on faith and reason is reminiscent of that of Leibniz, which I had earlier discussed,[8] I said:

These contemporary theists maintain that one's faith position on the existence and nature of deity need not be altered by any reasoning concerning the problem of evil, so long as it can be shown that no outright inconsistency is present in the believer's theistic position. And the believer can show this simply by suggesting possible hypotheses which remove the alleged inconsistency, even if these hypotheses are not considered probable.[9]

I had also quoted Plantinga's statement that "to rebut the charge of contradiction the theist need not hold that the hypothesis in question is probable or even true."[10] I then argued that, while that attitude may have been justifiable at the time of Leibniz and especially earlier, when the existence of God was not widely questioned, an approach based on that attitude is not adequate in our time. We need "a 'global argument,' the purpose of which is to show that a theistic interpretation can illuminate the totality of our experience, including the experience of evil, better than nontheistic interpretations."[11] For that purpose, the hypotheses reconciling God with evil must be plausible, not simply possible. It was to this discussion that I referred in saying that the hypothesis about Satan and his cohorts "returns us to the previous point about the general illumination that theism needs to provide to render itself plausible in our day." I was not, therefore, perpetrating confusion about Plantinga's position; I was disagreeing with it.

I will use Plantinga's response as the basis for explaining in more detail my reason for disagreeing. (Other issues raised in Plantinga's response are discussed in chapter 3.)[12] Plantinga calls his enterprise a "defense." Let us look more closely at his claim about what is needed for a successful defense:

> Griffin apparently thinks hypotheses about Satan and his cohorts implausible. . . . Their plausibility or lack thereof, however, has nothing whatever to do with their role in the Free Will Defense. That defense is aimed at establishing just one thing: that the relevant P and Q are jointly consistent. *Any* proposition, plausible or not, that is consistent with P and together with P entails Q will do the trick.[13]

But do we normally think that a successful defense of the consistency of two propositions has been rendered if the connecting hypothesis is highly implausible? That certainly is not the case in a criminal trial. In our system of justice, the burden of proof is indeed on the prosecuting attorney (just as the defender of theism puts it on the atheist), because the defendant is presumed to be innocent until proven guilty beyond a reasonable doubt. But this fact does not make the task of the defense attorney inordinately simple. The judge does explain to the jury that the defense attorney need not prove that the defendant is innocent; it is only necessary to introduce a reasonable doubt about guilt. But that phrase, *a reasonable doubt*, indicates the defense attorney's task. The judge takes pains to explain to the jurors that the mere existence of a *possible doubt* is not sufficient for acquittal. The doubt must be a *reasonable* one. No precise criteria can be given, to be sure, for distinguishing between a reasonable and a merely possible doubt, but an example can illustrate the point:

> Tom Jones, a well-known contractor in a small town, is accused of robbing the local bank. It is known that he had been out of work for several months, and that he had had difficulty making his payments. During the robbery in question, the mask fell off the robber's face momentarily, and several of the employees and other customers were certain that they recognized the robber as Tom Jones. The robber at that moment even called Sally the teller by name, telling her to hurry up. As the robber left, several people noted that he had a limp just like that of Tom Jones.
>
> At the trial, the defense attorney admits that there is considerable *prima facie* evidence against the defendant, Tom Jones. But, he claims, that set

of facts is consistent with the proposition that Jones is innocent. To show this consistency, he gives the following account: "On the morning in question, Tom Jones was abducted by aliens from another planet, who took him to their spaceship. One of them transformed himself so that he looked, and even walked, like Jones. He also telepathically took over the contents of Jones' mind, so that he knew everything that Jones knew, including the names of all his friends and acquaintances, such as Sally the teller. He then robbed the local bank." The prosecuting attorney then asks if the defendant would be willing to take a lie-detector test to support this story. The defense attorney replies that such a test would be irrelevant: before releasing Jones, the aliens had given him a post-hypnotic suggestion that he had robbed the bank and that he would remember nothing about the abduction, even subconsciously. On hearing that, the prosecuting attorney exclaims, rhetorically and triumphantly, "Then how did he tell the story to you?" "He didn't," replies the defense attorney calmly, "I made it up. But you must admit that it might be true. I have therefore shown that my client's innocence is consistent with all the facts. I therefore call on the jury to acquit him of all charges."

Would anyone say that the defense attorney had made a successful defense? Incidentally, being now less a "modern man" than when I referred incredulously to the hypothesis of Satan and his cohorts, I do not consider the type of events contained in the above story to be completely beyond the pale of possibility (except, perhaps, that any attorney would attempt such a defense). But if I were on the jury, I would not vote to acquit, and I doubt that Plantinga would either.

In any case, for the story to induce a reasonable doubt in the jurors, much more evidence would have to be introduced—that extraterrestrials could be on earth, that the powers attributed to them are possible, that a UFO had been seen in the area, and so on. Only if the defense attorney thereby turned the merely possible doubt into a reasonable one would we say that he had successfully defended his client against the charge that his innocence is inconsistent with the facts. Of course, if he failed to mount a successful defense, we would not necessarily say that the attorney was incompetent; we would more likely conclude that he had simply tried to defend the indefensible.

Why should anyone, therefore, think that Plantinga and others who take the same line have done anything worth doing, insofar as they invent merely possible hypotheses that show the existence of the God of traditional theism not to be logically inconsistent with the existence of evil? Does it have any relevance to the problem of evil as humans actually grapple with it?

To apply the analogy of the criminal trial to the question is already to give the traditional idea of God the benefit of the doubt. That is, to say that this God is presumed to be innocent (of nonexistence) unless proved guilty beyond a reasonable doubt is to assume that traditional theism has a privileged position in relation to atheism and nontraditional theisms. This assumption does not by itself make the efforts of the traditional philosophical theologian irrelevant to the problem of evil as it is widely experienced in our culture, because that assumption is still widely held. But these efforts do become irrelevant if they provide a defense based on hypotheses that are, to use Plantinga's words, "neither true, nor probable, nor plausible." If the argument of the philosophical theologian is really to be a defense of the God of traditional theism, it must at the minimum provide the basis for a reasonable doubt that that God is guilty of nonexistence.

Some critics of traditional theism have, to be sure, presented the case against it as if a strictly logical inconsistency were the crux of the matter. That presentation has provided defenders of traditional theism the opportunity for an easy victory. But what the critics should have meant, if they did not, is that there is no *plausible* way to portray the consistency of the existence of that God with the evil in the world. Only with this interpretation would the critics be speaking on behalf of the problem of evil as it is widely experienced in our culture; and only with this interpretation would the philosophical theologian's attempted defense of the traditional God have any relevance to the wider culture.

At the heart of my disagreement with Plantinga, it should now be clear, is the question of the task of the philosophical theologian. We are supported by our society, I assume, to think on behalf of this society about the distinctively cultural concerns of this society—that is, questions of meaning. Religious questions, dealing with matters of *ultimate* meaning, are the cultural questions *par excellence*. We are paid (not very much, to be sure, but enough to get by) and given time (usually not enough, but more than most others have) to reflect, speak, and write about these questions on behalf of society at large, and therefore in a way that could be helpful to others, if and when they hear or read our conclusions. I cannot see how anyone facing the problem of evil as a real problem (and not as merely a challenge to one's imaginative or logical ingenuity) would be helped by a "solution" whose truth, probability, and even plausibility are said to be "utterly beside the point." If we claim that the plausibility of our reflections is irrelevant, then *we* are irrelevant (beyond the narrow circle of our professional colleagues), not performing the cultural role our society has the right to expect of us.

As I indicated earlier, by referring to the difference between our cultural context and that of Leibniz, the task of the philosophical theologian is different in different times and places, insofar as widespread assumptions and questions are different. What I have said thus far has presupposed the appropriateness of assuming that traditional theism has a privileged position, so that its God is presumed innocent of nonexistence unless proven guilty beyond a reasonable doubt. Even given that assumption, I have argued, the free-will defense strategy proposed by Plantinga is inadequate. But if we take seriously the present cultural context, should we even make that assumption? Our present culture is rather pluralistic, and present trends suggest that it will become even more so in the coming decades. A considerable portion of the population, to be sure, accepts an idea of God that corresponds closely to the view Plantinga means to defend. But in most academic and other intellectual circles, atheism is the presumed orthodoxy. In liberal Christian and Jewish congregations, some form of nontraditional theism is probably the dominant view. In other circles, ideas of the Holy Reality deriving from Eastern religions are becoming widespread (to be sure, this development is probably more noticeable on the West Coast of California, where I reside, than in Grand Rapids, Michigan, or Notre Dame, Indiana, where Plantinga has spent the recent decades). In this pluralistic context, the most pertinent way to formulate the cultural question about the problem of evil is not: Can the God of traditional theism be defended against the suspicion of being guilty of nonexistence beyond a reasonable doubt? It is instead: Which of the available views provides the most consistent, adequate, and illuminating account of reality in general, and of the relation between evil and the Holy Power in particular?

Given this question, traditional theism would have to begin on all fours with a number of other views. In this context, the Plantingan type of defense would play no role in the discussions. The proponent of atheism, for example, would make no impression by simply pointing out that, given a wildly implausible hypothesis, the goodness and complex order of the world are not inconsistent with atheism. The atheist's task would be to show that one can, from atheistic premises, produce an account of the world that is intrinsically more convincing than the accounts that begin from different premises. In the same way, theists, whether traditional or nontraditional, would not presume that the burden of proof was on those who rejected their form of theism, but on themselves to show that their basic hypotheses lead to a more satisfactory interpretation of experience, all things considered, than do the others.

This is, admittedly, a much more demanding task, to which the proponents of the recently dominant orthodoxies—traditional theism and neo-Darwinian atheism—will not easily be converted. But this is the task that is appropriate to our increasingly pluralistic situation. And within this understanding of the task of articulating and defending a comprehensive worldview, I have no doubt that process theism will fare much better than either traditional theism or modern atheism.

How far Plantinga is from this viewpoint is shown by his brief discussion of theodicy, that "different enterprise" in which one "might try to explain why it is that God permits the various sorts of evil we do in fact find." In this enterprise, "a good explanation will not be unduly implausible."[14] Plantinga begins to suggest that the premises of his defense could also be premises for a not unduly implausible theodicy, at least for those who believe in God:

> One who does not believe in God, for example, may find the existence of free, nonhuman, immaterial persons such as Satan quite implausible; one who already believes in the existence of at least one such free, nonhuman, immaterial person—i.e., God—may find it much less implausible.[15]

But Plantinga quickly leaves this line of discussion to say that, if one believes in God (in Plantinga's sense), theodicy is not really necessary:

> Now of course it may turn out that the theist cannot think of a plausible explanation for the evil we find. . . . And this can constitute a problem for him. Perplexed and disturbed about a horrifying evil in his own life or the life of someone close to him, the believer may find it hard to trust God, may come to question God's goodness or his concern, may even come to rebel against God. His perplexity about God's reasons for permitting evil can thus precipitate a spiritual crisis.[16]

The possibility Plantinga does not entertain is noteworthy: he continues referring to the person as "the believer," not dealing with one of the most common possibilities—that the person simply quits being a believer. This point, plus the disconnection between the problem of evil as experienced by ordinary believers and the intellectual task of philosophical theologians, is illustrated by Plantinga's next remarks:

> But as an *intellectual* or *theoretical* problem it does not come to much. If God is good and powerful as the theist believes, then he will indeed have a good reason for permitting evil; but why suppose the theist must be in a position to figure out what it is?

This account of traditional theism as holding a privileged, virtually invulnerable position in the minds of believers is reinforced by Plantinga's concluding remark:

And now suppose the best the atheologian can do by way of an antitheistic argument from evil is to point out that theists do not have an explanation for evil: then theism has nothing to fear from him.[17]

In Plantinga's portrayal, theists and their critics (as well as, implicitly, Buddhists, Hindus, and others) are not equal participants in a common quest for truth. If we can generalize from the portrait of the traditional theist, each group is concerned only to protect its own fortress. Rather than asking what we might learn from the others, we take comfort in the thought that we have nothing to fear from them—we will not have to modify our own position simply because others point out that it does not explain the obvious facts of the world. The atheist could then say:

> I do not know why there is order in the world, especially such complex forms of order as human beings, given that there is no Orderer, or why there is so much goodness, given that the universe is indifferent, so that it does not promote goodness. But I do not need an explanation. If the world is a product of impersonal efficient causes, and the world has order and goodness, then obviously those impersonal causes have a way of producing order and goodness; but why suppose that the atheist must be in position to figure out what it is? If the best you theists can do by way of a theistic argument from order and goodness is to point out that atheists have no explanation for them, then we have nothing to fear from you.

Each group could indeed play this game. But is this the way forward? Is this defensive game one that we should want to play if we believe in God as the creator of our minds, with their desire for consistent, adequate, and illuminating explanations?

In any case, my reflections on the problem of evil have been predicated on the belief that a plausible theodicy is needed. And to be truly plausible, a theodicy should be part of an overall worldview, the credibility of which is portrayed in relation to other positions and in terms of the general criteria of rational consistency, experiential adequacy, and illuminating power.[18]

B. DIVINE POWER AND THE TASK OF THEODICY

No necessary connection exists between Plantinga's doctrine of God and his purely defensive approach to the problem of evil. The Basingers, as we have seen, defend this idea of God but also advocate moving beyond defense to theodicy. Bruce Reichenbach, operating with essentially the same notion of God, also says that an adequate defense of this idea of God in the face of the problem of evil must involve an explanation that is shown to be not only possible but also true, or at least plausible.[19] Nevertheless, a connection does in general exist between one's position on the substantive question of the nature of divine power and the formal question of the task of theodicy.

Those who hold to the traditional doctrine of omnipotence, according to which God can unilaterally determine events in the world, believe that God could bring about an infallible self-revelation: any self-determining power of the human medium can be overridden, so that no error due to human fallibility need creep in, at least no error regarding essentials. And those who believe that God could do this conclude quite often that God has in fact done so, with the Bible, for Christians, usually being assumed to be the primary locus of this infallible self-revelation.

Those who approach the problem of evil from this perspective tend to believe that the truth of their doctrine of God is externally guaranteed: it is known to be true because it was revealed. The theological task, accordingly, does not include the task of showing that the idea of God advocated provides the basis for a worldview that surpasses or at least equals any of its competitors in terms of the general philosophical criteria of self-consistency, adequacy to all facts of experience, and illuminating power. Theologians of this type feel no need to argue for the intrinsic excellence of their theistic worldview, because they believe its truth to be certified extrinsically. Bruce Reichenbach, for example, says that he rests his belief in the omnipotence of God solely on the fact that this doctrine is implied by various biblical statements.[20]

This attitude tends to give the theologian a relaxed attitude toward the problem of evil. It may be taken rather seriously—seriously enough to write profusely about it, and to struggle sincerely to find plausible explanations for why the world, if it is the creation of omnipotent goodness, seems to contain not only evil, but so much evil, even evil that is horrendous, unequally distributed, and so on. But the attempt to find answers to these questions is not finally serious. Failure is not decisive: if no plausible answer can be found, no change in the theologian's belief about God is called for. The remaining problems are simply relegated to the category of "mystery." The assumption is made that there *must* be answers, because the concept of God that generates the problem of evil is known to be true, prior to and independently of any solution to the problem of evil. If we human beings do not yet know the answer, and in fact even if we will never know the answer (at least in this life), that is no cause for rejecting the existence of God or revising the inherited concept of God. It is sufficient to reflect upon the fact that God, being all-wise and all-good as well was all-powerful, *must* have a good reason for causing or permitting these evils. The task of developing a theodicy, then, is more academic than existential. It is "merely academic," as we say, because nothing about the theologian's personal existence hinges upon it. One answers as many questions as one can, but the fact that several questions remain without a plausible answer creates no crisis. Everything remains the same.

The mentality I have just described is, of course, not unique to the believer in an infallible divine revelation. All of us with firm convictions—especially convictions about big, worldview questions, where much interpretation is involved so that decisively disconfirming tests are not possible—are reluctant to change them. Even the scientific community—which had been thought to be uniquely empirical, always ready to change its theories in the light of new evidence—is now understood to function in terms of "paradigms." When some empirical fact does not fit the dominant paradigm, it is less likely that the paradigm will be revised than that the fact will be denied or simply put aside as an anomaly, with "anomaly" being the scientist's equivalent for the theologian's "mystery." The power of the paradigm, or of deep-seated convictions, I recognize to be strong in myself. Not believing, for example, that the future is already settled, at least in its details, and therefore not believing in the possibility of precognition (in the literal sense of *knowing* future events), I go to great lengths to provide alternative explanations for ostensibly precognitive experiences.[21] And with regard to theodicy, there are questions to which I do not have answers that I find wholly satisfactory, and yet this fact has not led me to drop my position in favor of another position or agnosticism. The difference between traditional theologians, therefore, and other thinkers is at most a difference in degree.

A difference in degree, however, can be a big difference, and the positions of many traditional theologians do tend to approach the point of being invulnerable to criticism in principle. Criticisms that seem to their critics to be overwhelming, both in seriousness and number, are dismissed, seemingly casually. A particularly good example of this phenomenon is provided by Stephen T. Davis. When confronted with a problem that his position creates, but for which he can suggest no plausible answer, he simply says, "I just don't know." Questions to which he has given this reply include why God created beings God knew would be damned; why God created moral monsters; why God did not intervene to prevent the Jewish holocaust; and why God does not prevent natural evils.[22] John Roth (who shares Davis' view of divine power but rejects the idea of God's perfect goodness) has characterized Davis' position as an "I Just Don't Know Defense."[23]

Although no one else with whom I interact in this book goes as far in this direction as Davis does, the same tendency is present in various authors to various degrees. The strongest example is surely Plantinga's defense devoid of concern for plausibility, but in the thinking of Bruce Reichenbach, Nelson

Pike, John Knasas, and David Basinger the same tendency seems to be present to a degree. Theodicy is not a crucial test of the self-consistency, adequacy, and illuminating power of a theistic worldview. It is, rather, in Pike's words, "a noncrucial perplexity of minor importance," because God's existence, goodness, and omnipotence are taken as axiomatic.[24]

My position, by contrast, assumes that we have no infallible revelation. That assumption is based partly on the fact that no such revelation seems to exist, but partly on the fact that my understanding of the God-world relation does not allow any such revelation to occur. God could not be the only cause on some moment of human experience, and could not unilaterally cancel out the error-producing causality of creatures. Every event, including every moment of human experience, is inevitably influenced by the environment out of which it arises, and exercises self-determining creativity besides. Neither of these forms of finite causality can be canceled out or overridden by divine causation. God's influence is always, in a sense, one causal influence among many; it cannot ever be simply *the* cause. From this perspective I assume that all ideas of God are human constructions. I do believe that the awareness of God's reality is based upon authentic experiences of the Holy Power of the universe, which in our tradition we call God. The ideas formed of God are not *simply* projections; they are not *simply* created out of whole cloth. But they are *largely* created, more constructed than given.

The truth of our ideas of God, therefore, cannot be simply assumed, but must be tested similarly to the way other ideas are tested. The fact that ideas of God are human constructions does not mean that they cannot be true, in the sense of corresponding somewhat well with reality; all of our ideas, including our ideas about sensory objects, are human constructions, and they can be more or less true. The implication of the realization that all ideas of God are human constructions is that no one idea of God should be treated as if it had a privileged position, meaning that it is presumed true unless proven false. As argued against Plantinga above, the theologian's task cannot be limited to defending one's inherited view of God against criticisms, as if to show that it cannot be disproved is to show that it is true, at least closer to the truth than other conceptions of the Holy Reality. After all, ingenious theologians of other traditions can surely do equally well in fending off disproofs of their tradition's idea of the Holy Reality. The recognition that all ideas of God are human constructions, so that none of them should be treated as innocent of falsehood until absolutely proven guilty, implies that the test of one's idea of God must be positive as well as negative. The truth of a particular idea of God can be argued only by showing that this idea leads to, or is an integral part of, a portrayal of reality that is more (or at least not less) self-consistent, adequate to our experience, and illuminating of our experience than other views.

Within this context, the presence of serious and multiple "anomalies" or "mysteries" in one's position counts against it. Besides not being positively self-contradictory, a position should be adequate and illuminating. To be adequate is to be at least minimally consistent with all the relevant facts of experience. To be illuminating is to go beyond bare adequacy to throw fresh light on things, to allow us to see features of the world or our experience that we had not seen before, at least as clearly and consciously, to give us an "aha!" experience, in which previous puzzles are solved. Every time we can avoid inconsistency only by giving an implausible hypothesis, every time we must say "I just don't know," we are pointing to some fact to which our theory is definitely not illuminating and perhaps not even adequate. Once we realize that our conception of God is not privileged, we cannot be indifferent to this absence of adequacy and illuminating power.

I will conclude this discussion by pointing to a disconcerting feature of discussions with those who believe their own doctrine of God to be externally certified by its revelatory origins. The criteria employed by those who consider their doctrine of God to be extrinsically validated in this way can be called "privileged criteria." By those criteria, nothing short of an outright logical contradiction, and sometimes not even that, counts seriously against the conception of God. The criteria of consistency, adequacy, and illuminating power can be called "nonprivileged criteria." The disconcerting feature to which I refer is that some authors use nonprivileged criteria when judging other thinkers' positions, but then employ privileged criteria with regard to their own position. We all tend to do this to some extent. But believers in the traditional idea of omnipotence seem to do it more.

Defenders of traditional theism can, to be sure, defend this practice on their part in terms of their basic assumptions; because they believe that their idea of God is derivative from God's own self-revelation, not from human speculation, they have the right, in fact the duty, not to treat this idea of God as if it were on all fours with others. For them to assume that this idea of God had to stoop, as it were, to the level of proving itself true in terms of human philosophical criteria would be for them to be disingenuous and unfaithful to their starting point. An idea that is truly from God, furthermore, should be above reason; the fact that it goes beyond what our finite minds can comprehend is part of the evidence that it is indeed from God. All this and more can be said.

I am not saying, however, that traditional theists are inconsistent in employing privileged criteria with regard to their own position and nonprivileged criteria with regard to other positions, such as mine. My point in this section is precisely this, that different substantive ideas about divine power tend to support different formal positions on the proper approach to the problem of evil. I mention this oscillation between two sets of criteria only, first, to point out that it does play a role in the discussions and, second, to register the fact that it *is* disconcerting. It prevents much of the discussion from being properly philosophical. In a properly philosophical discussion, as I understand it, one's own positions are to be judged with the same rigor, and in terms of the same criteria, as other positions are judged. One of the many reasons for opposing traditional theism is that it tends to discourage properly philosophical discussion of religious concerns.

Chapter 3

THE TRADITIONAL DOCTRINE
OF OMNIPOTENCE

In this chapter, I examine two criticisms of my characterization of the traditional doctrine of omnipotence. The first criticism, made by Bruce Reichenbach and the Basingers, is that the concept of "I omnipotence," which is contrasted with process theism's doctrine of "C omnipotence," is flawed, and does not apply to traditional free-will theists, such as Alvin Plantinga. The second criticism, leveled by Plantinga, Nelson Pike, and Stephen Davis, is that my account of the traditional doctrine of omnipotence does not really correspond to the views of most traditional theologians.

A. I OMNIPOTENCE, THE OMNIPOTENCE
FALLACY, AND PLANTINGA'S POSITION

The word "omnipotence," besides being fraught with various connotations—comforting to some, horrifying to others—is ambiguous. It can be taken literally to mean at least the following: (1) having power over all; (2) having all the power; (3) having all the power it is possible (for one being) to have. Less literally it can be taken to mean (4) having the most power, being the supreme power, being more powerful than everything else; this supremacy of power can be taken (as it is by Nelson Pike[1]) to mean (5) the power to overpower everything else. This meaning can be seen as an explication of the first literal meaning: having power over all. Perhaps even more important than the word's ambiguity are the connotations it carries in our culture and the images it evokes. It tends to suggest overwhelming, coercive power, and to evoke images of an almighty, crushing, cosmic hand, wielding the thunder and lightning, determining drought and death; in our time it evokes images of nuclear apocalypse.

Because of these connotations and ambiguities, and the widespread hearing of the word to mean simply having all the power, or at least the power to overpower everything else and therefore the power to control everything, I have decided since writing God, Power, and Evil that it is probably futile to try to salvage the word.

In that book, however, I did try to use the word positively. My strategy was to begin with the third of the literal meanings of omnipotence mentioned above: having all the power it is possible for one being to have. Then I distinguished between two ways of fleshing out that formal meaning, which I labeled "I omnipotence" and "C omnipotence," indicating thereby that one concept is coherent, the other incoherent. It is incoherent, I argued, to say that God simply has all the power, either actually or potentially. And the view that God can simply override the power of creatures finally reduces, I suggested, to this monopolistic view. Put otherwise, it is incoherent to attribute to God omnipotent coercive power, meaning the power unilaterally to bring about events in the world. Once it is realized that this concept is incoherent, the way is opened to reconceiving omnipotence. The term can be used for power that is not controlling, all-determining power. One can in fact speak of "persuasive omnipotence," indicating that the greatest power one being could possibly have is persuasive power. The term "omnipotence" can be used because the other concept of omnipotence, being incoherent, provides no standard by which to call a God with "merely" persuasive power finite or imperfect.

Although I am now less convinced of the wisdom of this approach, and suspect that we should simply abandon the notion of omnipotence rather than trying to reconceive it, I still believe that this approach, in philosophical discussions, has some rhetorical advantage. The distinction between two concepts of omnipotence can be useful in raising the question of whether the traditional concept is really meaningful. In any case, in this discussion of critiques of my distinction, I continue to employ the language of omnipotence for process theology's understanding of divine power as well as for the traditional understanding.

Although my distinction between I and C omnipotence has been astutely criticized by Bruce Reichenbach[2] as well as the Basingers,[3] I respond primarily to the critique by the Basingers because, besides the fact that it is probably better known, it is also more extensive so that response to it will better bring out the various issues. The Basingers' critique is contained in the essay by them that was mentioned in chapter 1, in which they defend the position of Alvin Plantinga. This critique is part of an argument that, as carried through by David Basinger, will be examined in chapter 5, which is that a free-will theodicy based upon the traditional doctrine of omnipotence can be as adequate as a process theodicy. The Basingers' discussion is seriously flawed through distortions of my meaning, distortions sometimes based on misquotations. But their critique, along with Reichenbach's, does reveal that some of my formulations need to be improved.

My definition of C omnipotence is based on the idea that to be actual is to have power, both the power of self-determination and the power to exert causal influence upon others. Any world that God could create would therefore necessarily be composed of beings with this twofold power of self-determination and efficient causation. To say that this twofold power is possessed by the finite beings comprising the world means that it cannot be withdrawn or overridden by any other being or beings. Given this definition of what a "world" is, an "omnipotent being," meaning one with *all the power it is possible for one being to have*, could not, if a world exists, simply have *all the power*. Nor could an omnipotent being completely determine the activities of the other beings, because "it is not logically possible for one being completely to determine the activity of another entity that by definition has activity that is underived from any other being."[4] An omnipotent and perfectly good being, therefore, not being able unilaterally to determine any state of affairs in a world, could not possibly guarantee the absence of all genuine evil in any world, because what happens will necessarily "be partly due to the worldly entities themselves."[5] Calling this view C omnipotence, I pointed out that the C can stand for *coherent* and *creationistic*, for these reasons:

> It is the only view that is coherent if one is talking about the power a being with the greatest conceivable amount of power could have over a *created*, i.e., an actual, world. If the world is an actual creation, and not simply a complex idea in the divine mind, or simply aspects or "modes" of God, then all-powerful cannot mean having all the power. And if there are many centers of power, then no state of affairs in which these entities are involved can be completely determined by any one of them.[6]

With this review, we can see that the Basingers' account of C omnipotence distorts it. They say:

> The proponent of "C" omnipotence maintains that it is not logically possible for God to unilaterally control the activities of self determining [sic] beings, even if such activities are intrinsically possible.[7]

Whereas I said that God could not unilaterally control the activities of *actual beings*, they speak of *self-determining* beings.

With their rewording, my controversial definition becomes tautologous for anyone who is an incompatibilist, meaning one who believes that an individual's freedom (in the sense of self-determination) is incompatible with its being fully determined by another being (God) or beings (the past). The Basingers' statement of C omnipotence in fact makes compatibilism *the* issue: one is an exponent of C omnipotence in their view if one affirms self-determining finite beings and is an incompatibilist. On this basis, they call Plantinga an exponent of C omnipotence.

Some of my statements, however, do provide openings for their interpretation, because these statements, taken by themselves, do not take account of the distinction between the free-will and the all-determining versions of traditional theism. One of these statements is the following: "The logic of C omnipotence would then involve the *denial* of the principle that God can unilaterally effect any state of affairs that is in itself intrinsically possible."[8] That statement, taken out of context, could open the door to designating any incompatibilist free-will theist an exponent of C omnipotence, because of the following point on which my argument turns: a state of affairs in which a human being performs an act freely is an intrinsically possible state of affairs (if one is not a determinist), and yet it is a state of affairs that God as an omnipotent being could not unilaterally effect (if one is an incompatibilist). This is a purely logical point: if God unilaterally effects an act or in any way infallibly causes the human being to perform it, the human being by definition has not performed it freely.[9] Because Plantinga affirms this principle— indeed, I used him as one of my chief witnesses on its behalf[10]—it could seem that he would be thereby advocating C omnipotence.

When taken in context, however, it can be seen that Plantinga's position is not an exemplification of what I meant by C omnipotence. For one thing, my next sentence says: "Although an actual world without genuine evil is possible, it is impossible for an omnipotent being to guarantee such a world." This statement does *not* say: If an actual world happens to have some beings that, besides being actual are also self-determining, then an omnipotent being cannot guarantee that this world will be devoid of genuine evil. My statement indicates instead that this guarantee is impossible in *any* actual world (because any actual world would necessarily be comprised of self-determining beings). That is a point that Plantinga does not hold. He believes that an actual world without self-determining beings is possible, and that God could have guaranteed a world without genuine evil by creating such a world.

The proper meaning of C omnipotence is also clearly indicated by the more general context, in which the "omnipotence fallacy" is the main topic.

This fallacy consists in moving from the statement that, if a particular state of affairs is intrinsically possible, an omnipotent being can (unilaterally) bring about that state of affairs.[11] The argument is fallacious because it oscillates between a *possible state of affairs* and a *possible action* (bringing about a possible state of affairs), thereby committing the four-term fallacy.[12] To have a formally valid argument, I said, one would need to add premise Q: "If a state of affairs among a multiplicity of actual beings is logically possible, it is logically possible for one being unilaterally to bring about that state of affairs."[13] (I will come back later to an inadequacy in this statement.) To accept *that* premise, I continued, one would need to accept premise X: "It is possible for one actual being's condition to be completely determined by a being or beings other than itself."[14] There is nothing here about actual beings that are *also* self-determining beings; the statement is about actual beings as such. I argued that we should reject X and thereby the idea that *any* actual being's condition could be completely determined by a being or beings other than itself. This rejection of X and therefore of Q would mean in turn that we should reject the idea that an omnipotent being could unilaterally bring about any state of affairs in an actual world. The mere fact that a state of affairs is intrinsically possible is not a sufficient basis for saying that God can bring it about; whether God can bring about any state of affairs among the creatures is partly up to them.

The Basingers claim that Plantinga "cannot be justly accused of committing the omnipotence fallacy."[15] Their claim, however, is contradicted by the following statement, which I had quoted from Plantinga as a prime example of the fallacy:

> An omnipotent being . . . can perform (roughly) any logically consistent action; hence either it is a logically necessary truth that evil exists or else God is able to eliminate any case of evil whatever. No reputable theologian, so far as I know, has held that the proposition *There is evil* is logically necessary; accordingly, I shall assume henceforth that God can eliminate every case of evil whatever.[16]

That statement exemplifies the omnipotence fallacy as clearly as possible. From the assertion that a state of affairs devoid of evil is logically possible, it moves to the conclusion that, because God can perform any logically consistent action, God can (unilaterally) bring about a state of affairs in which no evil exists. Plantinga can make that move because he believes that there can be actual beings that can be completely determined by God. This belief means that he accepts premise X: "It is possible for one actual being's condition to be completely determined by a being or beings other than itself."[17]

The Basingers base their claim that Plantinga does not commit the omnipotence fallacy on the assertion that he *rejects* X. But they can make this
claim only by again changing my wording. They reword X to read:

> It is possible for one actual self-determining [sic] being's condition to be
> completely determined by a being or beings other than itself (GPE
> 264).[18]

As can be seen, that is a direct quote of premise X, except that, as before, where
I say simply "actual being's" the Basingers insert the term "self-determining"
into the statement. That addition, of course, changes the whole meaning. Although Plantinga believes that actual beings that are not to any degree self-
determining can and do exist, and in fact that most actual beings are of this
nature, he is, thanks to the insertion of the qualifier "self-determining," portrayed as rejecting premise X and as therefore affirming C omnipotence.

The opposite of C omnipotence in my discussion is *I omnipotence*, which
follows from the acceptance of premise X (with *my* wording). It is the view
according to which an omnipotent being *can* unilaterally effect states of affairs among actual beings (assuming that those states of affairs are logically
possible). The "I" can stand for incoherent, I said, because "such a definition
is incoherent if it refers to an omnipotent being's dealings with an actual
world." Or the "I" can stand for idealistic: this form of omnipotence is coherent only if worldly entities are thought of as ideal beings in the divine mind,
because the only beings in our experience whose activities we can unilaterally determine are the ideas in our own minds.[19]

The Basingers find my treatment of Plantinga in relation to I omnipotence confusing. On the one hand, I had cited Plantinga as an advocate of I
omnipotence, as just discussed. On the other hand, I quoted Plantinga as a
witness against the application of the logic of I omnipotence to human beings. John Mackie had made this application by wondering why an omnipotent God would not have made free but sinless human beings, saying (in the
paradigmatic example of the omnipotence fallacy): "If their being of this sort
is logically possible, then God's making them of this sort is logically
possible."[20] Plantinga pointed out that this assertion is inconsistent if it
means that "God creates free men and brings it about that they always freely
do what is right."[21] We cannot indict God for the fact that human beings do
not remain sinless, because whether free beings "would always do what is
right would presumably be up to them."[22] Having cited Plantinga as exemplifying the omnipotence fallacy and as thereby affirming I omnipotence, and
also as protesting against the application of I omnipotence to human beings,
I concluded: "Plantinga evidently affirms the logic of I omnipotence in general, and applies the doctrine of C omnipotence only in relation to human

beings."[23] The Basingers call this description "exceedingly confusing," because, they say, " 'I' omnipotence, as it is first defined by Griffin, is a universal statement, and universal statements obviously admit of no exception."[24]

The Basingers' depiction of my description of Plantinga's position as exceedingly confusing is exceedingly exaggerated. I had built the possibility of an exception into the idea of I omnipotence from the outset. Several pages earlier, in discussing whether we should accept premise Q ("if a state of affairs among a multiplicity of actual beings is logically possible, it is logically possible for one being unilaterally to bring about that state of affairs"), which is said to be entailed by I omnipotence, I said: "It has been accepted by all traditional theists (although some have excluded states of affairs among some actual beings, such as human beings, from its scope—see pages 271–72 [that should have been 270–71], below."[25] That page reference is to my discussion of Plantinga as affirming I omnipotence in general and C omnipotence in relation to human beings. Accordingly, the revision of the formulation of I omnipotence required by this exception is easily inferred. The revised formulation could read: "I omnipotence" involves the doctrine that an omnipotent being can unilaterally effect any intrinsically possible state of affairs among at least some type of actual beings. In other words, one affirms I omnipotence if one believes that *any* (in the sense of *some*) state of affairs in the world can be unilaterally brought about by an omnipotent being. Whether or not one affirms that this is true not only of some but of *all* (intrinsically possible) states of affairs is an important, but secondary, question.

Nevertheless, although my meaning can be ferreted out from the text without much difficulty, some of my formulations do create unnecessary confusion, and should be improved. In the first place, consider premise Q:

> Q: If a state of affairs among a multiplicity of actual beings is logically possible, it is logically possible for one being unilaterally to bring about that state of affairs.[26]

Taken by itself, without the qualifying statement cited in the previous paragraph, this formulation is clearly inadequate. It seems to say that *any and every* such state of affairs could be brought about by one being, such as an omnipotent God. But that is just the point that is denied by traditional free-will theists such as Plantinga. A state of affairs in which three persons freely exchange phone numbers is a logically possible state of affairs, but no one being, even an omnipotent God, could unilaterally bring about that state of affairs. This is true, in any case, for all of us who reject the idea that divine determination and human freedom are compatible. Rather than giving that inadequate formulation and then qualifying it in a later sentence, I should have given this formulation (which can be called Q_i for improved Q):

Q_i: It is logically possible for one being unilaterally to bring about a state of affairs among a multiplicity of actual beings.

This improved formulation does not say that *any and every such* (logically possible) state of affairs can be thus brought about, only that at least some such states can. This reformulation makes the principle relevant to traditional free-will theists as well as to all-determining theists.

I also should not have said that Plantinga "applies the doctrine of C omnipotence . . . in relation to human beings," because that statement can easily be taken to mean that he affirms the doctrine of C omnipotence, which he does not. Rather than implying that Plantinga affirms the doctrine of C omnipotence in relation to (what he takes to be) a restricted class of actual beings (namely, self-determining ones), I should have said that the *reasoning* applied by advocates of C omnipotence to the relation between divine power and nondivine actual beings is applied (at least generally)[27] by Plantinga to the relation between divine power and (what he takes to be) a restricted class of actual beings—namely, ones that have been given the additional capacity (beyond actuality) of self-determination. Plantinga, in spite of the Basingers' claim, does not accept C omnipotence. Because he accepts X ("it is possible for one being's condition to be completely determined by a being or beings other than itself"), he accepts Q_i. By virtue of affirming Q_i, Plantinga can be seen to be an exponent of I omnipotence, holding that God can unilaterally effect states of affairs in an actual world.

Another concept needing an improved formulation is the concept of *I omnipotence* itself. This concept was defined as "the traditional doctrine that an omnipotent being can unilaterally effect any state of affairs, if that state of affairs is intrinsically possible." As the Basingers point out, my formulation was ambiguous, being open to two readings:

I_1:   There exists no intrinsically possible state of affairs devoid of evil that an omnipotent God cannot unilaterally bring about.

I_2:   There exist intrinsically possible states of affairs devoid of evil that an omnipotent God can unilaterally bring about.[28]

Because my formulation was open to the former reading, it is adequate for only some traditional theists. It is adequate for omnipotence as understood by traditional all-determining theists such as Thomas and Leibniz, who believed divine determinism to be compatible with human freedom, and those such as Luther and Calvin, who denied human freedom; but it is not adequate for traditional free-will theists, such as Plantinga, who affirm human freedom and reject compatibilism.

Plantinga, in fact, says: " I enthusiastically reject what David Griffin calls 'I-omnipotence.' "[29] He is able to do this by reading it in the sense of I_1. After citing my definition, he interprets it thus:

Perhaps another way to put this is to say that God has I-omnipotence if and only if every state of affairs possible in the broadly logical sense is such that it is within God's power to cause it to be actual. But then, surely, God does not have I-omnipotence. For while the state of affairs consisting in Eve's freely taking the apple is possible, it is not within God's power to cause it to obtain.[30]

I_2, which corresponds to Q_i, brings out more clearly what I intended. It allows for the existence of some intrinsically possible states of affairs— namely, the acts of self-determining beings (taken to be a restricted class of actual beings)—that God cannot unilaterally bring about, while I_1 does not. Many antitheists, such as John Mackie, have criticized theism on the assumption that it is committed to the doctrine of omnipotence expressed in I_1. This doctrine, however, is rejected in favor of I_2 by Plantinga and other traditional free-will theists who believe, in the Basingers' words, "that God could have unilaterally 'brought about' a world containing no evil if he had chosen . . . to actualize a possible world containing no self-determining individuals other than himself."[31] Mackie's criticism therefore fails. But I_2, it should be noted, is still a statement of I (incoherent) omnipotence.

From the Basingers' point of view, in which incompatibilism versus compatibilism is the main issue, Plantinga's rejection of I_1 means that his view of omnipotence is closer to mine than it is to that of Leibniz and most other classical or traditional theists. Plantinga and I are so close, the Basingers think, because our position "differs with Leibniz (and most other classical theists) on the fundamental question of whether freedom necessarily limits God's power."[32] That is, because Plantinga and I both reject compatibilism, we hold that creaturely freedom, which we both affirm, entails that God does not and cannot simply cause everything.

From my perspective, however, while I am always happy when persons show good sense by rejecting compatibilism, the "fundamental question" lies elsewhere. Although much of the Basingers' article is written as if they did not recognize this fact (and as if incompatibilism were the main issue for me, too), they finally do recognize it. They see that for me the fundamental question is "whether every actual world must necessarily contain self-determining entities and hence whether an omnipotent being can unilaterally bring about any world devoid of genuine evil."[33] The answer given to that question by Plantinga and most other traditional free-will theists, besides seeming incredible on other grounds, seems to me to make a plausible theodicy impossible.

I take up this issue in chapter 5. For now I turn to the question of whether my characterization of the traditional view of omnipotence is historically accurate.

B. DO TRADITIONAL THEOLOGIANS EXEMPLIFY THE "TRADITIONAL" DOCTRINE OF OMNIPOTENCE?

Alvin Plantinga, Nelson Pike, and Stephen Davis claim that what I call the traditional doctrine of omnipotence is not in fact exemplified by all or even most traditional theologians. I respond to the three of them in order.

In response to the Basingers' statement that most influential classical or traditional theists—for example, Augustine, Aquinas, Luther, and Calvin— have affirmed I omnipotence, Plantinga argues against the idea that there is "any one conception of God's omnipotence common to classical theists."[34] Plantinga's argument depends on the fact that he, like the Basingers, defines I omnipotence as essentially including (1) compatibilism and (2) a limitation to intrinsically possible states of affairs. On that basis, he holds that only some traditional theists, such as Leibniz, clearly affirmed it. He excludes Aquinas and Augustine on the grounds that they, he alleges, do not consistently affirm compatibilism. Luther's thought on this issue he does not know, he says, and he knows of no passage in which Calvin "discusses the question whether omnipotence consists in being able to actualize just any possible state of affairs" or from which we can infer this view. However, I reply, if I omnipotence is the doctrine that God can unilaterally effect states of affairs among actual beings, all these thinkers assumed it.

Furthermore, I had shown that all these theologians had affirmed it with regard to human acts (even though this is not essential to I omnipotence). Plantinga raises doubts about Augustine on the basis of *De Libero Arbitrio* (*On Free Will*). But I had shown that, after this and other early writings, Augustine clearly affirmed I omnipotence in the compatibilist sense.[35] While conceding that Aquinas "at any rate pays lip service to the claim that God has I-omnipotence," Plantinga thinks that Aquinas rejects it implicitly by denying that God can restore a fallen woman to virginity. In a peculiar argument, Plantinga says that the question is this:

> Can God now bring it about that Miss X is a virgin—i.e., that she is not now and never has been a fallen women? *That* state of affairs—*Miss X's being now a virgin*—is indeed possible, but Aquinas concludes that it is not within God's power to cause it to be actual.[36]

But for Aquinas the question here is whether God can change the past—or, more precisely, whether God can bring it about that what happened did not happen. In Aquinas' view, that question is in the same category as whether God can make a round square. His denial is therefore in no way a denial that God can unilaterally bring about all intrinsically possible states of affairs. With regard to Calvin, I had quoted passages in which he said that God is the sole cause of all motion, that the "plans and intentions of men" as well as the movement of inanimate objects are totally controlled by God, that a man cannot turn himself "hither and thither by the free choice of will," and that the distinction affirmed by some theologians between God's "doing" and God's "permitting" is bogus.[37] So, whether Calvin explicitly discussed the issue in a contemporary philosophy-of-religion manner, he clearly affirmed the idea that Plantinga uses as a litmus test for I omnipotence: that all human acts can be unilaterally determined by God. I also showed that Luther's views on this issue are the same as Calvin's. One can, to be sure, argue that they (especially Luther) are, like Plantinga, incompatibilists, denying that divine determination is compatible with human freedom. But this judgment does not mean that they, like Plantinga, believe that some intrinsically possible states of affairs cannot be unilaterally determined by God; it only means that they deny human freedom (Luther the more consistently).

All these theologians, therefore, hold essentially the same view, saying that God can and in fact does unilaterally determine all states of affairs in the world, including the "free" decisions of human beings, if such be affirmed. Furthermore, given what I meant by I omnipotence, even this much agreement is not necessary. All that is required is that God *could* unilaterally determine all events in an actual world. I defined the traditional idea of God as holding that "God controls, or at least could control, every detail of the events of the world."[38] For an incompatibilist such as Plantinga, if God unilaterally brings about all events in the world, then there can be no genuinely free acts; but if God were willing to forgo free acts on the part of the creatures, God could unilaterally determine all events.

Plantinga's claim that traditional theists do not share a common conception of omnipotence is based in part on the fact that Descartes, along with some medieval theologians, held that God could unilaterally bring about "*every* state of affairs, whether possible or not."[39] But the fact that some traditional theologians *went beyond* I omnipotence, defined as the view that God can unilaterally bring about intrinsically possible states of affairs among finite actual beings, does not conflict with the assertion that they affirmed it.

Although Plantinga is certainly correct that several different views of omnipotence can be found among traditional theists, they all affirm I omnipotence and thereby the view that God is the actual or potential controller of all events in the world. The different views are all variations on that common doctrine.

I turn now to Nelson Pike's critique, which focuses on my description of I omnipotence as the monopolistic view of omnipotence. On the basis of a quotation from Charles Hartshorne, Pike describes the monopolistic view as the view that God "has all the power." Regarding this view as a "somewhat surprising misconstrual on Hartshorne's part," he dismisses it with these words:

> Thus, when it is claimed in Christian theological texts that God is all-powerful, this is not meant to imply that God (in Hartshorne's words) "has all the power." Being omnipotent, God has the power to shatter the glass [sitting on my desk], but so do I and so does my son. The so-called "monopolistic view" of omnipotence is of no real interest in the present discussion. If it is unintelligible . . . this will not count as a criticism of what Griffin calls "traditional theodicy," nor will it have any real bearing on the adequacy of various positions taken in the contemporary, philosophical literature on the problem of evil.[40]

One "somewhat surprising" feature of Pike's discussion is that, although he is discussing *my* position, he bases his definition of the monopolistic view entirely on a couple statements from Hartshorne,[41] without examining how I define it. I do *not* describe it simply as the view that God *has* all the power, which would imply that God actually does everything. Rather, I say that, according to the traditional idea of God, "God controls, or at least could control, every detail of the events in the world."[42] I distinguish between traditional theologians from Augustine to Karl Barth, on the one hand, who held that "God actually controlled every detail of every event," and popular theistic faith and some contemporary free-will theists, on the other hand, who hold that God has granted freedom to at least some creatures but that "God can, at any chosen time, totally determine what will happen."[43] Accordingly, because this gift of free will is a gift of power, "in traditional theism the term [omnipotence] has this meaning: 'actually or potentially having all the power there is.'"[44] In this traditional view, "divine omnipotence means that God actually or potentially has a monopoly on power."[45] The "monopolistic view," therefore, is not to be simply identified with the view that God (actually) has all the power, so that the creatures have none. It is the view that "one being *could* simply have all the power."[46] This distinction is even reflected in Hartshorne's statement, quoted by Pike, that the traditional doctrine says that God "does or can do everything."[47]

Even if we ignore this distinction, and treat the traditional view as the view that God actually has all the power, Pike's statement that this view is not found "in Christian theological texts" is contradicted by much evidence that was presented in my book. Luther, for example, says that we have no

power of free will, because God predestines and does all things. Power belongs to *God's* nature, he says, so that free will is no more properly attributed
to us than is divinity.[48] Luther's famous assertion of the *Alleinwirksamkeit Gottes*
(sole efficacy of God) is echoed in our time by Emil Fackenheim's description
of God as the "sole power."[49] Calvin argued that no creatures have any intrinsic power with which they can harm us, because God is the cause of their
motion.[50] Calvin's views are echoed in our century by Karl Barth. Belief in
providence, Barth says, is belief in "God as the One who works all in all."[51]
God controls every creature in such a way that "all the activity of the creature is His [God's] own activity." Because God's causation totally governs the
other causes, God is the one true cause: the term "cause" does not designate
a genus of which the divine and creaturely causes are species. There is not
even an analogy between the two causes, Barth holds, because the divine
cause is self-positing, while secondary causes are grounded wholly from the
outside.[52] Pike evidently did not read my book very carefully before making
his statement.

Having claimed the monopolistic view to be historically insignificant,
Pike asserts that another view "has been widely enough held to warrant being
referred to as the *'standard* view' of omnipotence."[53] This so-called standard
view holds:

> If God is omnipotent, it is within his power to completely determine
> each of the activities of all other beings. . . . While the standard view of
> omnipotence does not appear to entail that beings other than God are
> devoid of power, it does entail that the exercise of power on the part of
> any finite being is . . . contingent upon God's willingness to refrain from
> exercising some power of his own.[54]

This view that Pike considers "standard" depends, as is clear, upon the
distinction between the possession of power and its exercise. In my discussion of Calvin, however, I cite his rejection of the view of omnipotence as an
ability to do all things that sometimes sit idle.[55] Calvin in fact spoke harshly
of those in his day who, like Pike, distinguish in God between "doing"and
merely "permitting"; Calvin says that such persons "babble and talk
absurdly."[56] Although Thomists were among the targets of Calvin's invective,
the Thomist view that God is *actus purus* is a denial of any unactualized po-
tency in God. Pike's contention that his is the standard view is further contradicted by the Thomist doctrine of divine simplicity, which entails that
God's knowing and doing are identical, so that the divine omniscience causes
all things.[57]

Pike's assessment that the "so-called 'monopolistic view' of omnipotence is of no real interest in the present discussion"[58] is also contradicted

by evidence found in my book. The version of the monopolistic view according to which God actually has a monopoly of power is reflected not only by Fackenheim and Barth, who were quoted above, but also by Charles Campbell, Anthony Flew, and Dewey Hoitenga. I quoted Campbell as saying that worship of God is impossible "once the infinitude of God has been compromised and forces independent of God and either actually or potentially hostile to Him have been admitted."[59] Flew says that the doctrine of divine omnipotence means that "absolutely nothing happens save by [God's] consenting ontological support. Everything means everything; and that includes every human thought, every human action, and every human choice."[60] Hoitenga rejects the claim of some theists that it is inconsistent to speak of God's *causing* us to do good *freely*, on the grounds that Augustine and Calvin did not think it inconsistent, and says that allowing any iota of independence to the human will would conflict with the theist's belief in providence.[61] Once it is recognized, furthermore, that the traditional or monopolistic view includes the view that God *potentially* has a monopoly on power, even if that potential monopoly has been given up (through a voluntary self-limitation), it is clear that this view is the one either presupposed or criticized by most contemporary philosophers of religion. Pike's claims are entirely erroneous.

Stephen Davis, on the basis of a more careful reading of the text, has made a more valid criticism of my use of the term "traditional theism," saying that I have used it too loosely.[62] On the one hand, he accepts my contention that "according to traditional theism, God either actually or potentially controls all things."[63] This definition allows for the distinction between the all-determining and free-will versions of traditional theism. But in some of my formulations (as discussed above) I did not have that distinction in mind and wrote as if traditional theism were to be equated with the all-determining version of it. In particular, as Davis points out, I have written in various places that traditional theism includes the idea that all causality is explicitly or implicitly to be attributed to God.[64] This would mean that God is responsible for all murders as well as all natural evils, and that there is no sin, in the sense of an act that goes counter to the (effective) will of God.[65] Davis says he and many thinkers who consider themselves traditional theists do not hold these beliefs.[66] He is right, and it is also the case that my own definition, according to which "the defining essence" of traditional theism is "the idea that God is the actual or potential controller of all events,"[67] does not imply these beliefs.

The problem probably arose because of an ambiguity in the word "traditional." Besides the definition just given, which allows for a free-will as well as an all-determining version of traditional theism, the term can be used to refer to the theism that was virtually universal in all traditional, in the sense of premodern, Christian theology. In this latter sense of the term, traditional theism would be all-determining theism, because the idea of a divine self-limitation, which allows for genuine freedom on the part of human and perhaps other creatures without the contortions of compatibilism, has become a widespread doctrine only since the eighteenth century. While writing some of my statements I was evidently thinking of "traditional theism" in the latter sense, forgetting that my definition allows for a free-will version of traditional theism, according to which God does not actually cause all events.

In any case, the qualifier "all-determining" needs to be inserted into those passages in which statements are made about traditional theism that apply only to this version of it.

The contrast between the traditional and the process doctrines of omnipotence depends upon contrasting assumptions about what it means to be actual. This point was made clear above by the reference to premise X, which says: "It is possible for one actual being's condition to be completely determined by a being or beings other than itself." This premise is presupposed by traditional theists and rejected by process theists. In Pike's attempt to defend his version of the "standard" view of omnipotence, and to show, against me, that it does not reduce to the monopolistic view, he launches an extensive critique of my reasons for rejecting premise X. I will examine this critique in chapter 6.

But first I must look at the logically prior question of whether a revised doctrine of omnipotence is needed. John Knasas has argued that traditional all-determining theism, at least a Thomistic version of it, can answer process theology's criticism that its doctrine of divine omnipotence is unintelligible. And Pike, Reichenbach, and the Basingers have all suggested that a traditional free-will theodicy can, without resorting to a concept of a "finite" and "weak" God, be as adequate as a process theodicy. I examine these claims in the next two chapters.

Chapter 4

IS TRADITIONAL ALL-DETERMINING
THEISM INTELLIGIBLE AFTER ALL?

A. THE PROBLEM

One of the central claims of my theodicy is that the traditional doctrine of omnipotence is unintelligible, incoherent. As such, it provides no standard by which to call the God of process theism finite in the sense of imperfect.[1] If the traditional idea of God is not a coherently and therefore genuinely conceivable idea, it does not stand in the way of holding that process theology's doctrine of God fulfills the Anselmian criterion of perfection—of being that which none greater can be (coherently) thought. The God of process theology can therefore be said to have perfect power.

John F. X. Knasas, in "Super-God: Divine Infinity and Human Self-Determination,"[2] seeks to disprove this claim by defending the coherence of Thomas Aquinas' version of traditional theism, especially his doctrine of divine omnipotence. Knasas' aim is to show that at least one way of talking about "a God above Griffin's, a super-God," is not incoherent.[3] His conclusion is:

It is hard to see how Aquinas' elaboration of the traditional concept of omnipotence would merit Griffin's label of "I-omnipotence"—meaning "incoherent omnipotence".... In Aquinas the traditional notion of God remains an intelligible standard by which to judge Griffin's process God finite and imperfect.[4]

I used the term "I omnipotence" for the traditional doctrine of omnipotence to indicate that it is an incoherent notion (unless it involves the idealistic doctrine that the world is nothing but a complex idea in the divine mind).[5] I based this claim on a combination of two ideas: (1) the idea that an actual being, to be distinguishable from a merely possible or ideal being, must have some power of its own, which finally implies that it must have some capacity for self-determination;[6] (2) the idea that a being's self-determination is not compatible with its being wholly determined by a being or beings other than itself (in other words, compatibilism is incoherent).

Traditional free-will theists, as illustrated by Alvin Plantinga, Bruce Reichenbach, and the Basingers, seek to overcome the charge that traditional theism is necessarily incoherent by accepting the second point while ignoring the first. That is, being incompatibilists, they deny that God wholly determines the actions of self-determining beings (generally assumed to be limited to human beings, at least among earthly creatures), while ignoring the claim that God's complete determination of the activities and states of *any* actual beings is incoherent. Thomas Aquinas, however, was a compatibilist and accordingly did not speak of any divine self-limitation in relation to self-determining beings. God's causality is as fully determining in relation to self-determining creatures, such as human beings, as it is in relation to all other beings. In defending the coherence of Aquinas' doctrine against the charge of being an example of I omnipotence,[7] therefore, Knasas must defend the notion that is rejected by the traditional free-will theists—namely, that human self-determination is compatible with God's complete determination of all creaturely acts.

While recognizing that this would appear at first to be an impossible task, Knasas believes that the secret lies in Aquinas' concept of infinity. He says: "I will defend the coherency of a super-God *vis-à-vis* Griffin's by elaborating the crucial role of infinity in Aquinas' conception of God and God's causality of human acts."[8]

To make clear the difficulty that must be surmounted by means of this idea of infinity, I should point out that Knasas does not challenge my contention that Aquinas, no less than other traditional theists, portrays an "all-controlling God".[9]

It is clear that Aquinas' philosophical conception of God includes the omnipotence targeted by Griffin's criticism. God's causality encompasses within its effects the free acts of rational creatures, and as so encompassed these acts are subject to God's providence and included

within his knowledge. . . . Moreover, for Aquinas God's causality is un-
failing. As the cause of the very existence of things, their act of all acts,
no actuality is outside of God's control and able to frustrate it.[10]

Unlike many defenders of Aquinas, Knasas does not try to claim that evil acts
are not caused by God but merely "permitted."[11] He agrees with my contention that within the framework of the theology of Aquinas no meaningful
distinction between causing and permitting can be made. After quoting
Aquinas' statement that "God's will is the cause of the act of sin,"[12] Knasas
says: "Aquinas' saying that God permits evil to be done is just another way of
putting it."[13]

Besides not mitigating God's all-controlling causality, Knasas also is
not, in general, a compatibilist. Unlike many modern philosophers, he does
not try to maintain that human freedom is compatible with all human acts'
being fully determined by molecular movements. He does not give a Pick-
wickian definition of freedom in order to make it compatible with genetic
and environmental determination; freedom is not, for example, consent to
destiny, or merely the absence of external constraint, so that one can do what
one wants (while what one wants is fully determined by the past). The freedom Knasas is talking about is real freedom; it is acting "with a real ability to
do otherwise."[14] An act is free in the sense of self-determining if, after the
act, it is true that the creature "could have done otherwise."[15] Freedom involves "truly selecting from a number of genuine possibilities."[16] Freedom in
this real sense, Knasas agrees with me, is not in general compatible with
being completely determined by other agents: if those agents fully determined that you would do X, it would not have been possible for you to do
Y.[17] Complete determination by others in general—that is, by other finite
agents—would exclude any selection from among genuine possibilities.

This clear, straightforward discussion, which is devoid of fudging and
equivocating, shows Thomism at its best to be superior in this respect to
most modern philosophy. But it also makes the difficulty of Knasas' task crystal clear. How can he make intelligible the idea that God's complete determination of human acts is compatible with their freedom? Can Knasas, by
virtue of the concept of divine infinity, do the seemingly impossible?

B. THE SOLUTION OF JOHN KNASAS:
INFINITE POWER AND COMPATIBILISM

Knasas seeks to defend the intelligibility of Aquinas' assertion that
"God's workings in the human will are not opposed to man being the master
of his own act," which means that "the determining of man's acts of will is
man's own."[18] Aquinas explicitly deals, Knasas points out, with the objection

that the will could not be "master of its act... if it were not able to act without God operating in it."[19] Knasas says that this objection is similar to mine. This is the one place where he may misinterpret me; I deny not that God influences human decisions, only that this divine influence fully determines them. In any case, the real question is: How could *fully determining* divine influence be compatible with human self-determination? In relation to this question, Knasas quotes this passage from Aquinas:

> The will is said to have dominion of its act not through exclusion of the first cause, but because the first cause does not so act in the will that it determines the will from necessity to one thing just as it determines nature; and so the determination of the act is left in the power of reason and the will.[20]

In other words, God fully determines all events in the world. But, while God determines each natural event "to one thing," so that the event could not have been otherwise, God determines the human will so that it, based on the reason, really selects among alternative possibilities. "God moves the will... preserving in it all the while the ability to do otherwise."[21]

Knasas admits that the consistency of this statement is not immediately evident:

> Is it possible to explain how the divine causality upon the created will does not take away the will's ability to do otherwise? As mentioned, the divine causality is unfailing, and so it is difficult to see how what is under it could be called "able to be or do otherwise."[22]

With regard to this problem, Knasas mentions my remark that God cannot "cause an event to occur which is both contingent and necessary, i.e., which occurs necessarily and yet could fail to occur."[23] My reason for this claim is that God cannot bring about something that is self-contradictory, such as a round square. For something to be contingent is, as Knasas says, for it to possess "the ability to be otherwise."[24] But if God's causality *unfailingly* caused an event to occur, then its existence was necessary and its nonexistence was impossible. The event had no "ability to be otherwise." To be both necessary and contingent is as self-contradictory as to be round and square. Or so I claim. But Aquinas, quoted here by Knasas, affirms compatibilism:

> Although the non-existence of an effect of the divine will is incompatible with the divine will, the possibility that the effect should be lacking is given simultaneously with the divine will. God's willing someone to be saved and the possibility that that person be damned are not incompatible; but God's willing him to be saved and his actually being damned are incompatible.[25]

As can be seen, while I equate "being infallibly determined" with "impossibility to be otherwise" and hence "necessary," Aquinas and Knasas distinguish them. For an all-controlling God to will X is incompatible with the nonexistence of X, we all agree. But they hold that for this God to will X is compatible (in some cases) with the *possibility* of non-X. X could not not have occurred; it had to occur; and yet its nonoccurrence was possible. How can that be an intelligible idea? The notion that God's power is infinite, infallibly bringing about whatever God wills, seems to rule out all contingency. The opposite, suggests Knasas, is the truth; it is precisely because of God's infinite power that divinely determined human acts can be truly contingent. He quotes Aquinas:

> For the patient must be assimilated to the agent; and, if the agent is most powerful, the likeness of the effect to the agent cause will be perfect; . . . Now the divine will is most powerful. Hence its effect must be made like it in all respects, so that there not only comes about what God wants to come about . . . but it comes about in the manner in which God wants it to come about—necessarily or contingently, quickly or slowly.[26]

This argument begins to be intelligible, Knasas says, when we realize that the divine will, called "most powerful" in this passage, is really *infinitely* powerful, because God's power, being identical with God's subsistent existence, is infinite.[27] Coming to the crux of the matter, Knasas then asks:

> What is it about infinite power that is compatible with a real contingency in its effects? The answer apparently is in Aquinas' thought that the divine infinity contains the perfections of all things.[28] Among these perfections are the natures that are created acts of willing. Under such an infinite deity, rational creatures not only can do, but can do otherwise. They can do, for the deity can bring into existence in them the finite nature that is a particular act of will. . . . They can do otherwise, because another act of will is likewise contained in the divine infinity and able to be given existence in the rational creature. The created will's ability to do this or that is assured by an infinite deity that contains the perfections of either act of willing. Under the divine causality, it is always true that the rational creature could have done otherwise. Just as the divine causality does not exclude in the creature a real ability to do, so too it does not exclude a real ability to do otherwise. It makes sense to say this provided the divine cause is regarded as actually infinite.[29]

The reason it "makes sense to say this" if and only if God is infinite is that, as stated earlier, although a finite agent's determination of another would leave no contingency in the other, an infinite agent's could:

> Only an infinite being, then, respects the indeterminacy of the will. Only it can ground the ability of the will to do this or that. Because of its determination, a finite being could not but exclude the will's indetermination. That determination would be perpetuated in the finite being's causality and so exclude any ability to be otherwise.[30]

If I grasp Knasas' argument, it is that a finite being, because of its finiteness, is determinate. When it exerts causation on another, it passes that determination on to it, because "the patient must be assimilated to the agent." The agent's efficient causation, having no indetermination in it, excludes any indetermination in the patient, therefore any possibility of self-determination. God, on the other hand, being infinite, is indeterminate. God's causation, which is identical with God's essence, contains possibilities other than those acts that will actually occur, at least with regard to the acts of rational creatures. So, although God wills that Jones will do X at time T, God's infinity also contains Jones's doing Y at time T, and perhaps also doing W and Z. Because of God's infinite power, God can instill in Jones the possibilities of doing W, Y, and Z at time T, so that those are *real* possibilities, even though it is eternally true that Jones will do X. Knasas does not blame me for not having grasped this notion. He says, in fact, that even "most Thomists have only dimly perceived the importance here of Aquinas' construing divine omnipotence in infinite terms. . . . Only Joseph Owens spotlights the insight behind Aquinas' constant reiteration of the harmony between God's efficacious willing and creaturely contingence."[31] He then quotes this passage from Owens:

> The mind can reason that every finite agent, because determined and limited in nature, determines the effect it produces to some definite and limited character. But subsistent existence, because absolutely unlimited in nature, does not operate under this restriction. . . . The explanation has to be poised on the nature of the primary efficient cause, which is unlimited and, accordingly, able to act without determining.[32]

C. THE PROBLEM REMAINS

We can read the words, but can we think the thoughts? Regardless of how unlimited a being's power is, it cannot make a round square. How can it, by analogy, create an event that is both necessary and contingent—that *must* occur (because God infallibly causes it to occur) and yet *might not* have occurred? Can those words evoke an intelligible proposition in us? That is the crucial question, because, the reader will recall, Knasas' argument is that Aquinas has a *coherent* concept of omnipotence, one that provides an "intelligible standard by which to judge Griffin's process God finite and imperfect."

Knasas, who is always honest, recognizes the difficulty. He tries to overcome it with these reflections:

> What seems to cause all the difficulty in grasping Aquinas' position is our thinking that we can represent to ourselves this infinite divine causality. Because all our positive concepts—those able to be brought before the mind's eye—are finite and determinate, we ineluctably think the infinite divine causality in finite, determinate terms, too. Small wonder God's causality appears to rub out contingency.[33]

Knasas shows with the following quotation that Owens agrees:

> The human mind, able to understand only the determined and determining motion that proceeds from finite natures, cannot form any proper concept of the unlimited motion that causes a will to make freely but infallibly the decision to which it moves it.[34]

But how do these statements show that the traditional doctrine of omnipotence is an *intelligible* concept? Do they not imply just the opposite? If we "ineluctably" think so that we "cannot form any proper concept" of infinite causality, then this concept would seem to be unintelligible in principle for human beings. More pointedly, how can one *know* that the phrase "infinite causality" refers to any (proper) concept at all? Why should one even suspect that it does? This is one place at which Knasas does not acknowledge the difficulty. He simply says:

> So, knowing that God's causality of the human act remains identical with his infinity, we can sensibly and rightly say that it moves the will without detriment to the will's ability to do otherwise.... Unfortunately when the above claim is made, the intelligibility with which our words is laden remains impervious to our mind's eye. We know the proposition has meaning *quoad se*. But the meaning remains unavailable *quoad nos*.[35]

If the intelligibility of the words "remains impervious to our mind's eye," so that we do not understand its meaning, how do we "know" that the words enunciate a proposition that has meaning in itself (*quoad se*)? Surely the mere fact that Aquinas says it does not in itself prove that it is intelligible; his writings are not, even in the Roman Catholic tradition, authoritative in the sense of belonging to divine revelation. We can ask what type of proposition this is supposed to be? Does it belong to natural theology, so that it is based on reasoning from common human experience? Or is it based solely on revelation, so that it is above reason (though not, Aquinas would insist, contrary to it)? If it were a proposition of natural theology, it would have to be intelligible to human reason, and this is what it is said not to be. It must then be a product of divine revelation. That this would be Knasas' answer is suggested by the fact that he cites Aquinas' approving quotation of St. Paul's statement, "It is God who worketh in us both to will and to accomplish."[36]

But this answer would be doubly problematic. First, it would be one thing to claim that St. Paul's statement expressed a revealed truth; it would be something quite different to claim that the Thomistic way of trying to explicate this idea belongs to revelation. Second, even if one were to make this claim, one would not thereby have *shown* the concept to be coherent and intelligible: one would have merely announced one's own willingness to assume, as an act of faith, that the words somehow point to a concept that is, in itself, coherent.

Recalling Knasas' conclusion that "it is hard to see how Aquinas' elaboration of the traditional concept of omnipotence would merit Griffin's label of . . . 'incoherent omnipotence,'" I must conclude that it is hard to see how it could be labeled anything else. Knasas made a valiant effort; but, just as even infinite power cannot make a triangle round, even the finest intellect cannot make an incoherent concept coherent. I therefore see no reason to revise the judgment that the traditional doctrine of omnipotence does not provide an intelligible standard by which to call the God portrayed by process theology imperfect, less powerful than a divine being might conceivably be. Knowing the impossibility of supertriangles (ones that are round as well as triangular), we do not belittle triangles. Knowing the impossibility of a super-God, we will not belittle God.

The conclusion that the all-determining version of the traditional doctrine of omnipotence is incoherent, and therefore cannot provide an adequate theodicy, does not by itself, of course, show that traditional theism as such cannot provide an adequate theodicy. Traditional free-will theists, being incompatibilists, reject the doctrine Knasas sought to defend. I turn now to the claim that the free-will form of traditional theism can provide an adequate theodicy.

Chapter 5

CAN A TRADITIONAL FREE-WILL
THEODICY BE ADEQUATE AFTER ALL?

In the first chapter I presented several arguments against the adequacy of the traditional free-will defense, as I had done in *God, Power, and Evil*, especially in the chapter on John Hick. I generally called it there the "hybrid free-will theodicy (or defense)," because freedom is not, as in process theology, thought to be inherent in actuality as such and thereby present to some degree all the way down, even in subatomic elements. Rather, freedom is thought to be a contingent feature of some finite actualities, so that an explanation of the world's evils cannot appeal to the necessary freedom and therefore uncontrollability of every level of existence. This type of explanation can be given only in relation to those beings to whom God is said to have given freedom. The evil arising in other portions of the creation must either be denied or explained in some other terms. In contrast with the approach of process theodicy, the result is a hybrid (rather than a thoroughgoing) defense in terms of freedom. Plantinga might be said to provide the basis for a thoroughgoing free-will defense insofar as he intends seriously his suggestion that all nonhuman evil could be due to the malevolently used freedom of "Satan and his cohorts," although in this explanation the freedom responsible for all natural evils would be external to the natural entities. In any case, in the present book I call this position the traditional (or classical) free-will theodicy (or defense).

In this chapter, I examine the claim of several critics that a nontraditional theodicy, such as a process theodicy, is not needed, because a traditional free-will theodicy can be at least equally adequate. This examination is organized in terms of my criticisms of this type of theodicy, which were discussed in chapter 1. One of the ten criticisms summarized there is that the traditional free-will theists tend, in spite of their apparent difference from all-determining theists on this point, to deny the reality of genuine evil.

A. CAN THE EXISTENCE OF GENUINE EVIL BE AFFIRMED?

One critic who finds my type of theodicy unnecessary is Nelson Pike. His analysis begins by examining John Mackie's claim that "God (an omnipotent and perfectly good being) exists" and "evil exists" are logically inconsistent. Mackie's claim can be defeated, Pike points out, by challenging either of Mackie's "quasilogical rules." Rule A is: "Good is opposed to evil in such a way that a (perfectly) good being always eliminates evil if it can." Rule B is: "There is no limit to what an omnipotent being can do," which "is meant to entail that it is within the power of an omnipotent being to eliminate all instances of evil."[1] Pike correctly sees that I attack Rule B. But he finds my theodicy unsuccessful (for reasons to be examined in chapter 7). He believes that an attack on Rule A, which Augustine made, provides "a more promising approach."[2] Pike says:

> Augustine's amazing message is that if God is omnipotent, then no matter how untoward the activities of finite agents may be, we must suppose that they are performed with God's permission. Somehow or other (in a way "unspeakably strange and wonderful") all things that exist or occur (including such activities) contribute to the ultimate good. . . . Since God is omnipotent, it is within his power . . . to prevent all instances of evil. He does not do so only because the evil actions of others are ingredients in the ultimate good.[3]

Pike believes that this theodicy is free of any logical contradiction between "God exists" and "evil exists."

Of course it is, because it denies that there *is* any *genuine* evil. The "evil" that exists is said to be only apparently evil, in that it contributes to, rather than detracts from, the overall good of the universe. It is very disappointing to see Pike conclude his article by offering as a "more promising approach" than mine the one that I spent over half of the book criticizing, with no mention of this fact. I said in the Introduction that I insert the word "genuine" into the formal statement of the problem of evil to prevent precisely the oscillation between "genuine evil" and "only apparent evil" that Pike's approach exemplifies. I pointed out that this insertion helps us see that "the controversy is not really about the meaning of a 'morally perfect being'—

everyone agrees that such a being would want to prevent all genuine evil"—
but about whether there is (genuine) evil in the world.[4] The final section of
my chapter on Augustine was entitled "The Denial of Genuine Evil."[5] I
showed that the same answer was given by Aquinas, Maritain, Journet, Luther,
Calvin, Leibniz, Barth, Hick, Ross, and most of the personal idealists.[6] I argued that the controversy over whether the acceptance of evil and the acceptance of the God of traditional theism involves a logical contradiction
dissipates once the distinction between *prima facie* evil and genuine evil is
made.[7] And I mentioned Pike as one who solves the problem by invoking the
possibility that all *prima facie* evils are only apparently evil, which enables him
to dismiss the problem of evil as "a noncrucial perplexity of minor
importance."[8] I also suggested that, while the existence of genuine evil is
incapable of proof, it is not in need of proof, because the idea "that not
everything is as good as it could have been" is "one of those basic presumptions in terms of which we all live our lives, in spite of what we might verbally affirm."[9] I argued further:

> These basic presuppositions . . . must be used as the ultimate check
> upon the tenability of any proffered system of thought. For if we cannot
> help believing them, it simply does not make sense to doubt their truth.
> Accordingly, any position that denies one or more of them, whether
> explicitly or only implicitly, must be considered in that respect false.[10]

It is disappointing that Pike made no response to, and did not even acknowledge, this argument against his "more promising approach," which is presented as if I had never considered it.

In any case, I hold, as argued above in chapter 2, that the task of philosophical theology is to find positions that are not merely free from logical
contradiction, but that are also believable and livable. In the face of Auschwitz,
of millions of starving children, of agonizing lingering deaths, of brutality to
minorities and the poor beyond belief, of animal suffering uncompensated for
by any moral growth, of war after war—in the face of these and countless
other forms of evil, can Pike *really* believe, and therefore *live*, in terms of the
belief that everything that happens contributes to the ultimate good?

It could be, of course, that Pike does not claim to believe this, but
merely presents his "more promising" theodicy as a logical possibility. That
would be, however, a trivialization of the problem of evil, and of the task of
philosophical theology. It may be, however, that this Augustinian solution is
not Pike's preferred position; I will consider in chapter 7 an alternative suggestion he makes.

It also may be that Pike's positive suggestion should not be considered
an example of a free-will theodicy or defense. He evidently thinks of it as

such, indicating in his statement about "Augustine's amazing message" that evil is performed with God's "permission" (not agency). But the correct reading of Augustine, I argued above in chapter 3, is that God directly causes all events. It is, in fact, only on this assumption that Augustine could believe that all things work together for good, so that no genuine evil occurs. In any case, I turn now to a response more clearly representative of traditional free-will theism.

The Basingers, as I mentioned in chapter 3, believe that an adequate theodicy can be based upon Alvin Plantinga's idea of the God-world relation. They agree with me, against Augustine and Pike, that an adequate theodicy must affirm the reality of genuine evil. One of the strengths of the free-will defense developed by Plantinga and others, they believe, is that the freedom attributed to human (and perhaps other) agents allows genuine evil to occur even though God is good and omnipotent. If this is indeed so, then at least one of the necessary conditions for an adequate traditional free-will theodicy would be provided.

It does seem to be difficult, however, for advocates of the traditional view of omnipotence to admit the reality of genuine evil. I had argued in my chapter on John Hick in God, Power, and Evil, for example, that he ultimately denies the reality of genuine evil, in spite of his strong defense of human freedom, and a recent examination of Hick's theodicy has supported this judgment.[11] I had also, by equating Plantinga's "unjustified evil" with my "genuine evil," concluded from Plantinga's denial of unjustified evil that he in effect denies genuine evil.[12] The Basingers believe that this conclusion is incorrect,[13] and they may be right. I will, however, explain why, even if Plantinga explicitly says otherwise, we may have to conclude that his position implicitly involves a denial of genuine evil.

A traditional free-will theist certainly could consistently affirm the existence of genuine evil, while considering these genuine evils to be justified in an important sense. For example, such a theist might say that God, in choosing to create beings with the power of self-determination, thereby effected a voluntary self-limitation, giving up the power to control all events and thereby also the power to know in advance exactly what will occur. Because of this self-limitation on the divine omnipotence and omniscience, all sorts of genuinely evil things may occur, things that make the universe poorer than it might have been had free creatures used their power of self-determination better. These evils can be regarded as justified in a strong sense, however, on the grounds that a world in which free creatures exist is a better world, even with all its evils, than a world without such creatures. Because of the contingency allowed into the world through God's creation of self-determining beings, this "justification" of prima facie evils need not be the type of justification that denies that they are genuinely evil. That is, the justification does not say of each particular evil, such as the Nazi holocaust,

that it somehow contributed to making the world a better place than it otherwise would have been. Rather, the justification simply refers to the *possibility*
of that type of event, saying that a world with genuinely free creatures, and
therefore a world in which events such as the Nazi holocaust *can* occur, is
better than a world devoid of free creatures. If that were Plantinga's position,
then I would have been wrong to say that he denies the existence of genuine
evil. And that *is* Plantinga's position—except for one important difference.

In Plantinga's free-will defense, the existence of self-determining creatures does not mean any modification of the classical idea of omniscience,
according to which God knows the future (at least what is future for us). In
Plantinga's neo-Leibnizian vision of possible worlds among which God
chooses, God knew, in choosing our particular world to be the actual one,
how every free creature would use its freedom. From my perspective, as I
argued in the chapter on Augustine in *God, Power, and Evil,* that position is
incoherent. If God infallibly knows, whether "eternally" or with perfect "foreknowledge," how I am going to act tomorrow, then my actions are not genuinely free. While rightly rejecting the logic appropriate to I omnipotence
with regard to self-determining beings, Plantinga has retained what can be
called "I omniscience." While he is an incompatibilist with regard to divine
power and human freedom, he is a compatibilist with regard to divine (fore-)
knowledge and human freedom. If this view is incoherent, as I hold, this fact
is a serious mark against any theodicy based on this idea of God.

Furthermore—to come to the main question at hand—this view of
omniscience has implications for the existence of genuine evil. If God is perfectly good, and if God chose to actualize our particular world not only in
its general structure but in its every detail (which God foresaw), including not only (say) the Nazi holocaust in general but every barbarous inhumanity that occurred during it, can we consistently believe that some of the
details are genuinely evil? If God could have chosen a better possible world,
but did not do so, God would seem to be less than perfectly good. If we
(within this framework) insist on the perfect goodness of God, must we not,
with Leibniz, hold that this world, *in all its details,* is the best of all possible
worlds—at least *one* of the best? Plantinga's assertion that no evils are unjustified would then apply not just to the *possibility* that evils might occur but
also to the *concrete evils* themselves. And that would be to say that it contains
no genuine evils.

Plantinga evidently seeks to avoid this dilemma—of denying either the
perfect goodness of God or the existence of genuine evil—by denying that
the idea of "the best of all possible worlds" makes sense. In correcting the
Basingers' attribution to him of a defense based on this notion, he says: "I see
no reason to think there *is* any such world. Perhaps for every world God
could have actualized, there is another, containing an even better balance of

good over evil."[14] I discussed Charles Journet's version of this position in my chapter on Aquinas. I concluded that Journet had failed "to show how the fact that there is a meaningless notion of 'best world' and of 'God's doing his best' can cancel out the principle that God should do 'his best' by creating the 'best possible world' in the sense in which this *does* make sense!"[15]

Whether my critique would apply to Plantinga's version, I am not sure. In any case, it seems desperate to suggest that an omniscient being, conceived as one who could foreknow all possible worlds, down to their tiniest details, would not be able to know one of them to be the best possible world (or at least *one* of the best possible worlds). How could a being be all-knowing and all-wise without knowing *this?* It seems a desperate move to avoid the conclusion either that God is not perfectly good or that the world *is* perfectly good. I am not convinced, therefore, that Plantinga has not provided a defense of God's goodness by *in effect* denying the reality of genuine evil, even though he says otherwise.

This conclusion, if sound, does not necessarily mean that a traditional free-will theodicy, which the Basingers propose, could not be adequate. It might only mean that they need to distance themselves more from Plantinga's theology, adopting in its place a more consistent idea of the divine self-limitation, in which knowledge of future contingents is relinquished along with all-determining power. Or, to put the point more accurately, they would say that the divine self-limitation involved in creating genuinely free creatures included the impossibility of knowing the future. On this basis, the affirmation of the existence of genuine evil—which traditional free-will theists agree to be a necessary feature of any adequate theodicy—could be made.

I turn now to responses to some of the other weaknesses of traditional free-will theodicies that I summarized in chapter 1.

B. CAN THE EXISTENCE OF THEOLOGICAL FREEDOM BE JUSTIFIED?

I have argued that traditional free-will theists, holding that freedom does not belong to actuality as such, have to explain why God gave human beings real freedom, through which they can be so destructive. By real freedom I mean freedom *vis-à-vis* God, which I have called "theological freedom." On traditional premises, God *could* have created beings who would be like us in all ways, enjoying all the values we can enjoy—intellectual, aesthetic, interpersonal, creative—except that they would not really be free to act contrary to God's will, and thereby would not wreak havoc. They could even enjoy moral values, in that they could feel and believe that they were really free. Another form of this argument, expressed by those critics who concede that it is good to have *some* genuine freedom, is that God could have given us less freedom so that we could not be quite so destructive. If God could have created such beings, having no or at least less freedom *vis-à-vis* God, instead of ones who slaughter each other and now threaten most other forms of life as well, should God not have done so? Traditional free-will theists can, of course, provide answers that are convincing to some persons. But their position does allow the question to be raised, and their answers are widely found to be unconvincing.

One of the virtues of process theism is that it does not have to provide an answer to this question. By maintaining that to be actual is to be partially self-determining, even *vis-à-vis* God, it precludes the question as to why God gave us *some* theological freedom. And by maintaining that the *empirically* observable correlations between value and power are *metaphysically* rooted, furthermore, so that beings with more capacity for intrinsic value *necessarily* have more self-determining power, it even precludes the question as to why God gave us such a dangerous degree of freedom. Process theology holds that God could *not* have created beings with no freedom, or even with less freedom than we have, who would nevertheless enjoy the various kinds of values we can enjoy. Actual beings with no freedom *vis-à-vis* God are metaphysically impossible. Beings with less freedom than we have would necessarily have the capacity to realize far fewer values. Beings with no more freedom than chimpanzees would be limited (roughly) to the types of values chimpanzees can enjoy; beings with no more freedom than cats would be limited (roughly) to felinelike values. Once this correlation is grasped as a necessary correlation, the angry, indicting question usually stops. Most persons, seeing the choice to be between *dangerous* human beings or *no* human beings at all, do not blame God or the universe for having brought forth such dangerous creatures.

I have connected process theology's answer to this question to its affirmation of creation out of chaos rather than out of absolute nothingness. The Basingers, in their attempt to show that process theology has no advantage over a properly formulated free-will theism on this issue, appropriately quote the following passage:

> Traditional theism denied that there are any necessary because uncreated principles governing the interrelations among worldly actualities, and hence God's relations with them, other than strictly logical principles. This rejection of uncreated and hence necessary principles fits with the doctrine that the existence of finite actualities is strictly contingent, and that they were created out of absolute nothingness. If it is not necessary that there be finite actualities, and if in fact they have not always existed, it makes no sense to talk about necessary principles governing their mutual relations.[16]

The Basingers say that the claim in the final sentence "is questionable in relation to Plantinga's position." They explain:

> Plantinga does believe that God has the power to create or not create
> finite, self-determining entities, but he strongly denies that the relation-
> ship between finite, self-determining entities and God's control over
> them is, therefore, not a necessary one.[17]

But the Basingers have ignored the fact that my first sentence speaks of
necessary principles *other than strictly logical principles*. The principle in Plantinga's thought to which they refer—a self-determining being cannot be totally determined by another being—is a strictly logical principle (similar to
"a totally red object cannot be partly yellow"). It therefore provides no exception to my correlation between the necessary existence of self-
determining finite beings and the existence of (not simply logical)
metaphysical correlations between value and power. They thereby have provided no qualification of my point that all the basic principles of the world
(other than strictly logical principles) are, according to traditional free-will
theism, unilaterally determined by God. God therefore could have created
beings who would be like us in all respects except for having no, or at least
much less, freedom to violate God's will.

The Basingers next challenge the claim that, on the premises of traditional theism, it would be "possible to have creatures who could enjoy all the
same values which we human beings enjoy, except that they would not really
be free."[18] They object that robots and humans could not enjoy "the same
values in relation to freedom" because "in a world of robots there would be
no actual freedom" and therefore "no real value for the robot to experience."
This objection reflects two confusions. First, I was speaking of the enjoyment
not of freedom as such but of "a wide variety of bodily, moral, and religious
values"[19]—for example, thinking theologically, worshiping deity, being
friends, falling in love, raising a family, and appreciating objects of great aesthetic delight. According to traditional theism, beings could enjoy all those
values while not really being free *vis-à-vis* God. In fact most traditional theists had declared or implied that to be our actual condition. In the second
place, one could (on traditional premises) enjoy the *feeling* of being free without really being free (*vis-à-vis* God). I had in fact said about the hypothetical
beings of this nature who would always do right: "Since they would think
they were free, they could even enjoy the smug satisfaction derived from
complimenting themselves on their moral virtue."[20]

The Basingers' third objection involves the question of divine deception. "Could a wholly good God totally and continually deceive individuals
with respect to the true nature of their supposed self-determination, even if it

were for their own good?"[21] This is surely a good question. Without meaning, or even wanting, to determine its validity, I point out three desiderata.
First, pressing this objection implies the moral indictment of the God of Augustine, Luther, and Calvin. According to these theologians, our feeling that
our actions are partially self-determined is ultimately an illusion, because
these actions are ultimately determined wholly by God. That implication,
may, of course, be agreeable to the Basingers, who reject the all-determining
form of traditional theism. However, and second, it would seem that Plantinga's God would also come under their indictment, insofar as (1) Plantinga's
defense assumes that nonhuman animals have no freedom vis-à-vis God and
(2) the Basingers would agree with me that at least some animals seem to
presuppose that they are partly free. (Problems involving nonhuman animals
are surely not trivial in the light of the fact that the human species is only
one of several million species.) Third, as suggested in chapter 1: even if we
agree that the traditional God's deception of otherwise humanlike beings
would be morally questionable, the traditional God's failure to engage in this
deception is also morally questionable. In other words, because He has I
omnipotence, the God of traditional theists is "damned if He does, damned if
He doesn't." (The male pronoun is fully appropriate for this God.) Process
theism, with its doctrine of C omnipotence, avoids this dilemma. By denying
that God could have created otherwise humanlike beings with no freedom,
process theists need not answer the difficult question as to whether that
choice would have been preferable.

The Basingers think otherwise. They claim that process theologians
cannot ask "whether the creation of truly free individuals by the Plantingan
God was worth the risk, given the potential for evil involved," because we are
forced to admit that "the same basic question can be asked of the process
God." To support this claim they quote my statement that "the question as to
whether God is indictable for the world's evils reduces to the question as to
whether the positive values enjoyed by the higher forms of actuality are
worth the risk of the negative values, the sufferings."[22] But that is precisely
not "the same basic question" that is directed toward the God of Plantinga and
the Basingers. The type of omnipotence that their God is said to possess
implies that all "the positive values enjoyed by the higher forms of actuality"
could be enjoyed even though these higher forms of actuality were not truly
free. This lack of freedom vis-à-vis God would mean that "the risk of
the negative values, the sufferings," would be eliminated, or at least greatly
reduced.

The only values that could not be realized in this type of world would
be those that require humanlike creatures to be really free rather than only
seeming to themselves to be free. These values, as I argued in my critique of
John Hick's theodicy, seem to reduce to values for God alone.[23] For this God

to insist on our having true freedom, if it is not metaphysically necessary, therefore seems selfish. In process theodicy, by contrast, with its *necessary* correlations between freedom and value, *none* of the "positive values enjoyed by the higher forms of actuality" could be enjoyed without the risks made inevitable by a correlative degree of dangerous freedom. The question of whether human freedom is "worth the risk" within this context is accordingly a radically different question from whether it is worth the risk within the context of traditional free-will theism. To regard these two questions as the same is to miss the whole point of the process theodicy.

C. CAN GOD'S NONINTERVENTION TO
PREVENT EVIL BE JUSTIFIED?

The Basingers then turn to another criticism I had raised against the traditional free-will defense, quoting the following passage:

> God could, on this hypothesis, occasionally violate human freedom for the sake of an overriding good, or to prevent a particular[ly] horrible evil. Of course, in those moments, the apparent human beings would not really be humans, if "humans" are by definition free. But this would be a small price to pay if some of the world's worst evils could be averted.[24]

The Basingers raise three considerations designed to suggest that this argument's "initial plausibility" may be deceiving.

First, they suggest, we have no way of knowing that God has not already profitably violated human freedom in the way suggested. The Basingers are certainly correct about that (assuming the truth of traditional theism). That answer nevertheless leaves the problem of evil where it was, with many persons believing that, if God *could* have done so, God *should* have violated human freedom in several other instances. That answer, in short, does nothing to mitigate the rage against God to which persons who have imbibed the traditional picture of divine omnipotence are often led.

For their second caveat, the Basingers say:

> Although it is easy from our perspective to identify, in isolation, certain "free choices" which we believe should have been vetoed by a Plantingan God, what must actually be demonstrated to make Griffin's contention a strong one is that the entire world system (the different possible world) of which such a violation would be a part would in fact result in a significant increase in the net amount of good in comparison

to the actual world. But it is difficult to see how this could be established in any objective sense.[25]

One problem with this caveat is that it implies that I would have to be God in order to criticize the traditional theist's picture of God! A second problem is that, in making this caveat, the Basingers have forgotten what the question at issue is. This question is *not* whether one can prove beyond any doubt that every traditional free-will theodicy is false. The question at issue, as defined by the Basingers, is only whether a traditional free-will theodicy is necessarily less adequate than a process theodicy. For that purpose, one does not need to provide an "objective demonstration" of genuine evils that are unjustifiable, assuming the existence of the traditional theist's God. A final problem with their second caveat is that it seems to presuppose what they were earlier at pains to deny—that this *is* the best of all possible worlds and is therefore devoid of genuine evils.

The Basingers' third caveat is that my criticism "has a questionable 'utilitarian' ring to it." They explain:

It may well be the case that God so respects the "humanity" of each particular individual that he will seldom, if ever, override those decisions which are significant in an individual's own life history, even if the actualization of such decisions will negatively affect large numbers of people.[26]

But that is just to repeat the problem. Those who rage against the God of traditional theism are taking issue with that God's priorities. They are complaining that God should have been, in some particular case, more "utilitarian," using the divine power to achieve good ends—that is, to prevent horrible ends. The point can also be made by turning the Basingers' argument from "respect" against them: those who rage against God are often implying that, for example, out of respect for the humanity of the Jews of Europe, God should have temporarily interrupted the freedom of the Nazis to treat them inhumanly. As long as persons believe that God *could* interrupt the freedom of human beings to violate the freedom of their fellows, a large number of them are going to believe that God *should* have done this in particular cases where it obviously was not done.

Bruce Reichenbach also seeks to answer the question of why God has not interrupted human volition more often to prevent some of the worst moral evils that have occurred. His explanation falls back on the argument that "worst evils" is a comparative notion, so that if God did eliminate the evils we consider the worst, the next worst evils would then be the worst, and we would demand that they should have been eliminated, and so on. But this elimination, he says, would require the elimination of all human freedom.[27] We finite beings cannot possibly know where that line is beyond which further miraculous interruptions to prevent moral evil would begin destroying the world's function as a theater for moral action and development. Only God would know where this line is, and it is possible, Reichenbach adds, that the present state of affairs represents that point.[28]

This argument may have a certain plausibility in the abstract, but can one find it plausible in the face of concrete evils, such as the Nazi holocaust, or the brutal rape of one's daughter which leaves her impaired the rest of her life? This argument will surely do nothing to quell the rage created in persons by the thought that God could have intervened in a particular situation but chose not to—a rage that can often be overcome only by turning to atheism.

The Basingers conclude their rebuttal of my criticism by saying: "it appears that this criticism has more psychological appeal than logical or evidential support."[29] But surely "psychological appeal" is what theodicy is all about! The question is: Can the ways of God be justified to human beings? And that is a psychological question. If a theodicy does not have psychological appeal, it has failed. Logic and adequacy to empirical realities are usually central factors in determining whether a position has psychological appeal, not criteria to be set in opposition to it. In any case, theodicy is not primarily a game played by philosophers of religion, in which one wins simply by showing that no rigorous disproof of one's idea of God has been produced. The question is whether that idea of God lends itself to an explanation of the world, including its evils, that is psychologically convincing to thoughtful men and women.

That the Basingers generally agree with this point is shown by the fact that they call for a move beyond a free-will defense to develop a free-will theodicy. They make this call, it may be remembered, in response to a third argument I raised against traditional free-will theism's ability to handle the problem of evil. This was the argument that it could not explain natural evil except by an implausible appeal to "Satan and his cohorts."[30] The Basingers correctly say that my argument is that "process theology presents a much more plausible explanation for natural evil than can classical theism." Their response is to distance themselves from Plantinga's appeal to Satan as a possible explanation, while adding that a plausible explanation for natural evils can also be provided on the basis of "a Plantingan free-will position."[31] I turn now to this question, to which Reichenbach and the Basingers give a similar answer.

D. CAN NATURAL EVILS BE EXPLAINED?

Reichenbach means his position to be adequate to natural evils, meaning those not caused by human beings. He asks:

How can a God characterized by omnipotence, omniscience, and perfect goodness be directly or indirectly the cause of debilitating diseases
such as cancer, arteriosclerosis, muscular dystrophy, poliomyelitis; natural disasters such as earthquakes, tidal waves, floods and tornadoes;
inherent defects such as Down's syndrome, sickle-cell anemia, spina bi-
fida . . . and a host of other evils?[32]

Reichenbach suggests an answer in terms of a threefold position derived from F. R. Tennant's *Philosophical Theology*. This threefold position is
(1) that it is good that our world is governed by natural laws, because only
in such a world could moral agents develop, (2) that somehow the possibility
of all these evils must be made necessary by the natural laws God chose to
govern our world, and (3) that any other system of natural laws would doubtless necessitate the possibility of equal or worse natural evils.[33]

As Reichenbach says, no one can prove this hypothesis to be untrue.[34]
But the question is: Do we find it plausible? Is it plausible that the *God of
traditional theism* would be so constrained? Has Reichenbach not in effect denied the doctrine of omnipotence he is defending if he says that God could
not create a world of natural laws that would not produce cancer or something equally bad? I will explore this question further by bringing in the
argument of the Basingers, who follow Reichenbach in appealing to F. R. Tennant's position. The Basingers quote a passage from Tennant's *Philosophical Theology*, after which they add this commentary:

It can be argued that every possible world containing free moral agents
must be a world characterized by regularity. If this is so, however, there
is a definite sense in which God's power even in nature must be seen as
limited in such worlds. God cannot unilaterally bring it about that
events in nature be perfectly correlated with the needs of specific humans. To achieve such a correlation would necessitate a myriad of special interventions by God in nature, and this would conflict with the
necessity for regularity in nature which is in turn necessary, given
God's intention to create free, moral creatures. . . . The upshot of this
is clear. The classical theist can (and *must*) develop a notion of "C"
omnipotence in regard to divine power in nature.[35]

This is an intriguing argument. The Basingers are suggesting that traditional free-will theism, properly and consistently thought through, would
end up being essentially the same, at least in implications, as the process
form of nontraditional theism. It would affirm C omnipotence, even in relation to nonhuman nature, saying that God could not intervene in natural

processes now and then to prevent particularly horrible forms of evil. There are, however, serious problems with this suggestion.

First, it contradicts the very meaning of C omnipotence, which says that God cannot interrupt the causal powers of creatures *for logical and/or metaphysical reasons.* When the Basingers say that God cannot intervene, they mean for moral and/or teleological reasons: God cannot interrupt only because of "God's intention to create free, moral creatures."

The Basingers themselves raise a second problem against their argument: "We can admit the need for a uniform system of natural laws, but why must this system contain horrifying, seemingly gratuitous evils—e.g., tornadoes, earthquakes, cancer, etc.?" The answer, they suggest, is that we cannot have the benefits of nature as a determinate, law-abiding system "without the unbeneficial by-products which logically follow from this very order." To illustrate, they quote Tennant's statement that water's "obnoxious capacity to drown us . . . is as much a necessary outcome of its ultimate constitution as its . . . thirst-quenching and cleansing function."[36] On the basis of this argument, that "the good cannot be obtained without the bad," the Basingers conclude: "If the very natural order that makes life possible logically implies evil, God cannot be blamed for the presence of these evils."[37]

Although this answer is similar to that of process theology, it does *not* work within the context of traditional theism, according to which God's efficacy is not restricted by anything other than purely logical principles—that is, principles forbidding self-contradictions. Given their defense of traditional theism, the Basingers have to speak of the unbeneficial by-products of the basically good order as *logically* following from that order. But *do* these by-products follow logically? "A thirst-quenching, nondrowning substance" is not logically self-contradictory, unlike "a round square" and "a married bachelor." Although we probably cannot imagine, given our experience with this world, a substance that would quench our thirst without having the capacity to drown us, the empirical connection between these two qualities is not a logical connection, unlike that between "being a parent" and "having a child." Furthermore, if God's omnipotence is limited only by logical principles, and if God created the world only for the sake of moral beings, why do we need water at all? There is no logical connection between "moral agents" and "needing thirst-quenching substances"—angels presumably do not need wine coolers or Perrier water.

To argue that the good features of our world cannot be had without the bad features is not to take the traditional view of omnipotence seriously. James Ross, who does take this view seriously, is clear about this point. I had quoted him as saying that God could have avoided the evils of pain and ugliness in our world, as well as its sin, without losing anything important: "Whatever end was to be attained in this creation could have been attained in some other in which these evils are not present."[38] The Basingers are implicitly denying the traditional view of omnipotence in their attempt to defend it.

I am not, of course, denying their substantive point, that nonmoral evils "exist as unwanted, though unavoidable, by-products of an otherwise good natural order." That point is essential to my own theodicy. I am only denying that one can legitimately make this claim within the context of traditional theism, with its view of omnipotence, according to which the only absolute (as distinct from conditional) necessities to which the divine creative activity must conform are purely logical principles.

Does this denial mean that I am rejecting the argument of the venerable F. R. Tennant, to whose writings the Basingers, following Reichenbach, repeatedly appeal in making this argument? Not at all. In one of the passages quoted from Tennant, he says: "We cannot have the advantages of a determinate order of things without its *logical or its causally necessary* disadvantages."[39] This passage shows that Tennant, unlike the Basingers, did not try to maintain that the unbeneficial by-products were all *logically* implied by the type of order necessary to produce moral agents; some of them are (only) *causally* necessitated. But to believe that God's activity must conform to some causal necessities seems to imply the existence of some metaphysical principles, other than strictly logical principles, that are beyond divine decision. In other words, Tennant's position might be the same as mine on this issue.

A close reading of his *Philosophical Theology* shows that this is indeed the case. Tennant, defining God as *essentially* the world-ground, holds that God has always had a world.[40] God did not, therefore, select our world, with its most basic principles, out of a number of possible worlds. What is possible in the most fundamental sense in our world is therefore not a result of a divine choice, but is determined by the nature of God and of God's one world.[41] God's power is accordingly not an "empty capacity" that could choose other "conceivable modes of action" than that operative in our world.[42] What is this relation between creatures and God's mode of action that could not be otherwise? Tennant accepts a "pluralistic spiritualism," in which all monads are "spiritual agents" with "relative degrees of spontaneity culminating in human freewill."[43] If we denied this spontaneity, he says, we would have to attribute evil to God.[44] He does speak of the spontaneity of creatures as "delegated," but it is not delegated in the sense that it could be canceled by God.[45] This spontaneity, according to which creatures are themselves creators, means that divine omniscience does not include foreknowledge of the future, except insofar as certain aspects of the future will simply be the outcome of present causes.[46] This spontaneity also means that the traditional view of omnipotence must be rejected, although Tennant says that he affirms "such 'almightiness' as theology can predicate of the Deity without self-stultification."[47] Tennant does speak misleadingly of God's "self-limitation" in respect to both omniscience and omnipotence,[48] but it is clear from his position that no optional giving up of greater powers is thereby implied. Besides the points I have already cited, his affirmation that "the mode of God's being and activity" is constituted by "the sum of eternal truths"[49] implies that this mode could not have been otherwise.

The free-will solution to the problem of natural evil that the Basingers, like Reichenbach, derived from Tennant is therefore a solution that belongs to, and makes sense only within, the context of a nontraditional theism that consistently presupposes C omnipotence, and that therefore employs a thoroughgoing (rather than a hybrid) free-will defense. It cannot be meaningfully employed within the context of traditional theism, with its doctrine of I omnipotence, which permits only a hybrid free-will defense.

At the conclusion of their essay, the Basingers argue that they have virtually reconciled process theism with traditional or classical theism, when the latter is "worked out coherently." Their discussion, while "starting with classical premises," they say, "still ends up with process-like conclusions regarding divine power."[50] This coherent form of traditional theism, including as it does "a notion of 'C' omnipotence in regard to God's relationship to both humans and nature," is said to involve "a notion of omnipotence practically identical to that of the process theist."[51] Through this reconciliation, they purport to have shown, on the one hand, that a coherent form of traditional theism can provide a solution to the problem of evil that is not "less adequate than the process approach."[52] They have, on the other hand, defended the process deity against the charge that it is less powerful than the greatest conceivable being by showing that "there is not a coherent alternative to which the process deity falls short."[53]

I can agree with their conclusion only in part. I do agree that their discussion illustrates the point that traditional theism does not provide a coherent view of divine power to which the God of process theology falls short. I also agree that an adequate theodicy can be developed only on the basis of a doctrine of C omnipotence consistently applied. I cannot agree, however, that they have shown that a doctrine of C omnipotence can be developed while retaining traditional premises: to affirm C omnipotence is to affirm that God cannot—metaphysically cannot—unilaterally determine the activities of any actual beings, and this affirmation is a direct denial of classical premises. I also cannot agree that they have shown that, while retaining traditional premises, one can provide a theodicy on the basis of a free-will defense that is not less adequate than a process theodicy. What they did show—to conclude with an agreement—is that theologians who are not process theists can work out an equally adequate theodicy by adopting "a notion of omnipotence practically identical to that of the process theist." This is possible because it is what F. R. Tennant did. If the Basingers would accept his view of omnipotence, they could legitimately adopt his theodicy. They would then, of course, no longer be traditional theists; but surely that is a small price to pay in order to have an adequate theodicy.

E. EVOLUTION, ANIMAL PAIN, AND OTHER REMAINING QUESTIONS

Several other problems with a free-will theodicy built on traditional theism that I have raised were not treated in the responses by Reichenbach and the Basingers. One of these problems is how to reconcile this theism with evolution. Reichenbach accepts the scientific picture according to which our world developed through a long evolutionary process originating with a big bang.[54] He does not explain, however, why a God omnipotent in the traditional sense would use this method to create a world. This question is especially pressing in the light of his anthropocentric justification for the fact that the world is governed by natural law instead of continual miracle—namely, that moral agency could develop only in such a world.[55] But as I have asked many times, if the whole creation is merely a stage for the human drama, and if God is not constrained by other than logical principles, why would God spend some fifteen billion years simply setting the stage? I have yet to see an answer to this question, even from the ingenious Basingers. And without an answer, they can hardly claim that their position is illuminating of the facts.

Evolution, it should be stressed, is not simply one more fact among others: the idea that our world has come about through an evolutionary process—the principles of which are surely thus far poorly understood—provides the overarching context for all the sciences. An answer would be possible, even within an anthropocentric framework, on the assumption that reality has inherent in it, besides purely logical principles, some metaphysical principles, such as the variables of value and power summarized in chapter 1. According to these principles, no complex world such as our own could be brought into existence except through a long, slow, step-by-step process. The appeal to Tennant by Reichenbach and the Basingers is implicitly an appeal to such an explanation. To make this appeal explicit would be to give up traditional theism, and thereby to be freed of the other problems as well.

One of those other problems involves animal pain. Although it is not mentioned by Reichenbach or the Basingers, it was one of the chief problems I had raised in relation to John Hick's version of the traditional or hybrid free-will theodicy.[56] Even if one could somehow justify all present-day animal pain as an aid to human moral and spiritual development—which I consider an appalling suggestion—the problem would remain of explaining all the animal pain that presumably occurred in the hundreds of millions of years prior to the rise of human beings. To suggest that such pain might not have occurred in those days would be to lose the contact with plausibility that Reichenbach and the Basingers wish to maintain.

And yet other problems remain for a traditional free-will theodicy: the inevitable belittling of the importance of enjoyment vs. suffering in relation to the issue of sin vs. virtue; the resulting callousness in the face of suffering; the fact that so much suffering promotes not virtue but its opposite, which makes belief in life after death absolutely essential for a successful theodicy; and finally the sheer unbelievability of the contention that every form of evil (even if not every instance thereof) somehow contributes to the overall good of the world. Answers to these problems may, of course, be implicit in the appeal by Reichenbach and the Basingers to Tennant's principles, but, if so, this would simply reinforce my contention that traditional free-will theism can produce an adequate theodicy only be becoming nontraditional.

F. SUMMARY OF THE ARGUMENT THUS FAR

I have thus far in this book argued that a plausible theodicy must be provided if theism is to be credible in the face of evil; that my description of traditional theism, especially its doctrine of divine omnipotence, has not been shown to be incorrect (although some reformulations were necessary in some places); and that neither form of traditional theism has been successfully defended against the claim that it cannot provide a plausible theodicy. A nontraditional approach to the problem of evil has therefore not been shown to be unnecessary.

The next question is whether the Whiteheadian-Hartshornean form of nontraditional theodicy I have developed is itself adequate, or can be made adequate—at least more adequate than the traditional theodicies. (The possibility that a still more adequate theodicy might be provided by one of the other forms of nontraditional theism is a question to be explored, or course, by advocates of those other positions.) The remainder of this book is devoted to examining various questions that have been raised, from various perspectives, about the adequacy of process theodicy.

Chapter 6

THE COHERENCE OF PROCESS THEISM'S CLAIM THAT GOD CANNOT COERCE

I begin this examination of the philosophical and theological adequacy of process theodicy with the central negative claim of process theism: the claim that God cannot coerce. In the present chapter, I examine allegations that this claim does not hold up even within the context of process philosophy. In the following chapter, I examine allegations that, even if the claim is consistent with the basic starting point of process philosophy, it should not be accepted as true, because process philosophy's basic starting point is not well founded.

The present chapter is organized into three sections. In the first and second sections, I deal with two widespread confusions about the contrasting terms *persuasion* and *coercion* as applied to divine power. The first confusion involves the belief that these terms correlate, respectively, with final and efficient causation. The second confusion involves the difference between the metaphysical and the psychological meanings of the distinction between persuasion and coercion. In the third section, I examine, as a test case of the coherence of the position, David Basinger's claim that the God of process theism could coerce. The point of Basinger's claim is that process theists are therefore faced with the same problems that we lay at the feet of traditional free-will theists.

A. THE RELATION OF PERSUASION AND COERCION TO FINAL AND EFFICIENT CAUSATION

Bruce Reichenbach, in a chapter entitled "Is God Omnipotent or Finite in Power?",[1] argues that I have not made a good case for the idea that God can be understood to be perfect in power, hence worthy of worship,[2] even though omnipotence in the traditional sense is not ascribed to God. Reichenbach's claim is that the God of process theology is finite in the sense of having less power than a conceivable being could have.[3]

Reichenbach examines my argument for God's perfect power or omnipotence in terms of the following six propositions taken to be metaphysical or necessary truths:

(f) There is an actual world.

(g) To be a world is to contain actual occasions or actual entities.

(h) All actual members of any world are or are composed of actual occasions or entities.

(j) All actual occasions or entities are self-determining beings.

(k) The only power an omnipotent being can have consistent with there being self-determining beings is persuasive power.[4]

(l) God possesses unlimited persuasive power.[5]

Reichenbach focuses his attention on k, saying that, if it is not true, then a being with greater power than the God of process theology could conceivably exist—namely, an omnipotent being with both persuasive and coercive power.[6]

Reichenbach attacks proposition k by saying that God, even on the principles of process theology, should be able to exercise efficient as well as final causation. To support this point, he quotes a statement in which I say:

To say an actuality has creativity is to say that it has power. The nature of this creative power is twofold—the power of self-creation and of other-creation. In the language of causation, it is the capacity to exercise final causation and efficient causation.[7]

Reichenbach then adds that, because God is an actual entity,[8] God also should have both creative powers—the power of efficient causation as well as the power of final causation. "In other words," Reichenbach concludes, "a being greater than a being solely possessive of unlimited persuasive power can be conceived—namely, one possessing both persuasive and coercive powers."[9]

Reichenbach's conclusion is based on the fact that he has equated *final causation* with *persuasive power* and *efficient causation* with *coercive power.* Both equations are wrong.

As indicated by the statement of mine quoted above, *final causation* is used synonymously with *self-creation* or *self-determination.* In my usage, which is also Whitehead's, final causation is correlated with "concrescence"; it is synonymous with what is sometimes called *immanent causation,* meaning causation exerted *within* a single actual entity. It is to be contrasted with "transition," or efficient causation, which is sometimes called *transeunt causation,* and which is the causal influence exerted *between* actual entities—that is, by one actual entity upon another.

Given this usage, the influence exerted by God upon the world cannot be, as Reichenbach thinks, an example of final causation;[10] it must be an instance of transitive, efficient causation. As I pointed out, "the power involved in the problem of evil is a relational concept. It is God's power in relation to something distinct from God, i.e., the world."[11] An actual occasion's own subjective aim is correctly correlated with its final causation, but its *initial* subjective aim (or simply the initial or ideal aim), through which God influences it, comes *via* efficient causation. (Certain statements quoted by Reichenbach that appear to indicate that I equate persuasive power with final causation, and that I refer to God's action in the world as "persuasive final causation," are not from my writings.)[12]

Having equated final causation with persuasion, Reichenbach then equates efficient causation with coercion. With that equation in mind, he is baffled as to why I think "self-determination and coercion (efficient causation) are mutually exclusive."[13] He is understandably baffled. For one thing, he notes that Whitehead, in a passage I quoted, specifically indicates that efficient causation and self-determination are compatible.[14] For another, he notes that, if the two were not compatible, and the actual world were made up exclusively of self-determining actual entities, there could be no efficient causation in the world, which process theology denies.[15] Accordingly, my position, as interpreted by Reichenbach, means that I not only contradict a passage from Whitehead that I had cited for support, but that I contradict one of process theology's basic tenets. Reichenbach accordingly concludes: "There is good reason to doubt the truth of (k) even on the process schema."[16] This conclusion means that my process theodicy is based on "a finitist concept of God: there is a being conceivable with greater power, i.e., one that possesses both efficient and final (persuasive) causal powers."[17] Although that statement by Reichenbach makes explicit (parenthetically) only the equation of final with persuasive power, the other equation implies that, because God exerts efficient causation, God must exert coercive power in relation to the world. And he means coercive power in the strongest sense:

he assumes that the God of process theism could unilaterally bring about states of affairs in the world.[18]

Reichenbach is not the only one to equate persuasion with final causation and coercion with efficient. The same equation is found in an article entitled "Some Problems in Process Theodicy" by Nancy Frankenberry, who is herself an advocate of one form of process philosophy.[19] Frankenberry's article, I should point out, was published in 1981, and she has long since left behind the misinterpretations contained in it. I deal with it, nevertheless, for two reasons. First, its argument that process theism has not "made good its claim to have solved . . . the problem of evil"[20] stands available in the public domain and has thus far, to my knowledge, gone unanswered. Second, if an astute thinker within the process tradition could misunderstand such a crucial point, this point must be in special need of clarification.

Frankenberry portrays process theology's doctrine that God works exclusively by persuasion, never by coercion or controlling power, as meaning the denial that God exerts efficient causation on the world. She says, for example:

Entirely absent from the literature of process theology is any discussion of the possibility that God's power might be conceived as causally efficacious without its being completely determinative, thus allowing the creature more or less ontological power of self-determination.[21]

When I encountered that statement, I found it puzzling, because the possibility she finds "entirely absent" in the literature could well be said to be the main point of my writings on the God-world relation, including *God, Power, and Evil*.[22] A theological account according to which both God and the world are "conceived as exercising efficient causality" would, she says, seem to be a promising option. "It has not, however, been explored," she claims.[23] And yet that is the option that I and most other process theologians had been exploring for years. What is amiss?

The problem is that Frankenberry, like Reichenbach, equates efficient causation with coercion, and final causation with persuasion. Accordingly, she takes the doctrine that God acts only persuasively, never coercively, to imply the denial that God exercises efficient causation. I and most other process theologians, by contrast, follow Whitehead in equating final causation with self-determination, which occurs *within* an actual entity, in its concrescence. Efficient causation occurs *between* entities, being the causal efficacy of an actual entity upon others.[24] Because God is distinct from the world, God's influence upon the world is efficient causation. It is, of course, *persuasive efficient causation*, not coercive efficient causation, a distinction I discuss in the next section.

Once the confusion on this point (along with that to be discussed in the next section) is overcome, the basis is removed for her thesis that process theodicy's "emphasis on God's persuasive, rather than controlling power is [not] without serious problems."[25]

It is equally important, however, to ask why confusion on this point is found not only in Bruce Reichenbach and other critics of process thought, but also in Nancy Frankenberry and other thinkers within the process tradition. (Reichenbach's confusion was supported by quotations from another process thinker who spoke of God's influence on the world as final causation.[26]) The confusion seems to result from the way "efficient causation" has been understood in the West, combined with some features of Whitehead's discussion of God, some essential and some modifiable.

In most systems of thought in the West, *efficient causation* has been conceived deterministically. Insofar as God was thought of as an efficient cause, God was generally thought of as wholly determining the creation, as (unilaterally) *effecting* it. And the efficient causation exerted by material particles has been thought fully to determine their effects (at least until the rise of quantum physics, and even since then efficient causation has generally been conceived deterministically above the quantum realm). Given that connotation, Whitehead's denial that God's power is all-determining could easily be heard as the assertion that God does not exert efficient causation.

Whitehead's God clearly does exert causation of some sort, however, and a term is needed to contrast this type of causation with deterministic causation. Final causation is the other type of causation to which Whitehead refers. God must, it is evidently inferred, influence the world by final causation.

This inference is supported by the past usage of "final causation," combined with Whitehead's doctrine as to how God influences each worldly occasion. While "final causation" can refer to the act of aiming at an end (*finis*), it can also refer to the end or goal itself: the end aimed at is the final cause. Given this second usage, God, conceived as the goal of the world, toward which it aspires, could be thought to act as a final cause. Aristotle's God is often said to be a final cause, not an efficient cause.[27] Whitehead's God, in providing each finite occasion with an "ideal aim" or "initial aim" (or "initial subjective aim"), could be thought to provide each occasion with a final cause (although actually the occasion's final cause is its *subjective aim*, which is evolved out of the *initial* subjective aim by the occasion itself; this distinction is necessary to prevent divine determinism). It is a short step to conclude that God acts by means of final causation. Indeed, Whitehead himself drew attention to the similarity between his view of God's action and Aristotle's, and referred to God, in a passage more poetic than precise, as "the lure for feeling, the eternal urge of desire."[28] Given all this, the fact that some have assumed that Whitehead and Whiteheadians equate persuasion with final causation, and therefore deny that God exercises efficient causation, is understandable.

Another feature of the development of Whitehead's idea of God, which I consider a defect to be overcome, has also probably contributed to the confusion. Whitehead spoke of God as a single, everlasting actual entity, whose concrescence would never come to an end. Because actual entities in general exert efficient causation only after they reach "satisfaction"—that is, after their concrescence or final causation is completed—the implication would seem to be that God could exert no efficient causation, only final. (God should be treated, Whitehead says, as the chief exemplification of metaphysical principles, not as an exception to them.)[29] And yet Whitehead assumes throughout that God does directly influence every actual occasion in the world. Although Whitehead says this, and clearly implies and even says that God exerts efficient causation,[30] the fact that his God could not be an efficient cause in the *same sense* as other actual entities, and *should not* have been able to exert efficient causation at all, surely muted this emphasis. It is possible for readers not to notice that God is portrayed as exercising efficient causation.

Reflection on these possible causes for the confusion about the nature of divine causation should lead process theologians to take more pains to make clear what is being said. I had, for example, spoken repeatedly of divine causation as "persuasive efficient causation" in the longer manuscript from which the final chapter of *God, Power, and Evil* was reduced. Had that term been prominent in the discussion as published, much of the confusion might have been averted.

In any case, once the confusion is cleared up, the point stands that God's final causation is God's own act of self-determination, while God's persuasive causation is God's exertion of efficient causation on the world. There is no basis, therefore, for the false deduction that, because God like every other actuality must exercise efficient as well as final causation, God must be able to act coercively as well as persuasively.

This clarification by itself does not, however, eliminate the basis for all possible confusions about this issue. One could still ask why, if God does exert efficient causation, this should be limited to *persuasive* efficient causation. Why cannot God also exert coercive efficient causation? After all, we can exert both types, so it would seem that God, having perfect power, should be able to do so too. How could God's power be perfect if it failed to include a form of power we have? One could even appeal to the notion that we are created in the image of God. Should not this notion, which process theology accepts, imply that God's power would be understood by analogy with our own? God would therefore exercise final causation and both forms of efficient causation—persuasive and coercive. This question has been asked by David Basinger and Nelson Pike.

The claim that God does not coerce (within process theism) can be challenged in yet a slightly different way. Frankenberry has, for example, concluded from the idea that God exerts efficient causation that God must "exert a measure of controlling power." (I had used "controlling power" synonymously with "coercive power.") This conclusion is not based simply upon her equation of efficient causation with coercion, but also upon her point that, in ordinary parlance, persuasion and coercion are not absolute opposites but refer to a spectrum of interactions in which coercive and persuasive elements are inextricably intermixed. "Between 'persuasion' and 'coercion' would seem to be a whole shaded range of power. . . . Most frequently, the two comingle in indefinable doses."[31]

Clearing up this latter challenge to the claim that God does not coerce involves a distinction between the metaphysical and the psychological meanings of the distinction between persuasion and coercion. Articulating the metaphysical meaning of the distinction will provide the basis for answering the former question—namely, why God cannot coerce in the metaphysical sense.

B. THE METAPHYSICAL AND PSYCHOLOGICAL MEANINGS OF PERSUASION AND COERCION

One source of the confusion surrounding the claim of process theism that God's power is persuasive, not coercive, can be found in the fact that the distinction between persuasion and coercion, which I follow Whitehead in using in a metaphysical sense when referring to divine causation, is more ordinarily used in a psychological sense. In the *metaphysical* sense, the distinction between coercion and persuasion is an absolute difference. Coercion and persuasion are the two types of efficient causation. In *coercion* the effect is completely determined by the efficient causation upon it. In *persuasion* the effect is not completely determined by the efficient causation upon it; the effect, meaning the causally influenced individual, partially determines itself. So understood, the difference is absolute: it is the difference between *none* and *some*, which is an absolute difference. The being upon whom the efficient causation is exerted either exercises some self-determination, or it exercises none. If it exercises none, the efficient causation is coercive; if it exercises some—whether a lot or only an iota—the efficient causation is persuasive.

Given the Whiteheadian worldview, coercion in the metaphysical sense could be exerted only on an aggregate, such as a billiard ball, which has no self or unity of experience and therefore no power of self-determination. Coercion in this metaphysical sense cannot be exerted on individuals, because, *qua* individuals, they have some power of self-determination. Coercion can, of course, be exerted upon what Hartshorne calls "compound individuals," *insofar* as they are treated *qua* aggregates—that is, as bodies. A father can, for example, pick up his young daughter and carry her from the room against her will. Insofar as he affects her *qua* individual, however, her behavior cannot be coerced—that is, unilaterally determined. He can get her to leave as an individual only by persuading her to do so.

Coercion on aggregates can also be exerted only by another aggregate. The billiard ball can be coerced, for example, by the cueball, the cuestick, or a player's hand. Coercion in this metaphysical sense can occur only when aggregate acts on aggregate. An individual cannot be coerced by an aggregate. For example, no matter how starved a person's body may be, it does not dictate to the mind or soul what response to make to the presence of food: the person can choose to starve to death. Likewise, an individual cannot coerce an aggregate. The billiards player, for example, moves the billiard ball by means of his hand.

It may seem, on first analysis, that our influence upon our own bodies (as in moving the hand) is an example of an individual's coercing an aggregate. The body is, to be sure, highly responsive to the mind's wishes for it. But even this causal relation between a human (or any animal) psyche and its body, which is an especially intimate case that has been produced over billions of years of evolution, is a persuasive relation. This fact becomes clear when the body is impaired by injury, drugs, alcohol, or weariness. And we say that some persons are more "coordinated" than others. The mind has the power to influence its body, not unilaterally to determine its motions. This fact becomes clearer when we focus on our influence not on our muscular system but on our physiological system as a whole. The mind has some power, for example, both to cause and to heal an ulcer, but this is the power to influence, not to determine.

Coercion in the metaphysical sense occurs only if the efficient causes totally determine the effect; if the causal relation is not completed, by contrast, until the effect makes a self-determining response, however trivial, then the causal relation is an example of persuasion, in the metaphysical sense. Coercion and persuasion in this metaphysical sense are, then, different in kind, not degree.

It is the distinction between persuasion and coercion in this metaphysical sense that is relevant to the problem of evil. This problem was generated by the assumption that God has the power to coerce the creatures of the world—that is, unilaterally to determine states of affairs among them. Only with this assumption does the existence of evil seem to conflict with the existence of a good God. Without this assumption, the evils of the world can be understood to result from the self-determining activities of the creatures, activities that God cannot unilaterally control. God cannot exert coercion in this metaphysical sense because God is an individual, not an aggregate, and therefore necessarily relates to the creatures of the world as individuals. This position lies at the heart of process theodicy.

Why is it that God cannot coerce, even though we can? Because we are local agents, with bodies between us and the rest of the world. Insofar as we can persuade our bodies to carry out our wishes, we can use them to coerce other bodies. But God, being a universal rather than a local agent, does not have a localized body. Insofar as God does have a body, it is the whole universe of finite things, including our souls and bodies. There is no localized divine body between the divine soul and us with which God could manipulate our bodies. God cannot coerce, then, because God is not one finite, localized agent among others, but the one universal, omnipresent agent.

We *are* created in the image of God, and can therefore employ categories such as "causality" and "body" analogically. But analogy is not identity. The difference between the finite and the infinite, the local and the universal, must be kept in mind. The tragedy of traditional theism is that, while it insisted on this distinction with regard to many issues, even pushing it too far on some (thereby abandoning analogy for equivocation), it did not apply it with regard to the *nature* of divine causation—that is, to the *kind* of efficient causation that can be intelligibly attributed to a nonlocalized agent. Although traditional theism insisted verbally that God is incorporeal, it in effect regarded God as a ubiquitous Superman. The problem of evil, with the mass atheism it has created, is only one of the deleterious effects of this category mistake of cosmic proportions.

I come now to the distinction between persuasion and coercion in the *psychological* sense. It is a distinction between two types of persuasion in the metaphysical sense. The term "psychological" indicates that the terms are normally used in this sense almost exclusively in relation to human interactions, and that the causal influence is being exerted on the human being as a *psyche* and therefore as an individual. In this psychological sense, the distinction between persuasion and coercion is not an absolute but a relative distinction. There is, in fact, a continuous spectrum of forms of causation running from purely persuasive persuasion at one extreme, through mildly, moderately, and very coercive forms of persuasion in the middle, to extremely coercive persuasion at the other extreme.

To threaten to shoot persons unless they do as you wish is to be extremely coercive in this sense. A bank robber may get the tellers to turn over money by using a "persuader"—that is, by threatening to shoot them with a pistol. The use of the term "persuader" for a pistol is intentionally ironic, of course: threatening to shoot someone is generally considered an extreme form of coercion. But the ironic usage conveys a metaphysical truth: although threatening to shoot someone is coercion in the everyday, psychological sense, it is persuasion in the metaphysical sense, because the threatened person still has the power to decide how to respond to the threat. The bank tellers may have turned over the money "against their will" in one sense; but in another sense they gave up the money because they willed to do so. Their will not to be shot was stronger than their will to protect the bank's money. At the opposite end of the spectrum, purely persuasive persuasion would occur when an individual was moved to act wholly by the intrinsic satisfaction promised by the act itself. A bee is persuaded to land on the flower; a man is persuaded to introduce himself to a beautiful woman; a student is persuaded to continue reading a book by an exciting first page (rather than by the threat of a low grade on a test).

Most forms of causation between human beings, however, occur somewhere on the spectrum between purely persuasive and extremely coercive persuasion. A driver stops at a stoplight both because it is good for citizens to obey the law and for fear of receiving a citation. Most citizens pay their taxes, likewise, out of a combination of intrinsic and extrinsic motivations. A student writes a good paper both because the topic is interesting and for the satisfaction of doing one's best, on the one hand, and to avoid a low grade, on the other. We usually eat because of the mixture of coercive persuasion exerted by bodily hunger and of persuasive persuasion exerted by the anticipation of delectable food.

Frankenberry's contention that the language of coercion and persuasion, as used in ordinary parlance, usually points to a spectrum of forms of causation between pure persuasion and pure coercion, in which persuasion and coercion are inextricably intermixed, is therefore well grounded. The terms are ordinarily used in the psychological sense, not in the metaphysical sense in which coercion and persuasion are different in kind, not simply in degree. Given the ordinary, psychological associations of the terms, it is doubtless difficult to prevent these associations from coloring one's analysis of writings in which the terms are used in the metaphysical sense.

It may be that, for this reason, a different set of terms should be used for the metaphysical distinction between the two forms of efficient causation. I have, for instance, often used the term *unilateral determination* to indicate more clearly what I mean by the exercise of coercive or controlling power,[32] and I have sometimes used *evocative power* along with or in place of persuasive power (partly because it connotes better the Whiteheadian idea that the influence is not exerted upon a preexisting thing but serves to evoke its partially self-creating effect into existence).

In any case, once the distinction between the metaphysical and the psychological meanings of the difference between persuasion and coercion is seen, the fact that human interactions involve various mixtures of coercion and persuasion (in the psychological sense) provides no basis for rejecting the claim of process theodicy that God cannot coerce. That claim is concerned with coercion in the metaphysical sense, because that is the sense that generates the problem of evil.

Could God even exert coercion in the psychological sense? Not as I have defined it, because coercion in this sense depends upon a threat to exercise coercion in the metaphysical sense, generally upon one's body. This fact is most obvious in what I have called extreme forms of psychological coercion, such as threatening to shoot someone. But the various other forms of psychological coercion depend upon a threat, more or less explicitly, to inflict bodily pain or deprivation, such as putting one in prison or denying one a job through which money for food and shelter could be earned. Because God cannot coerce in the metaphysical sense, it also makes no sense to think of God as a coercive power in the psychological sense. That is, of course, no small point: the major reason for living in accord with the divine will has all too often been thought to be the divine threat of consignment to a fiery hell.

Even with all these distinctions, another is needed. No wonder the discussion of this point has been so confused and confusing! The discussion of this third distinction can, mercifully, be briefer.

C. PERSUASION AND COMPULSION

Still another term is needed because of one more ambiguity lurking in the idea that divine power is persuasive, not coercive. That distinction can be heard in yet another way beyond those that have been covered. It can be heard to suggest the relative strength of causes that are, in the metaphysical sense, persuasive. We could, for example, use that language to distinguish the power of bodily urges from that of moral ideals, saying that the former work coercively upon us, the latter persuasively. I suggest that for this distinction we follow Whitehead in contrasting persuasion with *compulsion*.[33] The causality would be more or less compulsive depending upon the strength of energy with which it impressed itself upon one's experience.[34]

The language that God's power is persuasive, not coercive, can be heard to mean that the divine efficacy is in all respects and in all cases at the extreme remove from compulsive efficient causation. But there is nothing in the Whiteheadian position that requires that this possible meaning of the expression be affirmed. Process theologians can legitimately differ about the extent to which the divine aims for creatures can be compulsive, thereby insistent and difficult to ignore. The sense that the divine effects are quite strong, at least in some respects or in some events, seems to lie behind the fact that some process theologians have demurred from the idea that God cannot coerce.[35]

This concern is at the heart of Frankenberry's critique. She says that we should "reconceive the nature of God's power as truly providing not simply ideal aims but also a creative energy which is nevertheless not entirely determinative."[36] That statement reflects her erroneous historical belief that Whitehead and most process theologians have refused "to lodge creative energy in God,"[37] and also her problematic theological belief that creative energy should not only be *lodged in* but also *equated with* God[38] (an issue I will discuss in chapter 11). Nevertheless, her critique has validity. There *has* been a tendency in process theology to present the divine causation as if it simply presented us with ideal aims devoid of any creative energy empowering us to realize these aims.

This tendency follows from yet another problematic feature of Whitehead's own doctrine, beyond that mentioned above (101). This feature is Whitehead's description of ideal aims as deriving from the primordial nature of God alone. This description is surely to be explained in large part historically, in that the "principle of concretion," which was Whitehead's term for God in *Science and the Modern World*, became the "primordial nature of God" in *Process and Reality* after the doctrine of God's "consequent nature" was added. Whitehead for the most part simply retained his original idea that God affects the world in terms of a primordial envisagement of the eternal forms. This idea probably also seemed to provide a solution, insofar as a solution was possible, to the problem of how God as a single actual entity could influence the world. This solution was evidently to attribute a "satisfaction" to God's primordial nature which could be apprehended as God's "superjective nature" by worldly actual entities.[39] In any case, the association of the ideal aim exclusively with the primordial nature, understood as God's unity of conceptual feeling,[40] gave a highly idealistic tinge to most of Whitehead's statements about God's causal efficacy. The ideal aim is often called a "conceptual aim." And, even when Whitehead acknowledges that our feeling of God, being a feeling of another actual entity, must be a *physical* feeling, he specifies that it is a *hybrid* physical feeling, meaning that we feel God only by means of God's conceptual feelings, not also by means of God's feelings of the past world (God's consequent nature).[41] The latter type of feeling would be a *pure* physical feeling. Although Whitehead indicates that a transference of creative energy occurs in both pure and hybrid physical feelings,[42] it would be easy to assume that such a transference occurs only in pure physical feelings, or at least that it is insignificant in hybrid feelings. From these assumptions one could easily conclude that God provides ideal aims for us without empowering us to realize these ideals.

Whitehead's own statements in places imply the need to go beyond his own characteristic way of speaking. He portrays God as both being influenced by and exerting efficient causation upon every occasion of experience in the universe. This portrayal can be made consistent with his metaphysics only if God is defined not as a single actual entity but as a "living person," meaning a serial society of divine occasions of experience. The necessity for that change is made even clearer by the fact that Whitehead saw the world as affected by God's consequent nature, which means by God's physical feelings of the world.[43] Whitehead's assertion here implies that our feeling of God cannot be simply a hybrid physical feeling, but must also involve a pure physical feeling, because it feels God as a whole. The implications of Whitehead's metaphysics, accordingly, and his own statements that reflect these implications, show that his doctrine needs revision. This revision allows for a more robust portrayal of divine efficient causation than is usually given.

In conclusion: the doctrine that the divine power is persuasive alone, not also coercive, is a very complex issue. Because of the various distinctions and connotations of the terms, misunderstandings could have been prevented, if at all, only by a much lengthier discussion in which the various distinctions were clarified. Although in some cases I think the critics could have read more carefully, most of the misunderstandings I attribute to the brevity of my discussion combined with the complexity of the issue. In any case, although the various criticisms have provided invaluable spurs to state the case more clearly and convincingly, they have not, once confusions have been overcome, provided any reason to revise the claim that the God of process theology cannot, in the metaphysical sense of the term, coerce.

As a further illustration and clarification of the confusions surrounding this point and the distinctions needed to overcome them, and also as a test of whether this point can stand up under sustained criticism, I conclude this chapter with an extensive examination of a critique by David Basinger. This examination will necessarily involve some repetition of points already made, but these issues have occasioned so much misunderstanding that the repetition may be helpful.

D. DAVID BASINGER'S CLAIM THAT THE PROCESS GOD COULD COERCE

In "Divine Persuasion: Could the Process God Do More?,"[44] David Basinger argues again, as he had done in the article written with his brother, against the view that "the model of divine omnipotence affirmed by process theism is superior to that affirmed by classical theists in the 'free will' tradition."[45] This conclusion is said to follow "once the process concept of divine persuasion is properly analyzed." This analysis is said to reveal the misleading nature of the process theologians' comparison between their God and that of classical or traditional theism, according to which the latter "possesses and exercises coercive power" while the former never coerces in the sense of "unilaterally bring[ing] it about that other entities must act in accordance with his will."[46] In this response, I consider whether Basinger's conclusions follow "once the process concept of divine persuasion is properly analyzed." I will suggest that they do not follow, because the analysis is improper.

Basinger begins by asking what process theists mean by saying that God never coerces. He rejects my claim that, from the perspective of process theology, "God never unilaterally brings about any state of affairs."[47] Basinger rejects this claim on the grounds that "God unilaterally lures each entity." Although his discussion here distorts what I mean by "states of affairs," and is misleading in other respects as well,[48] he does see that what process theists deny is that God's "luring ever insures (unilaterally brings it about) that God's ideal aim . . . is actualized." Basinger therefore proposes that what process theists mean is that "God never brings it about unilaterally that other entities must *act* in accordance with his will."[49] Although the way Basinger intends to use this reformulation is problematic, as will be seen later, it is fine in itself.

Basinger asks why the process God does not coerce in this sense. After citing a passage from Lewis Ford that seems to say that the reason is a self-limitation on God's part (which would make process theists vulnerable to the criticisms they level against traditional free-will theists), he says that most process theists "seem to agree with Griffin that divine noncoercion 'is not due to a decision on God's part which could be revoked from time to time.'"[50] He then examines my argument for assuming "that God is thus limited":

> To affirm that God could coerce (unilaterally control the actions of) another entity, Griffin argues, is to affirm that "it is possible for one actual being's condition to be completely determined by a being or beings other than itself."[51]

Basinger here correctly quotes the statement that was misquoted in the earlier article written with his brother (see page 60, above); but the problem of misquotation arises again as he proceeds:

> However, he [Griffin] continues, actual entities can only be completely determined if they are "totally devoid of all power—power to

determine themselves, even partially, and power to determine others, even partially."[52] But "talk of powerless entities [sic] is finally meaningless," we are told, "since it cannot be given any experiential basis"—that is, since we "know it is possible for an actuality to have power" but have no "direct knowledge that [powerless] entities are possible."[53] Thus, he concludes, it is necessarily the case that no entity, including God, can unilaterally control other entities.[54]

Having thus distorted my argument, Basinger provides some counterexamples whose effectiveness depends upon the distortion. He points out that a parent can pick up a child and put it in bed if it will not respond to persuasion, or a parent can forcibly separate two fighting children.[55] The distortion is that, whereas I had said "talk of powerless actualities is finally meaningless," Basinger changed "actualities" to "entities."[56] His bracketed insertion of "powerless" in place of "such" near the end of the sentence reinforced the distortion. What I said was:

> But the person who assumes the existence of *powerless actualities* does not even have any direct knowledge that *such entities* are possible. On this point Berkeley is absolutely right. Talk of powerless actualities is finally meaningless, since it cannot be given any experiential basis.[57]

As can be seen, "such entities" referred back to "powerless actualities," *not* to "powerless entities." I, no more than Whitehead or Berkeley, think that the notion of "powerless entities" is meaningless. Berkeley's whole philosophy depended upon the distinction between perceiving things, or minds, which have power, and perceived things, or ideas, which do not (as I pointed out in my discussion of Berkeley).[58] Whitehead's distinction between actual entities and eternal objects (or pure possibilities) is similar. (Possibilities can be efficacious only by virtue of actual entities in which they are embodied, either physically or mentally.)

Furthermore, and more important for the issue at hand, I distinguished between *individual* actual beings and mere *aggregates* of individuals, specifying that by "actualities" I meant the former. On the page following the one Basinger (mis)quoted, I said:

> First, I take it for granted that most will agree that only individual actual beings can have or exert power. Power is not exerted by mere possibilities . . . nor by mere aggregates of individuals. . . . (In the remainder of this chapter "a being" will be used to mean "an individual actual being" unless otherwise indicated.)[59]

This distinction is repeated in the following chapter. I stress that "only genuine *individuals* are considered actual entities," while, with Leibniz, "things such as sticks and stones . . . are regarded as *aggregates* of actual entities."[60] By ignoring all this, and rewording my statement, Basinger makes it appear as if I (absurdly) affirmed that all entities whatsoever possess the capacity for self-determination.[61] He can therefore easily produce counterexamples. Pointing out that a parent, being unsuccessful at persuading a child to go to bed, can simply pick up the child and put it in bed, he says we here have a case "in which a parent (one entity) unilaterally controls the behavior of a child (another entity)."[62]

A human being, as a psychophysical organism, I reply, is not simply one (actual) entity, but a structured society comprised of billions of actual entities. However, a human being is, unlike a stick or a stone, not a mere aggregate of actual entities. Because of that series of *dominant* occasions of experience we call the mind or soul, a human being is an example of that special type of structured society called a *monarchical* society. By virtue of the soul, the human being (or any animal with a central nervous system, for that matter) is a true individual in a way that a stick or a stone is not. Unlike a stick or a stone, the human being as a whole can make a self-determining response to causal influences. Accordingly, whereas the stone can be absolutely coerced, the human being, *qua* individual, cannot. The human being, *qua* body, however, can be coerced like any other aggregate. Just as someone can pick up a corpse, which is a mere aggregate, a father can pick up his child's body and carry it to another room—although the child's body, unlike the corpse, may kick and scream en route.

Basinger accordingly has provided a "counterexample" to the principle that *actualities* or *individuals* cannot be coerced only by speaking of the coercion of one *aggregate* by another. It is precisely from this type of example (one billiard ball striking another, one human arm twisting another, a bullet parting flesh and shattering bones) that we get the idea of absolute coercion, in which the affected entity makes no self-determining response to the efficient causation upon it. An aggregate is not the kind of being that *can* make a self-determining response.

Basinger gives some recognition to this distinction by seeing that the parental control in his example is not unilateral control, or coercion, because the children retain "the power to resist physically, the power to desire not to act in accordance with their parents' wishes."[63] But Basinger claims that this reply is irrelevant to the problem of evil. The form of coercion with which we are normally concerned, he says, is not the ability to eliminate others' power of self-determination altogether, but the power to prevent them from *acting out bodily* their antisocial desires. By analogy, when persons ask why God does not prevent moral evil, they are not generally suggesting that God should deprive the culprits of all power of self-determination, but only that "God ought to bring it about unilaterally that potential evildoers are unable to act out certain antisocial, dehumanizing desires."[64] Basinger then summarizes his case:

> For the process theist to argue that unilateral behavioral control is not really coercion unless such control also causes the being in question to be devoid of all power of self-determination is in a very real sense for the process theist to win the battle but lose the war. To define coercion in this fashion may allow the process theist to claim that God never coerces. But if it does not follow from the fact that God cannot coerce in this sense that he also cannot unilaterally control the behavior of other entities, then the victory is only verbal. For if a being—for example, a parent or God—can control the behavior of another being without coercing it (in Griffin's sense), then Griffin's argument is irrelevant to the type of unilateral control with which we are normally concerned. And the proponent of his argument, accordingly, opens himself up to the very same attack which Griffin levels against the classical free will theist: if God could occasionally stop individuals— for example, a Hitler—from performing extremely antisocial actions, why does not he do so?[65]

Basinger's conclusion follows only because he neglects the distinction between the human soul, on the one hand, and the billions of cells and other actualities comprising the human body, on the other hand. Unilateral behavioral control of another person's body *is* coercion in the absolute sense. When the parent uses his or her body to pick up the child, the child's soul is not coerced (in the absolute sense that is at issue here), but the child's body is. It is precisely this type of absolute coercion that could not, I maintain, be a possible way for God to act in relation to the world.

The reason for this distinction is that the parent has a body, which can be used to coerce another body, while God does not. That is, insofar as God has a "body," it is the world itself, which includes our bodies; it is not another body *between* God (as soul of the universe) and our bodies, with which God could coerce our bodies. Absolute coercion occurs when body acts on body, aggregate on aggregate. Only an aggregate, as distinct from an individual, is devoid of the power of self-determination; and only an aggregate can act coercively on another aggregate. If either the cause or the effect is an individual, the efficient causation will be a case of persuasion rather than absolute coercion. God's causal influence on our bodies, therefore, must be a case of persuasion, not unilateral determination. Precisely that part of the analogy between God and a parent that would be needed to make Basinger's argument work is the part that is denied. It does not follow, therefore, from the fact that parents can coerce their children's bodily behavior that God could do so.

Having made his argument at some length, Basinger then shows his partial awareness of the point I have just made:

> For process theism, what we normally identify as a human is really a society of enduring actual entities [he should say *enduring objects*]. . . . It might be argued, accordingly, that although one society of actual entities (a parent) can at times unilaterally control the spatiotemporal characteristics of other aggregates or societies (children), no specific actual entity (or aggregate) can, itself, control unilaterally the self-determined activity of the specific actual entities of which a society is composed.[66]

Saying that this position would still leave open the question of whether God can "unilaterally control the behavior of human aggregates" (as distinct from the internal activities of the billions of actual entities making up the body), he points out this possible reply:

> But perhaps God cannot exercise unilateral control over human behavior—that is, over the spatiotemporal characteristics of that enduring society of entities we call humans—even though we as humans can do so. Unilateral behavioral control, it might be argued, is only possible on the human level because we as humans possess "bodies" which have the ability to control unilaterally the "bodies" of other humans, and, thus, since God has no body, such control is not within his power.[67]

Basinger has thereby given the outline of an adequate answer to his own question. Although it would need to be fleshed out in more detail and with several examples to be clear and convincing, this answer explains not only why the God of process theism cannot coerce (completely determine the activities of) any actual entities, but also why this God cannot coerce the outer, bodily behavior of any beings, human or otherwise.

While that would have been an excellent place for Basinger to have concluded the article, he continues:

> Or, stated differently, it might be argued that we as humans can only be controlled unilaterally by the use or threat of physical force and, thus, since God cannot use physical force, it still holds that God can only persuade.[68]

The first part of this statement would require modification. (Our bodies can be coerced in this absolute sense by the use of force, and we, *qua* individuals, can be coercively persuaded by the use, or the threat to use, force on our bodies.) But it moves in the right direction, and its conclusion is correct.

Basinger, however, is not willing to accept this argument. He asks, "Why ought we grant that humans can be unilaterally controlled only by the use of physical force?"[69] In pursuing this question, Basinger makes his case by redefining "unilateral control." Here is one of his examples of what he calls unilateral control effected by psychological rather than physical force:

> Let us assume, for example, that one individual discovers that another individual is having an extramarital affair and threatens to tell the unsuspecting spouse if not paid $10,000. And let us further assume that the consequences of discovery are so undesirable for the adulteress that she sees no option but to pay the blackmailer. It appears in this case that the adulteress has in a very real sense been forced to act against her will.[70]

But this is precisely what is *not* meant by unilateral control or absolute coercion. The woman has to *decide* how to respond to the threat. When Basinger says that the adulteress "sees no option," he means that she decides that one of her options is the best. She in fact has several options from which to choose: she could tell her husband the truth, commit suicide, run away to another country, call the blackmailer's bluff, kill the blackmailer, or threaten to do so if exposed. Basinger in fact says: "It might be argued that the 'control' . . . is not really unilateral since the adulteress still retains the power to refuse to meet the blackmailer's demands."[71] And he admits: "In one sense this is true. Psychological manipulation, unlike physical manipulation, does not destroy the capacity of an individual to refuse to act in accordance with the wishes of the manipulator."

Undeterred, however, by the recognition that he is using an example of something other than unilateral control to prove the possibility of unilateral control, he continues:

> But it is not clear that, given the value system of the adulteress, she would in fact even seriously consider not paying the money. . . . In short, it is not clear that individuals can in fact always resist psychological manipulation. Such manipulation does in some cases appear in a very real sense to result in unilateral behavioral control.[72]

Basinger evidently believes that, by using a number of qualifiers, or weasel words ("not clear that," "seriously consider," "not . . . always," "in some cases," "appear," "in a very real sense"), he can justifiably use the term "unilateral" after admitting that it does not apply.

In any case, his conclusion is so weak that nothing of import follows for the problem of evil. After arguing that God should be able to coerce worldly entities in this sense—not "always," to be sure, but "on occasion"— he concludes:

> But if such unilateral manipulation is possible in even some cases, then the process theist is again open to a version of Griffin's challenge to the classical free will theist. If the process God could prevent (or minimize) some particularly horrible evils by the judicious use of psychological manipulation, why does he not do so?[73]

Leaving aside the metaphorical and emotive term "psychological manipulation," Basinger's question is whether God can sometimes influence persons to change their behavior. My answer is: "I hope so." For an example, Basinger asks whether God could "make the adulteress experience enough guilt . . . to insure that she stopped her illicit affair?"[74] If he means whether God, in that particular case, could unilaterally ensure she would stop by inducing sufficient guilt feelings, the answer would be no. But Basinger has worded his conclusion so that the question is whether *on occasion* adulterers would feel sufficient guilt to stop cheating on their spouses. To that question I would answer yes. I assume that guilt feelings, at least at times, are due to our awareness, at some level, of divinely rooted norms, which include truthfulness, fairness, and respect, and that persons quite often either desist from or never begin some practice because they feel it would violate these norms and induce intolerable guilt feelings.

Accordingly, when Basinger asks why God does not sometimes prevent or minimize some particularly horrible evils by using this power, my answer is: "I assume that God is doing so all the time." Basinger seems to think his question has the same force in relation to a process theodicy that my question has in relation to the theodicy of the traditional free-will theist. But the difference between "always" and "in some cases" is an absolute difference, the difference pointed to by the word "unilaterally." According to the traditional theist, God could in *all* cases unilaterally prevent particularly horrible evils, because God can unilaterally control finite happenings (even if this means momentarily overriding human freedom or its natural effects). When some particular evil happens, one can therefore conclude that God thought its nonoccurrence not sufficiently important to guarantee it. But in process theism, in spite of Basinger's efforts to try to make the word "unilaterally" applicable, God can prevent evils only insofar as the creatures use their power of self-determination to respond conformally to the divine persuasion.

Accordingly, when some preventable evil happens, the appropriate assumption is not that God did not do everything possible to prevent it, but that the creatures who caused or permitted the evil did not respond adequately to the divine initiatives.

As often before, Basinger had anticipated the answer to his question. He admits that he has perhaps too hastily concluded that the process deity should be able to coerce persons to act contrary to their wishes. After reviewing my argument for the existence of certain "necessary because uncreated principles governing the interrelations among worldly actualities,"[75] he says:

> As Griffin sees it, God does not have the option of coercing us, even occasionally, because he is compelled by metaphysical principles which he did not create but to which he must conform, to use persuasive power.[76]

Aside from the fact that I do not say that God is "compelled by metaphysical principles," as if they were alien principles (like the "nonrational Given" of Brightman's God) to which God only grudgingly submitted,[77] this conclusion is correct.

But a problem quickly arises. As a statement of the principle from which the conclusion follows, Basinger presents the following statement as a quotation from me:

> The freedom which is entailed by the capacity to enjoy human-level values is necessarily the freedom to disregard the initial aim proferred [sic] by God in favor of some other real possibility for that moment of existence [proferred misspelled in original text].[78]

Basinger then, on the basis of this statement supposedly from me, takes my position to be open to meaning that "we can be considered truly human only in those contexts in which we have the power to reject God's wishes," as if my position could be the same as that of traditional free-will theists. He continues:

> But it does not follow from the assumption that there exists a necessary correlation between human-level values and self-determination that God could, in fact, never coerce us (unilaterally control our behavior). For example, it does not follow from the assumption that Hitler only acted in a truly human fashion in those instances in which he was not coerced by God that God could not have unilaterally controlled Hitler occasionally.[79]

This is just the argument I had used against John Hick and other traditional free-will theists.[80] Would it not be ironic if my position were open to the same objection?

Basinger, unfortunately, has again been able to make his case only by misquoting me. Compare the supposed quotation above with what I actually said:

> Also, the increase in complexity means an increase in the number of novel real possibilities for actualization. In regard to the finite actuality's relation to God, this means more capacity to disregard the initial aim proferred [sic] by God in favor of some other real possibility for that moment of existence.[81]

In my statement, nothing about "the capacity to enjoy human-level values" is mentioned; no opening therefore is provided for Basinger's interpretation, according to which "there exists a necessary correlation between human-level values and self-determination."

The basic point that distinguishes the theodicy of process theism from that of traditional free-will theists is the hypothesis that God cannot unilaterally control *any* actual entities, because *all* actual entities, not just human ones, possess self-determination to some degree. All actual entities, therefore, have *some* capacity to disregard the initial aim proffered by God. According to my hypothesis about a set of necessary or metaphysical correlations between value and power, more complex actualities, which are able to enjoy more intrinsic value, necessarily have more freedom and thereby "more capacity to disregard the initial aim." Basinger's quotation, besides creating "human-level values" out of whole cloth, omits the comparative word "more," thereby leaving the impression that only human beings have *any* capacity to disregard the initial aim from God. And yet the centrality of the comparative word "more" can be seen from my immediately following sentences, in which it is used *ad nauseam*:

> Accordingly, God's stimulation of a more and more complex world, which has the capacity for more and more intrinsic value, means the development of creatures with more and more freedom to reject the divine aims. Increased freedom in relation to the world necessarily means increased freedom in relation to God.[82]

I say, therefore, not that only human-level values entail self-determinism, but that enjoying "the high-level values of which we are capable entails genuinely having a high-level power of self-determination, even *vis-à-vis* God."[83]

Basinger had correctly seen that, if the point stands that "God does not have the option of coercing us, even occasionally," his whole argument would collapse. That point stands.

But Basinger has yet another challenge to the principle that "God cannot bring it about that other entities are devoid of the power to act out their desires." For someone to establish this principle, he claims:

> It must be shown that there exists some eternal, necessary metaphysical principle which has compelled God to "create" only actualities who are free to reject his initial aim at all times. This Griffin has not done.[84]

Basinger has here shifted to a completely different type of argument, evidently without being aware of it. Up to this point, he had been attempting an *internal* critique of my position, arguing that my conclusions do not necessarily follow from my basic (Whiteheadian-Hartshornean) position. Now he suddenly claims that, to make my theodicy work, I must prove that that basic position is *true*. I must *show* the existence of the alleged metaphysical principle upon which my theodicy rests.

But how can one show the existence of such a principle? One can show this only very indirectly, I have argued, by showing that the metaphysical position to which it is fundamental provides a more consistent, adequate, and illuminating account of experience and reality in general than any metaphysical position starting from the contrary hypothesis. Every metaphysical position is a hypothesis, whose basic principles can be defended only in this indirect way. How could Basinger show the existence of the basic metaphysical hypothesis that lies behind traditional theism—namely, what I have called premise X ("it is possible for one actual being's condition to be completely determined by a being or beings other than itself")?[85] Only by showing that, by starting with this principle, he can produce a worldview that is more coherent, adequate, and illuminating than the worldview based on the contrary starting point. That is presumably what the debate between process theologians and traditional free-will theists is all about. I have attempted to show that the basic metaphysical principle behind my own theodicy is true in the only way in which I could, by showing that a theodicy based on it is superior to those theodicies that are based on its denial.[86] It is to misunderstand the nature of the whole enterprise to demand that I reverse this order and defend the validity of my theodicy by first independently demonstrating the truth of the basic metaphysical hypothesis on which it is based.

Basinger to some extent sees this point, but only to some extent. He suggests that the idea that God does not unilaterally control the actions of other entities may simply be taken as "a metaphysical given—a foundational belief—within the process system."[87] But what he means by this idea differs from the view sketched above in two respects. First, he supposes the stipulation that the God of process theology does not coerce to be compatible with the view "that another being with the capacities of the process God could coerce."[88] But that is emphatically *not* what is meant. The hypothesis, which I made as clear as I could,[89] is that creativity, which involves the power of self-determination as well as efficient causation, is the ultimate reality. As such it is necessarily embodied by every actual entity. The reason the being who fits the God-shaped hole in this metaphysics cannot coerce is not because this is arbitrarily stipulated of the being called "God," but because *no* individual can unilaterally control the activities of another individual, if all individuals embody creativity. If there is a "metaphysical given," it is not the noncoercion of God *per se*, but the ultimacy of creativity.

The second way in which Basinger's description of foundational beliefs differs from my position is that, for him, foundational beliefs are arbitrarily stipulated in the sense that they have epistemological immunity from outside criticism, on the one hand, and are devoid of objective supporting arguments, on the other. My position is not, however, that objective reasons cannot be given for the hypothesis that the ultimate reality is creativity (from which it follows that no genuine individuals can be completely controlled). In the first place, to show that one's starting point leads to a worldview that is more coherent, adequate, and illuminating than those rejecting that starting point *is* to provide an objective reason for holding it.[90] In the second place, I had provided an argument from experience: we have direct experience of actualities that embody creativity—meaning the twofold power to exercise self-determination and efficient causation—namely, our own experiences. We therefore know that actualities embodying creativity are possible. To assume that all actualities in any world would necessarily embody creative power does indeed involve a speculative leap. *But it involves less of a leap than the speculation that some actualities are, or could be, devoid of creativity altogether, because we have no direct experience of such entities and therefore no knowledge that such entities are even possible.*[91] Those who are unconcerned to have their basic terms and hypotheses rooted in direct experience may be unimpressed by this argument; but it *is* an "objective" argument, relying upon a direct appeal to common experience, not simply to some axiom of process metaphysics.

The substantive point of Basinger's critique is that the claim "that a being with the attributes of the process God could not at times coerce other beings in the sense in which we normally use the term" is doubtful. His formal point is that, therefore, "the process perspective on divine omnipotence is not in any obvious sense more adequate or satisfying than the perspective affirmed by classical free will theists." I have argued that neither point stands up to scrutiny.

Chapter 7

THE TRUTH OF PROCESS THEISM'S
CLAIM THAT GOD CANNOT COERCE

Even if the *coherence* of the idea that the God of process theology cannot coerce is sustained, one can still ask whether it is *true* that God cannot
coerce. The former question, treated in the previous chapter, is a question
within the context of process philosophy. It asks: Given the basic starting
point of this system of thought, does it follow that the being that fits the
God-shaped hole in this system cannot exert coercive power, understood in
the metaphysical sense as the power unilaterally to being about states of affairs in the world? The latter question, treated in the present chapter, asks:
Granted that the basic starting point of the system has that implication, is
there any good reason for accepting that starting point? Is there, accordingly,
any good reason to suppose that God—not simply the God of process theism but the God who actually created the universe of which we are parts—
cannot coerce? Put otherwise: Is there any good reason to believe that a God
with coercive power could not possibly exist, so that the power ascribed to
God by process theology is not less power than a God could have?

This chapter examines critiques of the basic starting point of the system, which is the denial of premise X. According to this denial, no individual
actual being's activities can be wholly determined by power beyond itself,
because every actual being has at least an iota of nonoverridable power to
determine its own activities. I first examine at considerable length an exten-

sive critique by Nelson Pike,[1] then look briefly at a critique by Bruce Reichenbach. There are also some responses in the notes to Stephen Davis, who has raised some of the same questions as Pike.

A. NELSON PIKE'S CRITIQUE: AN OVERVIEW

In "Process Theodicy and the Concept of Power," Pike rightly focuses on "the difficult, though foundational, metaphysical concept of power."[2] Through his analysis he seeks to refute the fundamental basis for my claim that a being with perfect power could not exert coercive power, and therefore could not unilaterally guarantee the absence of genuine evil in a world.

Pike places his critique in the context of what he considers to be three different views of omnipotence. The first is the "monopolistic view," which, as we saw in chapter 3, Pike describes as the view that an omnipotent being "has all the power."[3] The second is what Pike (tendentiously) calls the "standard view." According to this view, as we also saw in chapter 3, an omnipotent being does not necessarily have all the power, but does "have power enough to completely *over*power the others," so that "it would be capable of completely determining each of the activities of all of the others."[4] Pike correctly sees that I would say that this "alleged alternative really reduces to the monopolistic view."[5] The third view, which I adopt, he calls the "social view." It holds that "the greatest power a being could have is power to 'influence' the partially self-determined activities of others."[6]

Pike points out that the rejection of the first two views in favor of the third depends upon the metaphysical assumptions that "anything qualifying as a world would have to contain a multiplicity of actual beings,"[7] and that "each actual being has power—power to (partially) determine its own activities and power to (partially) determine the activities of others."[8] To accept these two ideas as metaphysical truths would not only rule out the monopolistic view; it would also mean that Pike's "standard view" reduces to it. This view, again, is that finite beings may have power, but that God could, whenever God wished, completely determine the activities of all finite beings. My reason for holding that this view reduces to the monopolistic view is my claim that to have power is not to be completely determinable by another. To say that God could overpower all finite beings, meaning that God could completely determine their activities, would imply that they really had no power, and that God therefore really had it all.[9]

Pike rightly sees that, in terms of John Mackie's statement of the problem of evil as a matter of logical inconsistency, I reject Mackie's quasilogical rule B, which says: "There is no limit to what an omnipotent being can do," which is meant to entail that "it is within the power of an omnipotent being to eliminate all instances of evil."[10] Pike then summarizes nicely (except for phrases that I have replaced with ellipses) my response to the problem of evil in terms of a definition of omnipotence according to which God is omnipotent if God can "bring about any state of affairs (S) which is such that [God's] bringing about S is logically possible":

> What the social view of omnipotence is telling us is that a world devoid of evil is not a possible value of S. . . . This is not because a world lacking evil is logically impossible. It is because if such a world were to come about, it could not be said to have been brought about by a single being capable only of influencing, rather than determining, the activities of others. It would be . . . a joint-production. . . . Part of the cause would be the self-determined element contributed by the others.[11] The upshot is that Mackie's challenge to . . . Christian theism fails. Quasilogical rule B is false.[12]

As Pike sees, this argument depends upon the rejection of premise X, which reads: "It is possible for one actual being's condition to be completely determined by a being or beings other than itself."[13] He also correctly sees that "included in an actual being's 'condition' are all of its activities."[14] Pike therefore inserts a bracketed clarification into the definition of premise X so that it reads thus: "It is possible for one actual being's condition [including its activities] to be completely determined by a being or beings other that itself."[15]

Pike then devotes most of his critique to the attempt to undermine my argument for rejecting this premise. The main problem with Pike's critique is that it is a philosophical version of the "divide and conquer" approach. That is, he takes my argument against premise X and divides it into three distinct arguments, each of which is then found to be inadequate.

My view is that actual beings, by virtue of being actual, *necessarily* have some power of self-determination that cannot be overridden. I therefore consider premise X, which presupposes the opposite metaphysical position, to be *metaphysically false*. Once it is made explicit that an actual being is necessarily a (partially) self-determining being, premise X involves a *logical inconsistency* (assuming incompatibilism—namely, that freedom in the sense of partial self-determination is not compatible with being fully determined by a cause or causes beyond oneself). I agree with Hartshorne, furthermore, that metaphysically false positions are not genuinely conceivable, so that metaphysically false positions are finally meaningless (even though we finite beings may never be fully capable of seeing this).

In Pike's analysis, this argument is divided into *three* arguments that are said to be not only *distinct* but *incompatible* with each other.[16] As if this mutual incompatibility were not bad enough, each one is also judged to be *unconvincing* in itself. Another noteworthy feature of Pike's analysis is that the importance of the argument for metaphysical falsity is belittled: the other two arguments are portrayed as more central. The idea that X is metaphysically false is said not to be argued in the text but only "hinted at",[17] the metaphysical argument is said to be inconsistent with my defense of omnipotence (as the *logical* limit of power); and the claim that X is "only" metaphysically false is said to be a weaker claim than that of its being logically false. Not only, therefore, is my argument divided into three distinct and incompatible ones, the heart of my argument is portrayed as almost an unessential addendum. With this preview, I turn now to the details of Pike's analysis.

B. PREMISE X AS MEANINGLESS

In asking exactly how premise X is said to be deficient, Pike says: "Griffin's official (i.e., fully explicit) answer to this question is that Premise X is *meaningless*."[18] Pike's contention, however, is contradicted by the statement he quotes at the conclusion of my argument: "Accordingly, premise X should be rejected not simply as false, but as meaningless."[19] This statement, which refers back to a discussion of metaphysical falsity, shows that the answer that X is false is as "fully explicit" as the answer that it is meaningless. I did *not*, however, make clear my view that being meaningless and being false finally coincide with regard to metaphysical (as distinct from contingent) issues, so my statement does provide some basis for the view that I have *two* distinct arguments. I will return to this issue later.

For now, the question is the worth of the argument that X is meaningless. This argument is that "the meaningful use of terms requires an experiential grounding for those terms," and that there is nothing that we would call actual that we experience to be devoid of power. We therefore have no "empirical basis for the meaning of 'a powerless actuality.'"[20] The existence of powerless actualities is presupposed, however, by premise X, as pointed out by this passage:

> For premise X to be accepted, actual (in distinction from imaginary or ideal) entities would have to be totally determinable, in all respects, by some being or beings other than themselves. In other words, they would be totally devoid of power—power to determine themselves, even partially, and power to determine others, even partially.[21]

The conclusion is that premise X should be rejected as meaningless.

Pike rejects this argument on the basis of three criticisms:[22] (1) it rests on an *ad hoc* premise (that "powerless actuality" is a meaningless phrase); (2)

it is implicitly inconsistent (treating "powerless actuality" as a meaningful phrase while affirming its meaninglessness); and (3) it rests on an invalid inference (from "B is determinable" to "B is devoid of power").

With regard to the first criticism, Pike argues that the requirement that terms to be meaningful must be based on direct experience is "much too strong to be adequate."[23] He says, "it is surprising to find a contemporary thinker relying on a theory of meaning as naively empirical as this," and suggests that the history of logical positivism illustrates that "no such theory could possibly pretend to capture the meaning of 'meaning.'"[24]

What logical positivism illustrated, however, was the *inadequacy of a superficial, sensationist empiricism*. In Whiteheadian-Hartshornean thought, which builds on the "radical empiricism" of William James, sensory perception is a derivative, not the fundamental, form of perception. Given this deeper, more adequate understanding of empiricism, the empirical criterion of meaning need not be surrendered to maintain contact with the presuppositions of common sense, ordinary language, and scientific practice. For example, Whitehead says that "Hume's demand that causation be describable as an element in experience is ... entirely justifiable."[25] He is able to honor this demand while speaking of causation (as real influence, not simply "constant conjunction") by recognizing a mode of perception deeper than Hume's sensory impressions. He calls this deeper mode, significantly, "perception in the mode of causal efficacy."

I do not know if Pike, with this wider notion of "empiricism" in view, would consider the empirical criterion of meaning "naively empirical." Whitehead, in any case, given the mathematical and speculative dimensions of his work, is generally not considered naively empirical. Charles Hartshorne, furthermore, is generally considered anything but excessively empirical; indeed, many persons seem to think that, in comparison with Whitehead, he is not empirical enough.[26] And yet Hartshorne endorses the empirical criterion. He says that "the principle of empiricism" is "the basis of intellectual integrity," and characterizes it as "the determination to abide by two rules." The first rule is that direct or perceptual experience is to be transcended only by imaginative experience. The second rule is that this extension is to respect clues given in perceptual experience.[27] When I speak of "direct experience," I mean what Hartshorne means by "perceptual experience" (which is not primarily sensory perception). I also agree, against some empiricists, that the discussion of meaningful issues often requires that perceptual experience be transcended by imaginative experience. But I insist with Hartshorne that this transcendence cannot involve a transcendence of all *analogy* with perceptual experience. We can talk meaningfully of supposed actualities that we have never consciously perceived, such as electrons, intelligent beings from another galaxy, and poltergeists. But if our idea of actualities comes from direct experience of actualities *with power*, and if we have no perceptual experience of actualities *devoid of power* (and Pike does not claim that we do), then we have no analogical basis for speaking meaningfully of possible worlds containing powerless actualities.

Pike wonders if the concept of a "powerless actuality" could be derived by extrapolation from experience, analogously to the way Whitehead derived the concept of a geometric point by extrapolation:

> Allow that we do not directly experience powerless actualities. Still, we do experience things having more or less power. . . . Attending progressively through a series of actualities exhibiting less and less power, via an act of extrapolation to the limit of the series, perhaps I can arrive at the concept of a powerless actuality. Is that right? I don't know. But it is not clear that it is wrong.[28]

This procedure *is* wrong because it crosses the line between "some" and "none," which is an absolute line, demarcating a difference of kind. The line separating *some power* and *no power* is precisely the line between an actuality and a mere idea, form, or possibility. In Whitehead's method of extensive abstraction, by contrast, no such line is crossed.[29] Pike is probably correct that persons in fact arrive at the idea of a powerless actuality in this manner, more or less reflectively. But that does not make the resulting idea an ultimately meaningful idea, and the fact that the line between "some power" and "no power" is crossed suggests that it is *not* meaningful, because no shred of analogy with experienced actualities remains.

The distinction between "idea" and "ultimately meaningful idea" brings us to Pike's second objection to my argument about meaninglessness, which is that it is based on an inconsistency. If the phrase "powerless actualities" were meaningless, Pike says, then any statement using this term would be equally meaningless, including my denial that I experience any powerless actualities. My inconsistency is that I call the phrase meaningless while understanding its meaning well enough to know what it is that I do not experience.[30]

Pike is correct that my discussion appears to be inconsistent, and that I provided no distinction with which to dissolve this appearance. Pike himself, fortunately, points in the right direction, distinguishing between "the ultimate meaning-status of the function 'X is a powerless actuality'" and "some kind of surface meaning" that it has.[31] My position, as indicated earlier, is that metaphysically false ideas are ultimately meaningless, but that this absence of ultimate meaningfulness is not always obvious, sometimes even after sustained thought.

I have found Hartshorne convincing on this twofold point. On the one hand, he says that "a philosophically false position is not really conceivable," and "necessary truths are those whose contradictory is nonsense."[32] On the other hand, he says that most a priori or necessary truths are not obvious, that metaphysics is that area of necessary truth "in which clarity and certainty are least readily attained," and that distinguishing real from merely apparent absurdity can be a delicate matter.[33]

To hold, then, that the phrase "powerless actuality" is ultimately meaningless does not prevent it from having sufficient surface meaning for us to have some idea of what is meant by it. Other examples of ultimately meaningless ideas with some surface meaning are the ideas of "going backward in time," "returning to the past," "an actual instant," and "an immutable consciousness of temporally successive events." Not every absurdity is as immediately and obviously self-contradictory as a "round square." We can therefore speak somewhat intelligibly about powerless actualities, asking whether to affirm or to deny their possible existence, even asking if the phrase is ultimately meaningless so that such alleged beings cannot exist in any possible world.

Although Pike tries to punch holes in my argument against the meaningfulness of "powerless actualities," he is not really concerned to defend the possibility of such entities. His concern is to use the surface meaning of both this idea and premise X to investigate "their logical connection . . . to the claim that actual beings are completely determinable."[34] In particular, he wants to break the logical connection I had suggested. The part of my argument he attacks is the phrase "in other words" in this statement:

> For premise X to be accepted, actual (in distinction from imaginary or ideal) entities would have to be totally determinable, in all respects, by some being or beings other than themselves. In other words, they would be totally devoid of power—power to determine themselves, even partially, and power to determine others, even partially.[35]

Pike asks:

> What shall we make of the idea that "there are powerless actualities" is just another way of saying ("in other words") that actual beings can be completely determinable? This would be true only if these two strings of symbols have the same meaning. This is precluded if the former has no meaning at all.[36]

Pike's conclusion does not follow. The two phrases can ultimately mean the same thing if they both are ultimately meaningless (while having a similar degree of surface meaning). And that indeed is my position. Or—to put the conclusion in other terms—to say that something is fully determinable by outside forces is to say that it is not an individual actual being.

Pike, however, while distancing himself from "powerless actualities," wants to affirm the possibility, and in fact the reality, of beings that are *actual* in the sense of having power but that are nevertheless *fully determinable by another.* We here come to his third and most important objection against the argument that premise X is meaningless. This objection is that the inference from "B is determinable" to "B is devoid of power" is invalid. Pike claims that one entity (B) could be completely determinable by another reality (A) without thereby being devoid of power to determine its own activities. One case of this, Pike says, would be when B has the power to determine its own activities but chooses not to exercise this power. For example, a father has the power to move his arm, but allows his daughter to move it for him. Through this example Pike believes that he has shown that we can distinguish between *having* power and *exercising* it, and that, therefore, "the 'standard view' of omnipotence does not reduce to the monopolistic view. These two concepts would be equivalent only if beings that are completely determinable are necessarily beings that are devoid of power."[37]

Pike's example, however, is not a counterexample to the claim that the activities of a (self-determining) actual being cannot be completely determined by outside forces. The main source of the problem is a pair of *category mistakes.* First, a complex society is treated as if it were a single actual entity; this is an example of what could be called the "fallacy of misplaced individuality." On the basis of this mistake, a second category mistake is made: an example of efficient causation (moving one's arm) is treated as if it were an example of self-determination. I will explain why each case involves a mistake.

By an "actual being," I indicated, I mean an occasion of experience. It is individual occasions of experience that exercise self-determination and then exert efficient causation upon others. The mind or soul is a temporal society of occasions of experience and is thus *in each moment* a single actual entity. Although a single occasion of experience is an "actual being" in the strictest sense, the mind or soul, as an enduring individual, can thereby also be considered a true individual, because at any one moment it consists of a single actual entity. The total human being, as a psychophysical organism, is an extremely complex society of billons of individuals: electrons, protons, neutrons, atoms, molecules, macromolecules, and cells can all be considered temporal societies of occasions of experience, analogous to the soul. I thus distinguished *genuine* individuals, whether momentary or enduring, from *aggregates* of actual entities, such as sticks and stones, or, for that matter, a human arm. Aggregates as such have no power of self-determination. I pointed out that by "a being" I would always mean "an individual actual being."[38]

In this light, we can see that Pike's example does not address this issue. To begin with, to move an arm is to move not an individual with self-determining power but a very complex society of individuals. An arm as such has no power of self-determination, which is clear if the arm is severed from the rest of the body or is the arm of a corpse. The arm of a healthy, living human being can, of course, provide much more resistance to an outside arm-mover than can a dead arm, but this resistance comes not from the arm's self-determination but from the *efficient causatiion* being exerted upon the arm by its owner through the brain and muscular system. In moving her father's arm, then, the daughter has not completely determined the activities of an "actual being," as I had defined it. For Pike's example to approach the point at issue, the daughter would need to be able to determine *all* the activities of *all* the arm's cells, and that of their molecular and subatomic constituents. This control would have to include not only their spatiotemporal movements but also their internal movements, meaning their activities of self-determination.

In Pike's example, the "entity" whose activities are allegedly being completely determined by an outside force is not the arm as such but the father. Pike's point is that the father has the power of self-determination—that is, the power to raise his arm—which he may choose not to exercise. Raising an arm (I reply) is not a simple act of self-determination by a single actual entity, however, but a complex series of acts of efficient causation upon a vast society of actual entities constituting the central nervous system and the arm muscles. The daughter in moving the arm has replaced a possible act of *efficient causation*, not a possible act of *self-determination*. This distinction is implicit in Pike's analysis. He tells us that the father "chooses" not to exercise his arm-raising power and "allows" his daughter to raise his arm for him. That decision-making power is what I, following Whitehead, mean by an individual's inherent power of self-determination. Only if the daughter could completely control whether or not her father would *want* to move his arm would we have an example of one individual's being able "to completely determine the activities" of another individual.

Taking choice as the primary form of self-determination is no peculiarity of process theology. In theological debates about "grace and free will," as I pointed out in *God, Power, and Evil*, the central question has been whether we have any freedom *vis-à-vis* God to decide for or against God's will. According to Luther and Calvin, for example, we cannot even choose to believe the gospel unless God has predestined us to believe it.[39] Augustine said that "God works in the hearts of men to incline their wills whithersoever He wills, whether to good deeds according to His mercy, or to evil after their own desserts."[40] Pelagians, Arminians, and traditional free-will theists such as Hick and Plantinga insist that we must have freedom of choice *vis-à-vis* God. Whitehead and process theologians insist not only that *we* have it, but also that *all* actual entities have it to some degree, and that this would be the case in *any* world. By ignoring the question of choice, Pike has ignored the central issue within my discussion, which has also been a central question within theology in general.

It is only because Pike treats a complex society of individuals as a single actual being, thereby committing the fallacy of misplaced individuality, that he is able to distinguish between "having" and "exercising" power. He sees an individual as being able to have power without exercising it, because a person can have the power to raise an arm without exercising it. The Whiteheadian analysis I was employing shows individuals, to the contrary, to be essentially active: it belongs to their essence to exercise their power of self-determination. They must exercise the power of choice, as Pike's example unwittingly shows: whether the father chooses to raise his arm, or chooses not to, he is still choosing. As the saying has it: "Not to decide is to decide." (Many choices are, of course, subconscious.) Because Pike takes the act of raising one's arm as an example of self-determining activity, he concludes that the exercise of such activity is optional. Raising one's arm, however, is really an instance of *efficient* causation—that is, the influence of one individual (the soul) upon other things (the cells comprising arm muscles *via* the central nervous system).

Although the power to influence others is as inherent to individuals as the power of self-determination, and its exercise as essential, the *way* in which this power is exercised is somewhat optional. This is especially the case in high-grade individuals, such as a human soul, which can consciously decide, to some extent, which kinds of causal power to exercise and which kinds to withhold. For example, I can decide whether to tighten my arm muscles or to keep them relaxed. But this does not mean that I could exist as an actual being if I were not making any decisions at all.

Pike's mistake is to conclude from the options we have with regard to *how* to exercise our power that the exercise of power *as such* is optional. But we cannot possess the power of self-determination and the derivative power of efficient causation without exercising these powers in some way. Once we see that, it is clear that we would not say that an individual whose activities could be completely controlled by another would have any real power in relation to that other being.

This may become clearer by examining Pike's second example, which is supposed to show that one being could be completely determinable by another without being devoid of power. In this case, A may have the power "to completely determine the activities of B" but choose not to exercise it, thereby leaving B the power to determine its own activities. Pike's example is that a father may have the power to restrain his daughter's arm and may yet allow her to move it herself.[41]

The same problems arise as with the previous example. First, the father's restraint of the locomotion of his daughter's arm does not come close to *completely* determining *all* her bodily activities. Second, the interesting question would be whether he could control her *desire* to move her arm, and this not with threats, which might produce a divided will, but by causing her not in any sense to *want* to move it. If the father could really control *all* her activities—all her desires, all her emotional reactions to events, all her decisions, as well as all her bodily movements—we would *not* attribute to her any power of her own. We would at least not do so while he was completely controlling her. And if he had the power to turn her off and on, we would not say that she had any power of her own, *in relation to him*, even in those times when he was not controlling her. All the power in the relationship would belong *essentially* to him; the situation would be essentially monopolistic. Accordingly, I had argued:

> If one holds that B's condition can be totally determined by A, this implies that B really has no power in relation to A. And if B represents the totality of the world, and A represents God, this means that God has all the power, while the world has none.[42]

Pike's attempted counterexample does nothing to undermine this point. He therefore has failed in his attempt to defend premise X by breaking its connection with the monopolistic view of divine omnipotence.

C. PREMISE X AS LOGICALLY FALSE

Having examined what he considered to be my distinct argument for the meaninglessness of premise X, Pike turns to what he considers a second argument, which is that premise X is logically false. Although Pike says that "this thesis is not explicit in Griffin's text," so that "no argument is given in its support," Pike for some reason "suspect(s) that it is this second thesis concerning the deficiency of Premise X upon which Griffin is really depending in his argument against the standard view of omnipotence."[43] Because I had unwittingly failed to give an argument to support what is, unbeknownst to me, my main thesis, Pike graciously offers one of his own construction.

Pike's proffered argument attacks what he calls a "strengthened version of Premise X," which runs:

> It is possible for A to completely determine all of the activities of B *even in the case where B is making whatever effort it can to determine its own activities for itself.*[44]

This "strengthened version" of premise X, Pike says, "is presupposed by the basic idea at work in the standard view of omnipotence, viz., that if A is omnipotent, A has the power sufficient to *over*power whatever effort B may make to determine its own activities for itself." The proffered argument, which concludes that this "strengthened" version of premise X is logically false, depends upon principle P: "If B makes whatever effort it can to do F and fails, B does not have the power to do F."[45] Pike then attacks P and concludes that any attempt to demonstrate the logical falsity of the "strengthened" version of premise X would fail.[46] Believing his proffered argument against premise X to be better than my own,[47] Pike presumes that in defeating his own argument he has defended premise X against my argument(s).

Although Pike is right that I would consider his "strengthened" version of premise X to be logically false, showing its inherently problematic nature does not require the introduction of principle P or any other outside principle. His premise is *contradictory* all by itself—that is, it is *self*-contradictory. If A is *completely* determining *all* of B's activities, then B cannot be making *any* "effort of its own" to determine its own activities for itself. Any *effort* B exerted would be part of its *activities* and would therefore by hypothesis be completely determined by A. Pike has again failed to realize that the choices, desires, and efforts of the individual are its central "activities."

Because this "strengthened version of premise X" is said by Pike to be presupposed by his so-called standard view of omnipotence, I can only consider that view incoherent. It reduces to the monopolistic view, and thus to the doctrine of I omnipotence, which is incoherent if it is applied to God's relation to an *actual* world. This view of omnipotence can be coherent only in the context of a monistic form of idealism, in which worldly creatures are really ideas in the divine mind. Our experience of completely determining the ideas in our minds gives us an experiential basis for speaking analogically of God as completely controlling worldly creatures. We can have a coherent view either by being monistic idealists who regard ourselves as mere ideas in relation to God, or by affirming our actuality *vis-à-vis* God and thereby God's inability to *over*power our power. We cannot coherently keep our actuality *and* God's overpowering power.

Pike's offer to make up for my failure to supply an argument for the logical falsity of premise X is based on his assumption that I needed some such argument. What led him to that assumption? He supports it by referring to a passage in which I summarized my reason for holding the possibility of genuine evil to be necessary:

This position follows from the meaning of "world" as containing self-determining beings, since it is not logically possible for one being completely to determine the activity of another entity that by definition has activity that is underived from any other being.[48]

The phrases "logically possible" and "by definition" in this passage are evidently the bases for Pike's opinion that the logical falsity of premise X "seems clearly to be underpinning [Griffin's] reasoning."[49]

My statement, however, rather than suggesting an argument for logical falsity distinct from an argument for metaphysical falsity, reflects instead the following view: if one accepts the metaphysical hypothesis that creativity, which involves the twofold power of self-determination and efficient causation, is the ultimate reality and is thereby necessarily instantiated in every actual being, then *any* world (meaning any plurality of actual beings) will be comprised of partially self-determining beings. Given that metaphysical hypothesis, it is not logically possible for any one being completely to control the activities of all the others. The argument for the falsity of premise X is not divisible into a logical and a metaphysical argument. There is one argument: a metaphysical hypothesis is suggested, and its logical implications are then drawn out.

Pike has misunderstood the nature of my argument, thinking it to be very different from Whitehead's approach. He says that Whitehead's theory that the world is comprised of actual entities, each of which possesses the twofold power of which I speak, was arrived at empirically. That is, the theory, which is arrived at through the method of descriptive generalization, "is to be thought of as a 'working hypothesis' finally to be tested by reference to empirical fact."[50] Whitehead's theory, Pike wants to emphasize, was "not advanced under the banner of a priori necessity" but was offered "as a contingent generalization whose truth could be established (if at all) only by straightforward a posteriori procedures."[51] On the basis of that summary, Pike asks: "How, then, did Griffin come up with the idea that 'actual beings are possessors of two-fold power' is true (as he says) 'by definition'?"[52] To say that this is true by definition, he complains, would imply that Descartes, by believing in physical substances with no power of self-determination, was "simply confused on a point of semantics—mistaken about the meaning of the phrase 'actual being.'" To say that "would be preposterous." Pike concludes: "Whatever the substantive metaphysical facts may be concerning the powers possessed by actual beings, they will surely not be discovered simply by consulting definitions."[53]

While finding it puzzling to be criticized as insufficiently empirical after having been earlier called "naively empirical," I will try, by way of response to this new charge, to sort out the issues. First, I *was* following the Whiteheadian method, which Pike evidently favors. I proposed a different "working hypothesis" than that accepted by traditional theists. Their twofold hypothesis—even if *they* did not consider it to be merely a hypothesis—was (1) that God could exist all alone, without a plurality of finite actual beings, and (2) that, if God chose to create finite actual beings, these beings could be wholly devoid of any power of self-determination in relation to God, so that God could totally determine all their states of affairs. My Whiteheadian-Hartshornean twofold hypothesis, by contrast, is that (1) a plurality of finite actual beings exists as necessarily as does God, and that (2) finite beings necessarily have some power of self-determination *vis-à-vis* God, so that God cannot completely determine their states. The question, then, is which of these working hypotheses survives better the confrontation with all the relevant facts of experience. Because the world's evil is the most germane fact, theodicy is the discussion in which the test of the relative adequacy of these two hypotheses comes to a head. As I said in the introduction to *God, Power, and Evil:*

> The present treatment of the problem of evil . . . is intended to be "philosophy" or "*natural* theology" in that I mean the constructive position to be advocated because of its ability to satisfy, better than competing views, the normal criteria of philosophic excellence, i.e., self-consistency, adequacy to the facts of experience, and illuminating power.[54]

The point of my book was to argue that the twofold metaphysical hypothesis at the root of process theism proves itself to be superior in these terms to the twofold metaphysical hypothesis presupposed by traditional theists (whether of the all-determining or the free-will type).

Second, the statement that actual beings have self-determining power "by definition" does not mean that this is a generally accepted definition, which one might encounter, say, in the *Oxford English Dictionary.* Dualistic and materialistic philosophers who have believed in actual individuals devoid of any self-determining capacity have therefore not been guilty of a simple semantic error.[55] The statement that actual beings are by definiton self-determining was made in the course of explicating a metaphysical hypothesis. Within this Whiteheadian working hypothesis, all actual beings *are* by definition self-determining. This is not an *ad hoc* stipulation; it follows instead from the basic principle of the system, which is that creativity, which involves the power of self-determination (concrescence) and the power of other-determination (transition), belongs to the "category of the ultimate" and is therefore instantiated in every actual entity.

Pike would evidently be critical of this procedure. He says: "Of course, one might always resort to metaphysics by fiat—pure stipulation concerning the meaning of 'actual being.' But, then, one could hardly be surprised if nobody pays very serious attention."[56] But every metaphysical hypothesis has to stipulate how its various technical terms are to be used. In the Cartesian metaphysics, for example, it is stipulated that physical substances are extended but nonexperiencing, while mental substances are experiencing but unextended. Some stipulations are merely implicit. I sought with my discussion of premise X to bring out an implicit stipulation of traditional theistic metaphysics—namely, that "it is possible for one actual being's condition to be completely determined by a being or beings other than itself." Rather serious attention has been paid to traditional theistic metaphysics in general, and to the Cartesian version in particular, in spite of these stipulations.

The serious question is not whether a metaphysical hypothesis stipulates (implicitly or explicitly) what it means by "actual being," but whether the stipulation seems plausible in the light of human experience. This is where Whitehead's "method of descriptive generalization" comes in. The traditional notion of a "completely determinable substance" and the Cartesian notion of an "extended but insentient substance" were based on the common human experience of entities such as stones. Descartes generalized his notion to all earthly creatures except the human mind; this generalization has seemed implausible to most persons, in that their pets seem different in kind from stones. Most premodern traditional theists generalized their notion of a completely determinable substance to all creaturely beings whatsoever, evoking the protest of Pelagians, Arminians, and modern free-will theists and atheists. Whitehead suggests that we generalize from a different starting point, taking "the percipient occasion" as "its own standard of actuality."[57] Rather than generalizing from stones, as materialists do, or from stones *and* conscious experiences, as Cartesian dualists do, he suggests (in the light of the difficulties encountered by both materialistic and dualistic metaphysical systems) that we generalize from a moment of human perceptual experience. The resulting hypothesis is that the actual world is comprised exclusively of "occasions of experience," which are understood by analogy with a moment of conscious human experience.

Working out this hypothesis requires lots of distinctions, such as that between individuals and aggregates, and that between higher-grade and lower-grade occasions of experience. The latter distinction requires judgments about which features of human (very high-grade) experience fade into irrelevance in the generalization to lower grades of actual entities.

The question is whether, once all the necessary distinctions and explanations are made, the hypothesis seems plausible. Even though the dualistic starting point may seem initially more plausible, can the Whiteheadian starting point prove itself finally more plausible by producing an overall theory about the nature of reality that is more self-consistent, more adequate to the various facts of experience, and more illuminating of those facts, than any dualistic system? And can it seem more plausible by these criteria than any known version of any other type of system?

As part of his justification for his starting point, Whitehead reminds us that "philosophy has always proceeded on the sound principle that its generalizations must be based upon the primary elements in actual experience as starting-points."[58] He then says that Descartes' "subjectivist bias" involves a great philosophical discovery. This is the principle "that those substances which are the subjects enjoying conscious experiences provide the primary data for philosophy, namely, themselves as in the enjoyment of such experience." This principle implies, for example, that "this stone is grey" does *not* express "a primary form of known fact from which metaphysics can start its generalizations." Rather, the primary starting point is "my perception of this stone as grey." Descartes, however, "missed the full sweep of his own discovery" and kept assuming that grey stones provided primary data from which to generalize.[59]

My own discussion of "powerless actualities" and "powerful actualities" embodies a similar point. We have direct knowledge of actual beings with the twofold power to determine themselves (partially) and to exert influence on others. These directly known actual beings are our own experiences. In deciding what we should mean by an "actual being" in general (or "actuality *qua* actuality"), should we not generalize from that one type of actuality we know most fully and immediately—the only one we know from the inside? We do not have any similarly immediate experience of anything that could provide an analogical basis from which to generalize about a type of actual being that is *devoid* of all capacity for self-determination. Our knowledge of a stone is certainly not as direct as our knowledge of our own experience. The knowledge of the stone is mediated through photons and the millions of cells constituting our visual and tactile sensory systems. "This stone as inert" is, accordingly, not a primary datum; the primary datum in this instance is "my self-determining experience which includes my perception by means of my body of this stone as inert."

Now for a third and final comment about Pike's criticism of the statement that actual beings "by definition" have some power of self-determination. Although this statement refers primarily to the definition of actual beings within the Whiteheadian metaphysics, I do also believe, as indicated earlier, that all metaphysical positions except one are finally inconsistent, therefore finally inconceivable, therefore finally meaningless. The goal of metaphysical exploration is to find the one genuinely conceivable and hence meaningful account. If the Whiteheadian view of actual entities is correct about the twofold power of all actual entities, then it would be true that any other definition of actuality *qua* actuality would be mistaken. There would be no possible worlds with actualities devoid of either the power of self-determination or the power of other-influence. In that sense (assuming the truth of the Whiteheadian position on this issue), one could say that the very meaning of actuality "by definition" involves the exercise of this twofold power.

If this is true, however, our insight is far too limited to see it clearly; metaphysicians therefore cannot simply presume this definition, proceeding deductively from it as an *a priori* given. They must show that this definition makes more sense of the actualities of our world than any other definition, and that other proffered definitions lead to inconsistency as well as inadequacy to the facts. I have suggested, for example, that Pike's view that actual beings can be fully determinable from without leads to these problems.

Incidentally, although many other commentators have, like Pike, contrasted Whitehead's more empirical approach with the more *a priori* approach of Hartshorne, this contrast is often overdrawn. There is a difference, to be sure. But Hartshorne's approach *is* empirical in one sense of the word, as I mentioned above. In saying that metaphysics uses an *a priori* method, he did *not* mean "independent of *all* experience" but simply "independent of the *contingent details* of experience." Metaphysical ideas are derived from the *generic traits* of experience. And Whitehead's approach does not presume metaphysical truths to be simply contingent generalizations. He said that a philosophical scheme should be "necessary," and he spoke of "ultimate metaphysical necessities" and of "characteristics so general that we cannot conceive any alternatives."[60] It is not contrary to Whitehead's approach, therefore, to assume that, if his account of the twofold power of an actual entity is true, it is necessarily true and without any alternative genuinely conceivable by us (although we may never be able to realize this clearly).

I have said in this section that the so-called logical falsity of premise X is not a point distinct from its metaphysical falsity. The logical inconsistency arises if "an actual being" is taken to mean "a (partially) self-determining being," and the meaning of "actuality *qua* actuality" is, of course, a metaphysical, not a logical, question. I have accordingly already discussed the metaphysical question at some length. In the next section, I turn to Pike's direct consideration of this question.

D. PREMISE X AS METAPHYSICALLY FALSE

After introducing premise X ("it is possible for one actual being's condition to be completely determined by a being or beings other than itself"), I say:

> Premise X, which speaks of actual beings, begins: "It is possible. . . ." But what kind of possibility is at issue? This is not an issue that can be settled by logic alone. Rather, this is a metaphysical issue. In fact, this is what many would consider the metaphysical issue par excellence, the

difference between actuality and the other types of "being," such as possibility. (Even if one proclaims their nondifference, this is a metaphysical claim.)[61]

Pike begins his section on "Premise X as Metaphysically False" by quoting this statement (except for the final, parenthetical sentence), and then says: "Exactly what the 'metaphysical issue par excellence' is supposed to be is not made clear in this passage." I had made quite clear, I would think, that it is "the difference between actuality and the other types of 'being,' such as possibility." In the subsequent discussion, I deny that "the meaning of perfect power or omnipotence can be settled apart from a metaphysical discussion of the nature of the 'beings' upon whom this perfect power is to be exercised." Those who assume otherwise, I say, produce "arguments that are formally invalid because devoid of necessary premises."[62] I suggest further that because "the metaphysical question of the nature of a 'world' is overlooked in most recent discussions of God and evil," most "writers assume that the meaning of omnipotence is easily established."[63] (Pike is, as will be seen, one of those writers.) Having made these formal remarks, I promise to turn to "the substantive or metaphysical issue at stake ... indicating thereby my reason for rejecting premise X."[64] (Not "*one* of my *three* reasons," but "my reason.") I then point out that for premise X to be accepted, "actual (in distinction from imaginary or ideal) entities would have to be totally determinable, in all respects, by some being or beings other than themselves."[65] I later discuss "what the term 'perfect power' or 'omnipotence' can mean if it is a metaphysical truth that actual entities as such have some power, and that any actual world would have to contain actual entities."[66]

Evidently struggling to find some shred of meaning in all this, Pike says that "the implication seems to be" that my rejection of premise X rests "on the idea that it is unacceptable for metaphysical reasons." While finding "precious little on this topic to work with in the text" (I would refer Pike to the pages just reviewed, plus pp. 268–74, 276–81, and 291–300), he attempts to "make this thesis clear."[67] But, creating my thesis out of his own position instead of my text, he fails. I will explain.

Whereas Pike believes that logical possibility is a distinct kind of possibility in itself, my point is that logical possibility about actualities as such cannot be discussed apart from some metaphysical assertions as to the nature of actualities. Apart from some account of what is *meant* by an "actuality," the question of whether it is "logically possible" for one actuality's activities to be totally determined by some other being cannot be answered. To give such an account is a metaphysical task.

Two distinct kinds of possibility are not involved here. If one answers the previous question in the affirmative (saying "yes, it is logically possible for one actuality's activities to be totally determined by another"), one has already, willy-nilly, given an answer to the question about the metaphysical nature of actuality. If one begins, as I do, by explicitly taking a position on the metaphysical question of the nature of actuality, no further question of "logical" possibility remains to be answered.

Logical possibility involves the absence of contradiction among propositions. If the propositions are biological ones, referring to the nature of living things on our planet, logic tells us what is not possible for such things, *given* the initial propositions about the nature of Earth-life from the science of biology. If the propositions are metaphysical ones, referring to the nature of actual beings *qua* actual beings, logic tells us what is not possible for actual beings in this or any world, *given* the initial metaphysical propositions about the nature of actuality. Logic tells us which arguments are *valid;* but whether we think a valid argument to be *sound* depends upon our judgment as to the truth of the metaphysical propositions serving as premises.

Because this all seems elementary, and because I thought the nature of my argument was clear, Pike's attempt to state my thesis that premise X is metaphysically false came as a shock. He says:

> I think that the finished view all but explicit in Griffin's remarks is as follows: There are possible worlds—i.e., logically possible worlds—in which the activities of some beings are completely determined by another. But these worlds are not metaphysically possible.[68]

In Pike's view, which he attributes to me, logical possibility is a distinct kind of possibility that defines possible worlds much wider in scope than those that are only (!) metaphysically possible. He therefore attributes to me the view that "Premise X is only metaphysically false (and not logically false)," meaning that it is "only metaphysically impossible (and not logically impossible) for one being's activities to be completely determined by another."[69] Given that view, combined with his insistence that "omnipotence" means having the *logical* limit of power, he concludes:

> There would be no apparent reason for supposing that it is not within the power of an omnipotent being to completely determine each of the activities of all other beings and thus to bring about a world devoid of evil. The fact that S is precluded by *metaphysical* principles provides no reason at all for supposing that X's bringing about S is not *logically* possible.[70]

For Pike, in other words, the fact that something is (merely) metaphysically impossible does not exclude its being *really* possible.

Pike tells us that his view is the usual one in a passage that explains why he assumes that a being with no limits beyond logical ones could surmount metaphysical impossibilities:

> Consider the status of what is usually counted as a metaphysical principle. Such a principle is presumably descriptive of fact, however foundational. Though it may be supposed stronger . . . than a mere physical law, it is still a substantive proposition whose negation is not contradictory and which is thus logically contingent. This is to say that however binding it may be, there are possible worlds in which it fails.[71]

Although I will take Pike's word that this is the way metaphysical principles are usually understood in his circles, it is not how I understand them.

I hold with Hartshorne that metaphysical principles do not merely describe "fact," if *contingent* features of existence are thereby indicated. To formulate a metaphysical principle is to intend to describe a necessary feature of existence, one that could not be otherwise. Metaphysical features of reality (if such there be) are eternal features, and, as Aristotle said, the eternal is the necessary. I have already indicated, furthermore, that I accept Hartshorne's view that the negation of a metaphysical truth is nonsensical.

Even apart from that point, I would not agree that there are possible worlds in which metaphysical principles, if they be truly metaphysical, are not exemplified. If it is a metaphysical truth that actual beings are partially self-determining, then there is no possible world in which the activities of some actual beings are fully determined by other beings. I do not, therefore, as Pike assumes, have to say that omnipotence is restricted to the metaphysically possible, *rather* than to the logically possible. The whole point of my discussion was that, given the metaphysical view that actuality as such involves some power of self-determination, it is *logically* impossible for any being, even an omnipotent one, completely to determine the activities of another actual being. To say, therefore, in Pike's words, that "the logical limit of power is restricted to power sufficient to bring about only [*sic*] what is metaphysically possible" does not, contrary to Pike, "involve a slip to the concept of something less than perfect power."[72]

Besides thinking that the metaphysical falsity of premise X would provide no obstacle to a truly omnipotent being, Pike believes that "Griffin's text provides nothing in the way of support for the assertion that the metaphysical principle upon which he is relying is correct." He emphasizes: "What is needed is an argument—some whisper of evidence."[73]

I have reviewed above the arguments I had given about experiential meaning and the comparative plausibility of competing metaphysical hypotheses in terms of consistency, adequacy, and illuminating power. Why does

Pike ignore all that? The clue comes from the first part of his sentence, which begins: "If we discount appeals that had relevance *only* when considering the claim that Premise X is meaningless or the claim that Premise X is logically false."[74] In other words, Pike not only decided that I had three distinct arguments against premise X, he also allocated all my metaphysical discussion to the first two, so that, when he finally got to the argument about metaphysical falsity, there was nothing left to count as support for this "third" claim. The lack in question is entirely of Pike's own unmaking.

Pike's assumption that I understand omnipotence as he does, that is, as consisting in the "logical limit of power" understood as power undeterred by (merely) metaphysical impossibilities,[75] is therefore false. I do, contrary to his supposition, "follow a route that would allow [Whitehead's] straightforward comment on the existence of evil in the Process Universe"—that is, that "although God is perfectly good and thus would prefer a world devoid of evil, it is not within his power [unilaterally] to bring such a world about."[76] Following this route does not imply, as Pike assumes, that God has "less than perfect power."[77] This is because I, unlike Pike, take metaphysical principles to be really metaphysical—that is, necessary, not contingent, principles.

I conclude that Pike has provided no good challenge to my contention that premise X should be rejected. This premise, which allows for the existence of beings that are actual but essentially powerless (because their activities can be totally determined by forces beyond themselves), is the premise presupposed by all traditional theism, including Pike's so-called standard view. Insofar as we have no good reason to affirm this premise, and do have good reasons to reject it, we have good reason to reject the idea that a divine being could totally determine the activities of the beings making up an actual world. The thesis that God cannot exert coercive power is therefore sustained.

But because this point is so basic, and so controversial, it will be good to examine an attack on my arguments for it leveled from a somewhat different perspective. Bruce Reichenbach has provided such an attack.

E. BRUCE REICHENBACH'S CRITIQUE AND THE EXPERIENTIAL CRITERION OF MEANING

Reichenbach, as we saw earlier, wants to show that the God of process theology is finite in the sense of having less power than some conceivable being. One of his attempts to support this point, we saw in chapter 6, fails because he falsely equates persuasive power with final causation. A second attempt involves an attack on my rejection of premise X.

Reichenbach correctly summarizes my argument against premise X in the following steps:

(22) No actual entity is devoid of power.

(23) If an actual entity can be completely determined by another, it must be devoid of power.

(24) ∴ No actual entity can be completely determined by another.[78]

He then identifies 22 as the critical premise and asks what reason I have for considering it a necessary truth. He presents my defense as two related arguments. The first argument he summarizes is the statement that "we do not experience 'any actual thing as being devoid of power.'" He dismisses this point as irrelevant to my position because it "is a bare assertion about the speaker's limited experience and lacks the requisite universality to establish (22) as a necessary truth."[79]

My argument actually has a somewhat different character. It is based on the empirical—or better, experiential—criterion of meaning, the principle that "the meaningful use of terms requires an experiential grounding for those terms."[80] Assuming that the reader accepts this principle, I ask: "What reality could one point to that would supply an experiential basis for the meaning of 'a powerless actuality'?" This thing, I claim, "would have to be directly experienced, and directly *experienced as being devoid of power*." I testify that "I do not experience anything meeting these criteria which I would term an actuality."[81] This is indeed "a bare assertion about the speaker's limited experience," as Reichenbach says. But then I state the point more broadly, in terms of the question of "whether we experience anything that we might term an actual thing as being devoid of power. I say that we do not."[82] I am here making a claim not only about my experience, but about what I assume to be the common experience of my readers and indeed of all humanity.

If Reichenbach believes that I have misread my own experience, or that my experience in this respect is parochial, the appropriate response would be for him to show why. The limited nature of my experience is beyond doubt. The relevant question, however, is whether my experience as reported in the above statement *reflects a limitation that is germane to the topic at hand*. The implicit question of Reichenbach or any other reader is: "Is there something in your experience that you would call an actuality and that you directly experience as being devoid of power? So long as no one provides a convincing positive answer to this question, then it seems that my conclusion follows—that "those who talk of actualities that are totally devoid of power do so without any experiential grounding for the meaning of the concept."[83] Of course Reichenbach and others may want to accept this conclusion without rejecting talk of powerless actualities, thereby explicitly rejecting the experiential criterion of meaning.

But assuming that most readers do not wish to liberate meaningful talk from the necessity of anchorage in experience, I will proceed to the positive side of my argument, which Reichenbach presents simply as a second but related argument. He quotes these statements from it: "I have direct experience of my experience itself as having some power to determine itself. . . . Accordingly, this provides me with an experiential basis for speaking meaningfully of an *actual* entity which I can then transfer by analogy to other things."[84] He dismisses this point by saying that it "depends upon the validity of arguing by analogy from my experience to that of actual entities," and by then adding: "Since this argument is identical in form to that which argues by analogy from the existence of my mind to that of other minds, it is fraught with all the same problems which plague the latter."[85] He also says that the argument is irrelevant in any case, because it does not establish principle 22 as a universal truth.

Reichenbach has again misunderstood the nature of the argument. The issue is not that of indubitable knowlege, as in the question of the existence of other minds; the issue is the meaningful use of language. And the issue is not whether we can go inductively from a particular, or set of particulars, to a universal, metaphysical truth. The issue is this: given two metaphysical hypotheses—one that says that all actual things are partially self-determining, and one that denies this, saying instead that at least some actual things are devoid of any power for self-determination—does the experiential criterion of meaning give us a reason to favor one hypothesis over the other? I argue that it does, saying that "one who speaks of actualities as having power has an experiential grounding."[86] I take it as reasonable to begin with my own present experience as an instance of an actuality, in that it is the thing of whose existence I am most certain. Then, because "I have direct experience of my experience itself as having some power to determine itself, . . . the meaningfulness of 'powerful actuality' is grounded in my immediate experience." If I think of other actual entities as having some self-determining power by analogy with my own experience, I am at least thinking meaningfully about them. "A critic might consider this analogical transference questionable," I point out. But, I continue:

> What is often overlooked is that, if this affirmation is questionable, the *denial* that other things considered actual are to be understood by analogy from one's own experience is *doubly* questionable. For I at least know that it is possible for an actuality to have power. . . . But the person who assumes the existence of powerless actualities does not even have any direct knowledge that such entities are possible. On this point Berkeley is absolutely right. Talk of powerless actualities is finally meaningless, since it cannot be given an experiential basis.[87]

Where is the critic who has provided a satisfactory response to this argument? Reichenbach, like almost everyone else, does not even attempt this, possibly, again, because he does not feel the force of the experiential criterion of meaning. There has been a widespread rejection of this criterion in recent philosophy, on the basis of the recognition that experience, understood in a sensationist manner, cannot ground the meaning of many terms that are clearly meaningful. The solution, however, is not to give up the experiential criterion of meaning, but to broaden our understanding of experience in the ways suggested by Whitehead and William James.[88] In any case, Reichenbach has provided no reason to doubt the truth of principles 22–24, and therefore of the principle that no actual entity can be completely determined by another.

In chapter 6, I examined several challenges to the *coherence* of the claim that the God of process theism could not exercise coercive power, at least in the sense that would give process theism a problem of evil similar to that of traditional theism. Those challenges were found to be based on misunderstanding or distortion. In the present chapter, I have examined challenges to the possible *truth* of the claim that a God with coercive power (in the stated sense) could not exist because an actual world must be comprised of beings whose activities cannot be totally determined by another. Those challenges have likewise been seen to raise no serious problems. Because these challenges have been articulated by some of the leading contemporary philosophers of religion who have devoted particular attention to the problem of evil, the conclusion to be drawn, I suggest, is that the basic negative claims of process theodicy are capable of withstanding critical scrutiny.

Chapter 8

FURTHER QUESTIONS ABOUT
DIVINE PERSUASION

Although the reader might well think that the two previous chapters dealt with every conceivable question, and then some, about persuasion and coercion in relation to divine power, some further questions do remain. Peter Hare, granting the advantages of affirming metaphysical limitations on divine causation, asks why a voluntary self-limitation might not *also* be involved. Hare asks, furthermore, whether the doctrine of God's great persuasive power is falsifiable. David Basinger, granting for the sake of argument that God perhaps cannot coerce, asks whether God *would* coerce if this were possible. Besides believing that either answer will lead process theists into difficulties, he means with his question to ask what the God of process theism thinks about the use of coercive power by human beings. The second part of his question, accordingly, is whether the doctrine of divine persuasion supports human pacifism. I deal with these three questions in order.

A. WHY NOT A DIVINE SELF-LIMITATION AS WELL?

The review of my position by Peter Hare, who had previously been a strong critic of process theism's treatment of the problem of evil,[1] is the most positive of all those treated here.[2] He says that my book demonstrates that traditional theism, with its idea that God essentially has a monopoly on power, is metaphysically impossible and morally unacceptable,[3] and that I had presented a better case for a Whiteheadian-Hartshornean form of non-traditional theism than he had thought possible.[4]

Nevertheless, Hare says, these facts do not demonstrate that, among the variety of nontraditional theisms, past and possible, process theism is superior.[5] Hare does not intend this point as a criticism;[6] he wants only to encourage theists to use "their theological imaginations in the construction of the many varieties of nontraditional theism that are possible."[7] Hare's questions suggest the reasons why he thinks process theism and its theodicy might be less viable than some other conceivable form of nontraditional theism.

Hare's first question is whether the limitations on divine power to bring about effects in the world might be due to a divine self-limitation as well as to metaphysical necessities. Hare recognizes the advantages of rejecting the position of traditional free-will theists, according to which *all* limitations beyond purely logical ones are voluntary and self-imposed; but he wonders why a both-and position would not be better yet:

> Must we assume that God is always using all the power to which he is metaphysically entitled? Does God sometimes in some ways give creatures more self-determination than he is metaphysically forced to? I see no reason why process theists need banish contingent self-limitation from God in their eagerness to show that there are non-contingent limitations. Among even saintly human beings it is sometimes morally inappropriate for a person to exercise all his powers of persuasion, and that may be so for God too.[8]

I already, in one sense, affirm the position for which Hare is calling. In bringing forth, through the evolutionary creative process, increasingly complex beings with increasingly greater powers of self-determination, God has given creatures more self-determination *vis-à-vis* God than was metaphysically required. The result has been the introduction by God of a contingent self-limitation on the power to control what will occur among finite things. Self-limitation in this sense, however, follows from the effective *use* of divine power (to evoke into existence beings with increasingly greater power of self-determination), not from a decision not to use all the divine power. What should we say about self-limitation in this latter sense, which is what Hare has in mind?

Some process theists, following Whitehead in thinking of God as a single, everlasting actual entity (rather than as an everlasting series of divine occasions of experience), and in thinking of God's influence on the world primarily or exclusively in terms of God's primordial nature (rather than in terms of God as a whole—primordial and consequent), might rule out Hare's proposal on metaphysical grounds, thinking it too anthropomorphic. While I, too, find uncomfortably anthropomorphic the idea that God could voluntarily decrease the divine power being brought to bear here and there, now and then, I could not rule out this idea metaphysically on the same grounds, given my neo-Whiteheadian conception of God (indicated in the two parenthetical additions in the prior sentence). In this conception, the analogy between the soul-body relation and the God-world relation is stressed. Because we can voluntarily limit the power of our mind or soul to influence at least some parts of our bodies, God should be able, it might seem, to limit the divine power in relation to certain parts of the world. Accordingly, there is an initial plausibility to Hare's twofold suggestion that the soul of the universe could sometimes use less power than it has at its disposal, and that it might be morally appropriate for it to do so, just as it is sometimes appropriate for saints not to employ the full range of their persuasive powers.

This initial plausibility fades, however, as soon as we reflect upon the reasons why it is sometimes morally inappropriate for saintly persons to exercise all their powers of persuasion in relation to other persons, and upon the relevant metaphysical differences between a saint and God (as conceived here). Saints, being finite, are not omniscient (even if they have extraordinary telepathic and clairvoyant powers), and therefore will often not know all the relevant facts. Second, in relation to some decisions, saints may be interested parties. Third, even in cases where they are not interested parties, they might be aware of possible bias, of perhaps not being equally sympathetic to the welfare of all those who will be affected by the decision. Saints also know, fourth, that it is important for persons to develop their own capacities for thinking issues through and learning how to make decisions on their own. For any or all of these reasons, saints might well refrain from exercising their maximum persuasive powers in many or even most situations. In at least some cases, this negative decision might be supplemented by a positive vision of a Spirit of compassionate wisdom effective in human lives, which can be trusted without reserve. The saint's self-limitation might therefore be exercised in order to encourage a creative void in which the persuasive power of this Holy Spirit could more effectively operate.

None of these limitations would, by hypothesis, apply to God, because of metaphysical differences between God and all creatures. There is never any ignorance of relevant facts. Because God is not one finite being among others, but the all-inclusive being who is affected, for joy or for pain, by the consequences of every decision, God is never an "interested party" in the narrow sense: because of God's equally empathetic identification with all creatures, no partiality distorts the divine judgment. God's influence, furthermore, does not inhibit persons from becoming creative and responsible, but is precisely the call to become more fully creative and responsible. And of course there is no reason to leave space for the working of a Spirit of compassionate wisdom—God *is* that Holy Spirit. These differences between God and a saint follow from taking seriously the notion of God as the all-inclusive soul of the universe, who knows the world with the same kind of immediacy, sympathy, and impartiality as we know the various parts of our bodies (although with a completeness lacking in at least our conscious knowledge of our bodies). Because God's aim is always for the best for all creatures, it would be inappropriate for God not to exert the maximum power possible to encourage the best possibilities always and everywhere.

So, in addition to the fact that a divine self-limitation might not be an intelligible idea, it would also seem to be inappropriate even if possible.

B. IS THE DOCTRINE OF GOD'S GREAT PERSUASIVE POWER FALSIFIABLE?

A second question raised by Hare is about the falsifiability of process theism. Remarking that "process theists seem to find it easy to use the logic of persuasive power to explain any and all shortcomings of the world," he asks: "Is there any imaginable state of affairs or gradual historical development that would be formally inconsistent with the existence of the deity of process theism?"[9] By answering this question, he adds, "process theists could clarify the empirical meaning of their religious beliefs." This answer "would be helpful also in increasing our confidence that God's values are just what process theists say they are."[10]

A process theist could dismiss this question by saying that it is based on confusion. One way to do this would be to distinguish between a metaphysical and a eulogistic meaning of "persuasion." In the *metaphysical* sense, persuasive power is simply influence that is not coercive—that does not unilaterally determine the effect, because the effect is partially self-determining (as well as being influenced by other efficient causes). Persuasive power in the *eulogistic* sense implies that the agent is generally successful in evoking from others a self-determining response that is in harmony with the agent's will. Whitehead's statement that God's power is persuasive is intended in the neutral or metaphysical sense; it makes the negative point that divine power is not coercive. The evil in the world, which suggests that many creatures are not persuaded, far from being a disconfirmation of God's persuasive power, is therefore evidence for it. By giving this answer, the process theist could dismiss the question.

While that answer might be appropriate in relation to Whitehead's position, however, it would not be appropriate for me, given the more Hartshornean line I have taken, insisting that the word "God" refers to a perfect reality, and saying in particular that perfection in our tradition includes perfect power. (This is the element of truth in Pike's belief discussed in chapter 7, that my position, through its adoption of Hartshorne's emphasis on divine perfection, differs from Whitehead's.) Given that meaning of God, something of the eulogistic meaning is added to the purely metaphysical meaning of persuasive power. The persuasive power of the God who created our world is said to be unsurpassable by that of any conceivable creator of a universe. If it seemed to us, therefore, that a consistently conceivable creator could have greater persuasive power, our conviction as to our creator's worthiness of worship would be diminished.

A second way to deflect Hare's question would be to say, with Hartshorne, that empirical falsifiability is an inappropriate criterion for metaphysical hypotheses.[11] Falsifiability was proposed by Karl Popper precisely as the criterion for distinguishing between empirical (scientific) and metaphysical statements. (Popper did *not* mean, incidentally, that metaphysical assertions, not being falsifiable, were therefore meaningless.) An empirical truth is one that is not metaphysically or necessarily true; it could therefore in principle be falsified by some conceivable observation. A metaphysical truth would hold in any possible world, and therefore could not in principle be disconfirmed by some conceivable observation. Hare's call for process theists to clarify the "empirical meaning" of their hypothesis is therefore, one could claim, a confused call. A metaphysical hypothesis, precisely by being metaphysical, could not, without contradicting itself, claim to have empirical meaning; if the hypothesis is true, it is true necessarily and therefore universally, and no conceivable observation could falsify it.

This second way of dismissing Hare's question would also be inappropriate. Hare has asked not for *conceivable* scenarios that would falsify process theism, but only for *imaginable* ones, and we can imagine all sorts of things that are not genuinely conceivable, such as traveling into the past or foreseeing the future. Also Hare recognized that a "global hypothesis of this sort can never, of course, be knocked down by a crucial experiment," and that confirmation or disconfirmation "is a matter of degree and a matter of cumulative evidence."[12] Furthermore, as Hare points out, if we process theists "draw inferences about God's values from what happens in the world," we cannot maintain that any imaginable world, in which very different types of things occur, would be consistent with the existence of the God of which we speak.

That it is not inappropriate to attempt an answer to this question of "what sort of imaginable worlds" would be inconsistent with process theism is shown by Hartshorne's response to a similar question about process metaphysics in general. While insisting that a true metaphysical position could not in principle be falsified by empirical facts, Hartshorne points out that such facts can discredit a false metaphysics.[13] Moving from the negative to the positive, he adds that, if his metaphysical position is true, then science should be expected to uncover more and more facts supportive of this position.[14] He provides several examples that undermine materialism and dualism and support his view that the world is comprised exhaustively of experiencing, partially self-determining events. He cites the evidence from quantum physics against the view that the elementary units of nature are inert and fully determined by the past;[15] the evidence that nature is a complex of events, not enduring substances;[16] the evidence that space and time are inseparable, which supports the process view that *everything* is related to time;[17] and the evidence that the difference between primitive life and so-called lifeless matter is merely one of degree.[18] From Hartshorne's discussion we can infer what sort of imaginable worlds would be incompatible with process metaphysics: a world in which the elementary units of nature were enduring substances, especially if they were inert and fully determined; a world in which space and other things existed independently of temporal processes; a world in which an absolute gap separated living and nonliving things, or sentient and insentient individuals, or else a world in which there were no sentient things whatsoever.

With Hartshorne's answer as precedent and preparation, we can list some imaginable worlds that would contradict process theism's view of God's values and persuasive power. (1) A world that had existed everlastingly, or at least indefinitely, in essentially its present form, with all the same species, would contradict the view that novelty and variety are important to the supreme power of the universe, or that this supreme power can transform habits after they have become firmly entrenched. (2) A world remaining everlastingly in a state of chaos, in which only the most trivial forms of experience occur, would be inconsistent with the view that God regards unnecessary triviality as an evil and desires experiences that combine harmony with intensity, or with the view that God can effectively persuade creatures to incarnate these desires. (3) A world that started to evolve toward increased complexity, but in which no habits became sufficiently widespread to be considered "laws of nature," would be incompatible with the view that greatness of experience can be enjoyed only on the basis of a fairly stable order, or with the view that God can effectively persuade large numbers of creatures with trivial powers of self-determination to incorporate similar ways of being. (4) A world in which otherwise humanlike creatures never showed any interest in novelty and intensity of experience, forever choosing the way of safety and harmony, would conflict with the view that harmony and intensity are somewhat balanced in the aims proffered by the divine eros. (5) Process theism would be contradicted if otherwise humanlike beings manifested no deep-seated passion for truth, beauty, and goodness; if what we have known as conscience were to fade away, proving itself to have arisen from purely contingent causes; and if persons could be selfish and unloving and yet truly happy.

In the light of these examples, let us look more closely at Hare's way of posing the problem. He says:

> In our everyday life we think it unreasonable to doubt that someone has great persuasive power simply because few are persuaded. . . . In arguing for a belief in [a man's] considerable persuasive power we do not think it always sufficient to say that the self-determining persons he is trying to persuade can always refuse to be persuaded.[19]

From the point of view of process theism, however, it is not true that few are persuaded. The evolutionary process, through which galaxies, planets, and living creatures have been created over the past fifteen or so billion years, evidences massive and continuing persuasion. The so-called laws of nature, which are, from the perspective of process metaphysics, really the most widespread habits of nature, indicate that large numbers of creatures *are* persuaded, at least at the level of subatomic particles, atoms, molecules, macromolecules, and cells. The fact that scientists for several centuries could assume these "laws" to be absolute shows how widespread the habits are. The fact that many reasonable persons are convinced that paranormal events cannot occur shows how widespread are the physiological habits of interaction even at the human level.

Hare might concede this point but say that he was really talking about specifically human decisions, those studied by the psychologist, not the interactions studied by the physicist, chemist, and physiologist. My fourth and fifth examples above were directed at this question. Comparing our world with an imaginable world run by the supernatural God of traditional theism leads us, to be sure, to focus on the great extent to which persons do *not* act in conformity with the values of an ideal participant. But if we look at the world without this supernaturalistic premise, should we not be amazed at the degree to which human beings do conform to what we would suppose a benevolent soul of the universe to will? I grant that there are very few persons who are close to being perfectly persuaded in most of the areas of their lives—there are not many saints. But I do not grant that there are any who "always refuse to be persuaded," or even many who approach that negative ideal.

Hare makes one statement in the midst of his case that I find puzzling. He says that we have reason to doubt that a man has much persuasive power "if we have independent evidence that the persons he wishes to persuade are not exceptionally resistant and yet he repeatedly fails to persuade them."[20] I do not know what he means by "independent evidence" in this regard. We have no way of isolating persons from the various regular influences on them—the power of their genetic inheritance, the power of the past in general, including the effects of family and culture, and the persuasive power of God. Furthermore, in suggesting that persons are not exceptionally resistant, Hare goes against the experience of centuries, which is reflected in the teachings of the various religious traditions under headings such as original sin, Satan, karma, and maya.

One of the ways in which my own thought on this subject has advanced since *God, Power, and Evil* involves the notion of the "demonic," which is briefly developed in chapters 1 and 11. The basic idea is that creativity, at the human level, when characterized by hate or indifference, can function like a cosmic power of evil, seducing and intimidating persons into forms of behavior that go radically against the divine creativity, which is always characterized by creative and responsive love. The power of the demonic can be stronger in particular times and places, and the demonic potential of human creativity has become especially strong and widespread in the modern age. It seems to me, therefore, that persons in general *are* "exceptionally resistant" to the divine persuasion, in comparison with other creatures, and that modern persons in particular have unique influences upon them that make them even more resistant.

I cannot, however, stop at this point, because I have also taken my doctrine of God one step further since the writing of the previous book. I have included in what I call the "generic idea of God" in chapter 1 the stipulation that God is the "trustworthy ground for hope in the ultimate victory of good over evil." If this feature is an essential element of the doctrine of God, then the affirmation of God's perfect persuasive power must include the prediction that human spirits will eventually be persuaded in a much more complete sense. That prediction is not verifiable or falsifiable by any of us in the present ("eventually" could mean millions or billions of years), but it *is* verifiable or falsifiable in principle. In any case, the point to be brought out is that the effectiveness of God's persuasive power in relation to humanlike beings should not be judged solely in terms of what it has achieved already. By analogy, it would have been very misleading to have judged God's effectiveness with life in terms of that first billion or so years during which nothing more impressive than blue-green algae had emerged.

The prediction that things will get better does not entail steady improvement, which the increased evil of the twentieth century would falsify. I have already said that the modern world, which began about the sixteenth century, is in many respects a particularly bad episode. And some persons place the "fall" much further back—for example, with the rise of patriarchy, or of agriculture. This prediction also does not mean that the current episode might not be fatal to the human race, whether through nuclear holocaust, some other technological marvel, or more gradual ecological pollution. We cannot treat "perfect persuasive power" as if it were functionally equivalent to coercive omnipotence, so that it could unilaterally prevent our planet's or our species' premature death.

What, then, does the prediction mean? It might mean merely that God will effectively persuade human beings to live in much greater harmony with the divine will in the long run, *if* there is a long run (thanks to human prudence and an absence of natural catastrophes, such as an encounter with a huge meteorite). Or it could mean that, thanks to a capacity evoked in the human soul to continue its journey with God after bodily death, there *will be* a long run. While the first of these two interpretations would be consistent with the affirmation that God's persuasive power is the greatest conceivable (because the soul's survival of bodily death may not be possible), the second interpretation is the one I now hold. It was the growth of this conviction, through empirical evidence, that allowed me to see a point that I had not seen while writing *God, Power, and Evil*—namely, that the meaning of God as the "trustworthy ground for hope in the ultimate victory of good over evil" belongs to the generic idea of God in our culture. I therefore now agree with those who maintain that a fully adequate theodicy must include an eschatology. In particular, it must hold out the prospect of an ultimate overcoming of the power of the demonic.

C. WOULD GOD COERCE? PROCESS THEISM AND PACIFISM

In "Human Coercion: A Fly in the Process Ointment?,"[21] Basinger assumes, for the sake of argument, that the power of the God of process theism is necessarily persuasive. He does, with a reference back to his previous article (which was treated in the final section of chapter 6), indicate that he considers this claim questionable. And he repeats enough of that earlier analysis (including some of its errors)[22] to indicate what he means by "coercion in the weaker sense," which is "power which can unilaterally restrict or destroy the ability of individuals to act in accordance with their wishes."[23] But he focuses here on the question: "Would the God of process theism occasionally coerce in the weaker sense if this were an option?"[24]

It is important to recall, from the discussion in chapter 6, that what Basinger calls "coercion in the weaker sense" is *not* what I mean by relative coercion in distinction from absolute or metaphysical coercion. What Basinger means is, in terms of my categories, not a weaker sense at all; it is a case of absolute coercion exerted upon the bodies of human beings (except insofar as he switches to psychological coercion, which is not unilateral control at all). The fact that it is exerted upon our bodily parts, instead of upon our psyches, does not make it any less coercive. So the question really is: Would God exert absolute coercion to control our bodily behavior unilaterally if God could do so?

The first response to make is that this question, if taken literally, is meaningless, therefore incapable of being answered. One cannot simply "add" coercive power in the metaphysical sense to the God of process theology and still *have* the God of process theology. A metaphysical position in which it were possible for the activities of any actual individuals to be completely controlled by causal power from beyond themselves would be a different metaphysical position, requiring a different notion of God (if any at all).[25] One therefore cannot meaningfully ask whether coercive power, "if it were available,"[26] would be used by the God of process theism.

That response should not be used, however, to ignore the issues Basinger raises by means of his question. If this question is not taken literally, it can be a useful heuristic device to understand better the position of process theologians. Basinger's question arises from the fact that process theologians (in harmony with most other theologians) believe that human *praxis* should be based on our understanding of God.[27] The question is: What does the process doctrine of God imply about the use by human beings of their power to coerce, including the power to coerce violently? To ask whether God would coerce is to ask whether the God of process theologians favors coercive activity on the part of human beings.[28] This question arises in part, Basinger claims, because process theologians speak out of both sides of their mouths on this issue.[29] He is interested in pressing the question because, he believes, either answer creates problems for process theism,[30] thereby weakening its claim to be superior to traditional free-will theism.

Basinger begins by citing statements that seem to suggest that process theists provide no clear answer to the question. On the one hand, several statements suggest that persuasion, being both morally superior and more effective than coercion, is the only suitable form of power for deity to use. God therefore would not use coercion even if it were possible. On the other hand, I and other process theists typically criticize the deity of traditional free-will theists for not using its reputed coercive power more often to prevent particularly horrendous evils. "Process theists cannot have it both ways," Basinger says twice.[31] Either a perfect being would not use coercion, in which case process theists cannot criticize the position of traditional free-will theists on this score; or else a perfect being would use it, if it were available, in which case persuasive power's alleged superiority is denied and God's inability to coerce is a serious limitation on the divine perfection. Which horn of this dilemma, Basinger asks, does the process theist want to grasp?

I grasp the second horn (with the proviso, mentioned above, that I do not grasp it firmly, because the question is ultimately meaningless), while denying its alleged consequences. As Basinger recognizes, I state clearly that the divine *modus operandi* is persuasion rather than coercion for metaphysical, not moral, reasons[32] (even if some other process theologians may seem to indicate that the reason is the moral superiority of persuasion). But Basinger still believes that I oscillate on the question of whether persuasion is unambiguously superior to coercion, so that God would not use coercive power if it were at hand (so to speak). He cites statements endorsed by me that describe persuasive power as "the greatest of all powers" and as "a greater power than the supposed power of absolute control."[33] And he quotes me as saying that persuasive power is "the ultimate power of the universe" which is "finally all-powerful."[34] He believes this claim to be in tension with my criticism of the God of traditional free-will theists for not using this power (more often) to prevent evil. If persuasive power is more effective, why criticize the traditional God for not using coercion?

Basinger's criticism here is reasonable; there does appear to be an inconsistency. The inconsistency is, however, apparent rather than real. It is one thing to say that persuasive power is the *greatest* form of power; it would be something else to say that it is the *only* form of power, which I do not say. There is no contradiction in saying that God has only persuasive power, and that this is the greatest form of power, while saying that human beings, who by virtue of their bodies have coercive power as well, should use this second form of power to achieve good ends. For example, a parent should snatch a child from in front of a speeding automobile (rather than letting the child learn a valuable lesson by being run over). In the same way, it is not inconsistent to say that, if (*per impossibile*) God had coercive power, God should sometimes use that power for good ends, especially for preventing particularly horrible ends.

It is, furthermore, one thing to believe that the power of love, which *is* power, is *"finally* all-powerful," meaning that it is ultimately the origin of all motion and goodness, and that it will be more effective *in the long run* than the power of brute force based on hate and indifference (which was the point of the passage quoted). It would be something else to claim that persuasion is *always* more effective than coercion *in the short run*, which I do not claim. It is not inconsistent, therefore, to believe that the power of love will be finally victorious, and yet to believe that, if a being of perfect goodness with coercive power existed, that being would have used this power to prevent many of the things that have occurred. Perfect Goodness is not only concerned about the long-run good; if it had the kind of power that is often more effective in the short run, its compassion for us, who generally live in the short run, would lead it to use this power to prevent those evils that are too great to bear and that defeat life rather than in any way promoting it.

Basinger believes that this answer forces process theists to admit that their God is imperfect. We agree that, in the case of human beings, the best results can be achieved by a combination of persuasion and coercion: good parents use the power of love, inspiration, and example to produce long-run good in their children, while using coercive power to protect them from dangers so that the children will *have* a long run. By analogy, then, we should agree that the most perfect deity is one who would and could use a wise mixture of persuasion and coercion. Basinger thus challenges Schubert Ogden's contention that God is "good for others to an extent than which no greater can be conceived."[35] Basinger replies:

> A God who would coerce but cannot may rightly be said to be good for others to the greatest extent possible, given that being's limitations. But such a God cannot be said to be good in the greatest *conceivable* sense, since, in principle, a God who could actually coerce would be capable of doing even more good.[36]

In thus replying, Basinger reveals that he does not grasp the fundamental claim of Ogden, Hartshorne, and most other process theists, that while "a God who could actually coerce" in Basinger's sense is verbalizable and may in some sense be imaginable, it is not genuinely *conceivable*. To enter into this issue, however, and to deal with Basinger's repetition of the stock charge of traditional theists that "the God of process theism is a 'weak' being,"[37] would be to repeat the points of the previous chapter or to anticipate the points of the next.

The unique issue Basinger raises with his question concerns the moral issue of the desirability of coercion at the human level. In Basinger's mind, those who maintain that a perfect being would not coerce, even if it had coercive power at its disposal, should "criticize any use of coercive power on the human level" in favor of exclusive reliance upon "pacifistic persuasion."[38] Those who maintain, as I do, that God's noncoercion is for metaphysical reasons, and that a deity allegedly having coercive power should use it to prevent unbearable evils, can be expected, believes Basinger, to use this position to provide theological justification for coercion, including violence.[39]

There is some logic to Basinger's correlations, and they hold true of many theologians. He correctly sees that most process theologians do justify war and violent revolution in some cases. I want to suggest, however, that his correlations do not necessarily hold. I will not try to lay out all the possible positions, or address all the implied issues; I will only suggest that process theology would not necessarily give less support to a pacific way of life than traditional free-will theism, and that it might give even more.

In the first place, to say that the divine *modus operandi* is persuasion, not coercion, for metaphysical rather than moral reasons is not to deny that persuasion is admirable and therefore worthy of emulation. It can be both necessary *and* admirable. I return to this point below.

In the second place, even to say that the deity of the traditional free-will theists should use its coercive power to prevent unspeakable evils is not necessarily to imply that human beings should be quick to use strongly coercive force. The reason is that deity would have many important qualities not shared by mortals. Being *omniscient* (even if this omniscience were coherent omniscience and therefore did not include knowledge of the future, except for probabilities), this deity would know when strongly coercive action was likely to produce more good than evil; human beings are very bad at estimating this in many situations, such as when facing the prospect of war. Being *impartially benevolent*, this deity's decision to resort to strongly coercive measures would not be colored by partisan bias; human beings seldom if ever impartially take into account the good of all those who will be affected in deciding whether to go to war. Being *impartially sympathetic* (assuming, for example, Abraham Heschel's idea of God as the Most Moved Mover,[40] or a Christian concept of deity for which the cross is symbolic of divine suffering), this deity would feel all the sufferings that are produced by any strongly coercive action taken and could therefore be trusted not to inflict any pain that is not worth the price. Human beings, having a very limited range of direct sensitivity (primarily their own bodies), typically plan *not* to feel the pain they inflict. For these reasons the claim that the deity of the traditional free-will theists, if it existed, should often use its coercive power does not necessarily imply antipacifism.

A third element necessary for a complete response to this question would be a discussion of the various types of coercion. Basinger says that "human coercion has absolutely no intrinsic value within a process system (in fact, is an intrinsic evil)."[41] That is a great oversimplification. Besides distinguishing between relative and absolute coercion, one would need to distinguish, under absolute coercion, among (1) neutral coercion, (2) positive coercion, which saves, and (3) negative coercion, which frustrates, harms, or destroys. Absolute coercion is neutral when the object manipulated is an aggregate that is not the body of a sentient being complex enough to feel pain and frustration of purposes. I exercise coercion in this neutral sense when I use a typewriter to type these words. No one considers this act intrinsically evil (except, perhaps, those who disagree with the words). Positive coercion occurs when the parent snatches the child from in front of the speeding automobile, when the lifeguard administers artificial respiration, when the chiropractor corrects a dislocation. No one is harmed by this type of coercion; it is wholly positive. Coercion becomes problematic only when it frustrates, harms, or destroys. If it is exercised solely for one of these negative purposes, it is wholly evil. But in most cases it is ambiguous, because the negative coercion is carried out for a purpose that is good, or at least thought to be good by the agent. To tie persons up, or confine them to prison, is evil in itself, because it frustrates their desires; but it may seem justified in order to prevent them from, say, harming other persons or aiding an effort that would usher in a worse form of government. To induce pain in someone is evil in itself, but it may seem justified in order to uncover secret plans that, if carried out, would bring pain and death to large numbers. Coercion that kills is, in most cases anyway, evil in itself, but it may be, in some situations, the only way to save the lives of others. It is only negative coercion that can be considered evil in itself. The question is whether process theism encourages or discourages coercion in this sense.

Most process theists have, as Basinger correctly reports, agreed with Whitehead and Hartshorne that negative coercion must sometimes be used, but that it should not be used beyond that absolute minimum needed to prevent intolerable antisocial actions. The crucial question is whether, besides having an internal police force, a society should be prepared to go to war at times. Whitehead and Hartshorne have both thought so, and most process theists have agreed with this judgment. If we look at particular situations that have arisen, furthermore, such as the immediate provocations that started World Wars I and II, it is difficult to disagree with that judgment (although several brave and intelligent persons have done so). But those immediate provocations occurred within a whole system of world order, and in response to a particular history of events, which created deep frustration, anger, and resentment. The more important question is not whether process theism should lead one to be an absolute pacifist within the present world order (although that *is* an important question), but whether process theism, if widely adopted, would induce in persons a pacific spirituality through which they would become passionately committed to creating a new world order in which war would not seem necessary.

I believe that process theology should and could evoke this type of pacific stance. This topic, on which I have written at considerable length elsewhere,[42] is too complex to discuss here; I will mention only an implication of process theology's vision of divine power. At the root of religious life is, I believe, a desire to be in harmony with the ultimate power of the universe—the power from which all order and goodness come, the power that is ultimately most effective. If we deeply believe that this power is the power of love itself, which is persuasive power (not coercive force allegedly exercised with a loving purposes), we will, willy-nilly, want to embody and emulate that form of power in our relations with others. Being finite creatures with bodies who need to interact with other bodies, we would not quit using neutral and positive coercion (although we might decide that less use of even these forms of coercion would be possible and desirable). But we would, seeing that the divine reality seeks to overcome evil with good through persuasion, want to do likewise. We would therefore engage in or consent to negative coercion only with extreme reluctance, and only as a last resort, after other possible solutions had been seriously and exhaustively explored. (I wrote this paragraph on the day after the Reagan administration's decision to send troops to Honduras on the flimsiest basis, which was one more act in a long series that have illustrated an almost religious commitment to seeking military solutions to social problems in that region.)

This pacific mentality will be supported to the degree that we become convinced that the persuasive power of love is truly the ultimate power of the universe in general, and that it will, in the long run, overcome the evil in human souls in particular. It is only if process theism is thus portrayed and accepted that it will induce the type of pacific spirituality of which I speak. The antipacifist Reinhold Niebuhr, for example, accepted the Whiteheadian-Hartshornean vision of God,[43] but he did not believe that divine persuasion (whether directly or indirectly through human persuasion) would ever obviate the necessity for war, and thus in effect did not take it to be the ultimate power of the universe.

Critics of process theology are partly right in saying that it needs a more robust vision of divine power than it has typically provided. The more robust vision we need, however, is not one in which a mixture of persuasion and coercion is used. Nor is it one in which God's reliance on persuasion in relation to human beings is merely a self-limitation, resting upon coercive power held in reserve that can be used from time to time (and may be used in an overwhelming way in the end-time). Those visions simply reinforce the conviction that the ultimate power of the universe is coercive power and thereby reinforce the propensity to use this form of power. The more robust vision we need is one that portrays persuasive power as the truly ultimate, the truly most effective, form of power, especially with regard to overcoming evil. We need to see that evil can be overcome only by good, not by evil. We need to see suffering-persuasive love as the supreme power of the universe, which alone can overcome human evil. For those of us who are Christians, this means that we need a truly Christian vision of God.

Chapter 9

JOHN HICK'S CHARGE
OF ELITISM

In the third, updated version of his *Philosophy of Religion,*[1] John Hick includes a section on "process theodicy."[2] He pays it the compliment of being, along with the Augustinian and Irenaean responses, one of the "three main Christian responses to the problem of evil."[3] Hick's section on process theodicy is a summary and critique of *God, Power, and Evil.* The interchange constituted by Hick's critique and my present response is not the first encounter between the two positions. Hick's position as developed in *Evil and the God of Love* was the subject of a chapter in my book. Although Hick has never replied to this critique,[4] he and I did, in an edited volume entitled *Encountering Evil,* criticize each other's positions and then respond to each other's criticisms.[5] Hick's criticism of my position at that time was minimal and external. Hick's treatment in the new edition of *Philosophy of Religion* is much more extensive. He presents a lengthy and careful summary of my position, then presents a new criticism. This time he does not simply make the standard external criticism that process theism has a "finite God," but instead seeks to criticize my theodicy on its own terms.[6] Whether he succeeds is another question.

A. HICK'S SUMMARY AND CRITIQUE

Hick's summary of my position is accurate and to the point. He begins by emphasizing the crucial difference separating process theodicy and his own: "in contrast to the notion of divine self-limitation, process theology holds that God's exercise of persuasive rather than controlling power is necessitated by the ultimate metaphysical structure of reality." The reason for this necessity is that "God has not created the universe *ex nihilo*, thereby establishing its structure."[7] Hick further points out that, because the ultimate reality for process theology is creativity, which every actual entity embodies, every actual entity exerts "dual efficacy," being partly self-creative and partly determinative of the future.[8] This dual efficacy is not delegated to creatures by God, he emphasizes, but is inherent to the world, so that "it is impossible for even God to hold a monopoly of power." God's power, therefore, "is necessarily limited, and the reality of evil in the world is the measure of the extent to which God's will is in fact thwarted."[9]

Hick also accurately summarizes the other main point of my theodicy, which is that no good can be realized without the possibility of a commensurate level of evil. More specifically, there are two basic forms of intrinsic evil, discord and needless triviality, corresponding to the two dimensions of intrinsic good, harmony and intensity of experience. By stimulating the evolutionary process, in which greater complexity and thereby greater intensity of experience become possible, God overcomes a chaos containing nothing but trivial experiences. But in so doing, God necessarily makes possible greater suffering, because experiences can now be more disharmonious and more intensely so. "Thus this particular conception of a limited deity still requires a theodicy."[10] The essence of this theodicy, in Hick's summary, is this: "God's goodness is vindicated in that the risk-taking venture" has produced "a sufficient quality and quantity of good to outweigh all the evil."[11] Furthermore, God, who experiences all the pain as well as all the joy of creation, and who thereby "alone knows the total balance of good and evil, finds that the risk was worth taking."[12]

Hick sees this theodicy as having two main appeals. First, it avoids the traditional problem arising from the belief in divine omnipotence. Because God is neither responsible for the fundamental structure of the universe nor able to interrupt the causal processes, "God does not need to be justified for permitting evil, since it is not within God's power to prevent it."[13] The second appeal of this theodicy is "its stirring summons to engage on God's side in the never-ending struggle against the evils of an intractable world."[14]

"However," Hick tells the reader: "despite its appeal, the process theodicy has been severely criticized." This comment is footnoted with a reference to *Evil and the Concept of God*, by Edward Madden and Peter Hare. Hick fails to tell the reader that their critique was written prior to my book, and that Peter Hare had more recently written a very positive review of my book. In any case, Hick continues: "One basic claim is that it involves a morally and religiously unacceptable elitism."[15] Although Hick's wording gives the impression that he is simply reporting someone else's criticism (apparently that of Madden and Hare), he is in fact presenting his own critique. In spelling out this charge of elitism (which constitutes his entire criticism), he suggests that the God of process theodicy is *not* "the God of the New Testament, understood as the Creator who values all human creatures with a universal and impartial love." Also, this God is "far from being the God of contemporary liberation theology, who is the God of the poor and the oppressed." Rather, the "God of process theodicy is the God of the elite, of the great and successful among mankind. He is apparently the God of saints rather than of sinners; of geniuses rather than of the dull and retarded and mentally defective; of the cream of humanity rather than of the anonymous millions."[16] Overcoming any pretense of neutral reporting, Hick tells his readers that "the starving and the oppressed, the victims of Auschwitz, the human wrecks who are irreparably brain-damaged or mind-damaged, and those others who have loved and agonized over them, can hardly be expected to . . . regard such a God as worthy of their worship and praise."[17]

The reader who has stayed with me this far knows that this characterization of my theodicy as elitist runs totally counter to everything I mean to be saying. The affirmation that the divine power is not all-determining, and *could* not be all-determining, provides the basis for saying that God does love all human beings equally and impartially in spite of the gross discrepancies in welfare and even in opportunity. If God were said, by contrast, to have the traditional form of omnipotence, it would be hard to avoid the conclusion that God loves some more than others.[18] In the light of the fact, for example, that whites have, in recent centuries at least, generally lived out their lives in much more favorable conditions than persons of color, William Jones has asked: *Is God a White Racist?*[19] One of the many appeals to me of the Whiteheadian-Hartshornean position is that it allows us to say, without equivocation or endless appeals to "mystery" or "paradox," that God does indeed love all persons equally, that God in no way favors white over black, North over South, West over East, men over women, Christian over Jew, rich over poor, oppressor over oppressed, fortunate over unfortunate. This position allows us to say that none of the present injustices in the world are sanctioned by God—indeed at the outset of *Process Theology* the denial of "God as Controlling Power" is followed immediately by the denials of "God as Sanctioner of the Status Quo" and "God as Male."[20] We can thereby say that belief in God, far from sanctioning present injustices, entails working to overcome them.[21] This implication is reinforced by the conviction that, because God suffers with all suffering, whatever we do "unto one of the least of these" we do unto God.

Given all this, it was a surprise, indeed a shock, to read Hick's charge of elitism. How could it be explained? Simple misunderstanding could not account for it, given the accuracy of Hick's summary of my position. One possible explanation is that Hick, in spite of his intention to criticize my theodicy on its own terms, has unconsciously read his own presuppositions into the premises. A second possible explanation is that, although I did not (consciously) intend my position to be elitist (who does?), it nevertheless *was* elitist in effect, and that Hick's position enabled him to see this, even if in a distorted manner. The element of truth that I find in the second explanation I have already treated in chapter 1. I explore the first explanation in the remainder of this chapter.

B. THE ROOTS OF HICK'S CRITIQUE IN HIS OWN POSITION

To have a strong point of view on a subject is usually a source both of vision and of blindness in understanding the viewpoints of others. It is a source of vision insofar as we are sensitized to many of the issues involved, so that we are likely to notice the nuances in the thought of others insofar as they provide answers to questions that we ourselves have raised. But our own viewpoint can also be a source of blindness. Even after having noted the various elements in the other's position, we are likely to retain the assumption that our own position defines the questions that must be answered. We may have noticed that the other person or tradition had a different set of ultimate assumptions about what is most real and valuable; yet we continue to employ our own ultimate assumptions about what is real and important. We therefore tend to evaluate the other position in terms of whether it answers the questions set by our own assumptions. I suspect that some of this has occurred in my own criticisms of Hick's theodicy, but I will here discuss only the way in which this dynamic seems to lie behind Hick's criticism of my theodicy as elitist.

The basic conviction on which Hick and I agree is that a successful theodicy must portray God as morally perfect. And we do not disagree on the criteria for moral perfection.

The basic conviction on which we do disagree concerns God's essential omnipotence. I hold that God's power is essentially persuasive, because all actualities necessarily have some degree of self-determining power, which cannot be coerced. To speak of divine omnipotence, if that dangerous term is even to be used, is therefore to affirm one's faith that loving persuasion is ultimately the most powerful force in the universe. Hick believes that God's omnipotence essentially involves coercive power, so that God's exclusive reliance upon persuasive power in relation to us is voluntary. I have dubbed his position a "hybrid free-will defense." It is a merely hybrid form of the free-will defense because it rejects the hypothesis that a plurality of partially free beings belongs to the ultimate nature of things, so that it cannot employ the full-fledged free-will defense that that hypothesis would allow.

Given Hick's conviction that God is totally in charge of the situation, a defense of God's moral perfection necessitates the belief that the world contains no unredeemable evil. There can be no injustice that is not ultimately righted, no failure that is more than temporary—at least with regard to matters that are truly important. (Unredeemed animal pain does not seem to trouble Hick; the universe was created for the sake of creatures capable of moral and spiritual growth, so only their condition is truly important.)

For Hick, God's goal is a commonwealth of morally and spiritually developed beings. From this premise, some corollaries follow. First, these beings with moral and spiritual capacities must have genuine freedom, because moral and spiritual virtues would not be authentic if they were coercively imposed. There must, accordingly, be a *divine self-limitation* in relation to these creatures.

Second, the world must contain genuine obstacles—such as sources of temptation, suffering, and doubt—or no possibility would exist of developing such virtues as self-control, patience, helpfulness, and faith. The goodness of the world is accordingly to be evaluated in terms of its purpose as a "vale of soul making," *not* on the assumption that it should be a "hedonistic paradise." Not only are moral and spiritual considerations more important than the "aesthetic" consideration of whether present experience is experienced as enjoyable; the existence of aesthetic evil—pain and suffering—is *necessary* for the world to be good for its purpose.

A third corollary is the necessity of *eventual salvation for all humans*. Because God had a completely free hand in creating our world, unilaterally determining its basic structure (including the nature of human nature), and still essentially has a free hand (the only limitation is a voluntary *self-limitation*), it would be a smear on God's perfection if some souls did not attain the moral and spiritual development for which they were created. If some were permanently crushed instead of spurred on by the obstacles created by God, God's goodness or at least wisdom would be impugned.

With Hick's own position before us, I will now look more closely at the various aspects of his charge that process theodicy involves "a morally and religiously unacceptable elitism." I will suggest that, in spite of Hick's excellent summary of the position, he has not really gotten inside it to see how the issues look from within. He has implicitly presupposed that my position, to be acceptable, would have to solve the chief problem created by *his* position, that of guaranteeing universal human salvation. And the basically negative reaction thereby produced in Hick evidently led him to misread some of the features of my position, so that a caricature results.

I begin by quoting the long passage from my book that is quoted in full (except for three words at the outset) by Hick as the primary basis for his charge of elitism:

...the question as to whether God is indictable is to be answered in terms of the question as to whether the positive values that are possible in our world are valuable enough to be worth the risk of the negative experiences which have occurred, and the even greater horrors which stand before us as real possibilities for the future. Should God, for the sake of avoiding the possibility of persons such as Hitler, and horrors such as Auschwitz, have precluded the possibility of Jesus, Gautama, Socrates, Confucius, Moses Mendelssohn, El Greco, Michelangelo, Leonardo da Vinci, Florence Nightingale, Abraham Lincoln, Mahatma Gandhi, Chief Joseph, Chief Seattle, Alfred North Whitehead, John F. Kennedy, Oliver Wendell Holmes, Sojourner Truth, Helen Keller, Louis Armstrong, Albert Einstein, Dag Hammarskjold, Reinhold Niebuhr, Carol Channing, Margaret Mead, and millions of other marvelous human beings, well known and not well known alike, who have lived on the face of this earth? In other words, should God, for the sake of avoiding "man's inhumanity to man," have avoided humanity (or some comparably complex species) altogether? Only those who could sincerely answer this question affirmatively could indict the God of process theology on the basis of the evil in the world.[22]

Hick next sets the stage for his criticism by reminding us that the majority of persons in all ages have lived in dreadful conditions, suffering from hunger, disease, and oppression. Hick then launches his criticism:

What makes it acceptable to God, according to the process theodicy, is the fact that the same complex process that has produced all this suffering has also produced the cream of the human species. For each one such "marvelous human being," perhaps tens of thousands of others have existed without any significant degree of personal freedom and without any opportunity for intellectual, moral, aesthetic, or spiritual development, their lives spent in a desperate and degrading struggle to survive. But God is apparently content that this great mass of human suffering has been endured and this great mass of human potentiality has been undeveloped because, as part of the same world process, the elite have fulfilled in themselves some of the finer possibilities of human existence.[23]

Although there are several problems with Hick's criticism,[24] the main problem is that he rips my statement out of the context in which it was made, treating it in abstraction from the dilemma posed. The three words at the outset of my statement that were deleted in Hick's quotation are: "In this context." The context is the supposition that the creator had only two options: (1) encouraging the creation to bring forth humanlike beings, with all the additional risks that would thereby be inevitable, or (2) forgoing humanlike beings altogether. In that context I was also assuming that the human journey might not continue past bodily death, so that the question of whether to have such beings had to be made solely in terms of the additional good and evil that would be possible within this world. The question then was: Assuming that this choice was in fact faced by the creator, could we honestly say, on the basis of what has occurred thus far, that the wrong choice had been made? Could we really say that the suffering and sin have been so horrendous that it would have been better if life on the planet had never risen above the level of the other primates?

Hick fails to point out to his readers that this is the question behind my statement, and he does not answer this question. Hick's whole discussion suggests that the God of process theology is morally defective for having brought forth the human race when so much suffering and stunted development was likely, and yet Hick never answers the question: Should God—assuming the dilemma as I presented it—have decided not to create humanlike beings altogether? Only if Hick were to answer that question in the affirmative, rather than ignoring it, would he have the right to suggest that this idea of God is "morally and religiously unacceptable."

What Hick has evidently done is to assume that that dilemma could not occur. After all, if we are speaking about God, who by definition (for Hick) is an omnipotent being whom only logic deters, then God could never face such limited options. For this reason, I suspect, Hick did not take the question seriously. He was tacitly presupposing all along that the only proper thing for God to do was to create human beings such that they would continue their journey past this vale of tears. He in fact says near the end of his critique:

> The situation would, of course, be transformed if a process theodicy were able to affirm the eventual successful completion of the creative process in a future heavenly fulfillment in which all are eventually to participate. Then the tragedy of human life, though real, would not be ultimate; it would be woven into what Dante called the Divine Comedy of God's creative action in its totality. Then it would be true that, in Mother Julian's phrase, all shall be well, and all shall be well, and all manner of thing shall be well.[25]

I think most of us would agree that it would be far better if this were the case, and that, if we had confidence that this would indeed be the case, we could be more enthusiastic about the goodness of the process in which we find ourselves living. In fact, in the appendix to *God, Power, and Evil*, after saying that I consider life after death possible, I said:

> I would add here that a future life in this sense would be in line with the general pattern of God's creative activity, according to which individuals at each stage are not only valuable in themselves, but are also preparations for forms of existence with greater value in the future. Also, insofar as much human life is characterized by more suffering than intrinsic good, the development of a postbodily psychic existence could be one more example of God's overcoming evil with good.[26]

And, after saying that I thought life after death should be an optional rather than an essential part of a Christian theodicy and of Christian faith in general, I added:

> The fact that this belief is optional does not mean that whether or not it is held may not make a tremendous difference in the nature of a person's faith. I personally believe that the inclusion of this belief can give one's faith additional dimensions of both vitality and peace, and that this belief also deepens one's sense of the importance of other human life and thereby one's concern for others, including the concern for human justice. Furthermore, hope that our present human life, besides having its present intrinsic value, is also in part preparation for a higher form of existence in the future, can add a final ground for affirming this present life. . . . Hope for a better future in [a transearthly existence] does add enthusiasm to one's Yes-response to past and present human life and hence to its creator.[27]

This statement shows that I did not disagree that, even with the account given by process theodicy, one's affirmation of the present life might be somewhat ambivalent, and that supplementing this theodicy with a portrait of life after death could overcome this ambivalence. Belief in life after death could, I suggested, make an otherwise adequate theodicy more than simply adequate. The question at hand, however, is whether the theodicy, without belief in life after death, *is* adequate. Hick fails to address this question within the context of my assumptions. My question is: "Assuming that God had to choose between A and B, which should God have chosen?" Hick answers: "C."

Within the context of Hick's assumptions, God would be morally reprehensible for creating a world in which so much evil is virtually inevitable, unless this were done with a view toward creating "a limitless final good to justify all the evil that will have occurred on the way to it."[28] But, if such a "limitless good" were not possible, or if it at least could not be guaranteed, as

I was presupposing, would God have been justified in urging the evolutionary process to bring forth human beings? Hick does not answer this question. He simply criticizes the God of *my* theodicy for being elitist because this God does not necessarily guarantee the universal salvation that is required to make *Hick's* theodicy successful.

That Hick is reading his own presuppositions into his critique of process theodicy is also apparent in another criticism. He suggests that my view is "reminiscent of nineteenth-century *laissez faire* capitalist theory, that though the weak may go to the wall, the system as a whole is good because it also produces those who are spiritually and culturally rich."[29] But the idea of *laissez faire* has meaning only in a context in which a central power could exert control but decides not to. That describes Hick's universe, with its self-limiting omnipotent being, not mine. In Hick's framework, God's *laissez faire* policy can only be justified if the cosmic trickle-down process works perfectly, so that *everyone* eventually becomes morally, spiritually, and hedonically rich. Hick is rightly outraged by doctrines within the context of the traditional idea of divine omnipotence that allow for any failures in the cosmic salvific process, such as the doctrine of hell as everlasting torment. But he then inappropriately transfers that moral outrage to process theodicy, in which the notion of a divine *laissez faire* makes no sense. As Hick himself correctly pointed out in his initial summary of process theodicy, God's use of persuasive rather than coercively controlling power is not due to a voluntary self-limitation. The question within this nontraditional context is: If the potentials of all persons for self-realization and happiness will be very unevenly realized, and if many will in fact have little or no chance of a fulfilling life, should God therefore have not created persons at all? Hick fails to address this question, criticizing this God in terms of a third option that this God, by hypothesis, might not have had.

Hick's failure to carry out his attempted internal critique of my theodicy within the terms of that theodicy itself is also shown by his discussion of aesthetic *versus* ethical criteria. He says:

> In suggesting that Griffin's process theodicy is elitist in a way that violates the basic Christian conviction of God's love for all human creatures, one is perhaps complaining that its ultimate principle is aesthetic rather than ethical. . . . In this respect it is in line with the ancient Stoic and Neo-Platonic analogy (which Augustine also used), according to which the universe may be good as a whole even though it contains considerable evil in its details.[30]

One disappointing feature here is that Hick raises this issue as if it were the final proof of his charge of elitism (it constitutes the final paragraph of his critique), and as if it had not already been answered. Although he had earlier referred the reader to the critique of process theodicy by Madden and Hare, he fails to mention that I spent several pages dealing with their critique on just this issue, and that that was a feature of my discussion that Hare found to be particularly good.[31] In any case, making the aesthetic criteria of harmony and intensity of experience more fundamental than ethical criteria does not decrease the importance of morality but increases its scope; it also reinforces the universality of God's love rather than violating it. Not only severely retarded humans but also nonhuman animals are capable of some combination of harmony and intensity of experience, even if they are not capable of moral and religious growth. We therefore have duties to them, even if they have no corresponding duties to us. More important for our present discussion, to say that the fundamental aim of the creative power of the universe is to promote the intrinsic goodness of experience itself, rather than only the distinctively moral and religious qualities of experience, is to say that God is concerned about all creatures, not simply human beings. From this standpoint, it is Hick's theodicy that is terribly elitist, because he speaks only of God's love for "all human creatures," leaving out the millions of other species.

Furthermore, Hick's attempted association of process and Augustinian theodicies because of the role of aesthetic considerations in both of them is farfetched. Augustine's aesthetic theodicy was not just that "the universe may be good as a whole *even though* it contains considerable evil in its details," as Hick puts it. Rather, Augustine's doctrine is that the whole is better *because of* the evil in some of the parts, just as a piece of music is often more beautiful as a whole because of some of its discords, which considered in themselves are *not* beautiful. This type of aesthetic theodicy, which in effect denies the genuineness of evil, was explicitly rejected in my book.[32] Hick's theodicy, according to which we can expect "a limitless final good to justify all the evil that will have occurred on the way," is actually much closer to the Augustinian position. As I had pointed out, Hick often seems, with St. Augustine, finally to deny the reality of genuine evil.[33]

I come now to the heart of Hick's critique. In spelling out his charge of elitism, Hick suggests that the God I portray cannot "be equated with the God of the New Testament, understood as the Creator who values all human creatures with a universal and impartial love."[34] What is it that counts against God's impartial love for all persons? It is that many individuals "are deprived of the opportunity of developing the moral and spiritual, intellectual and aesthetic potentialities of their nature." From this fact Hick draws his conclusion:

> The God of the process theodicy is the God of the elite, of the great and successful among mankind. He is apparently the God of saints rather than of sinners; of geniuses rather than of the dull and retarded

and mentally defective; of the cream of humanity rather than of the anonymous millions who have been driven to self-seeking, violence, greed, and deceit, in a desperate struggle to survive, or of those millions who have been crippled by malnutrition and have suffered and died under oppression and exploitation, plague and famine, flood and earthquake, or again of those—perhaps numbering about half the sum of human births—who have perished in infancy.[35]

This is an eloquent statement, suggestive of sincere compassion for the wretched of the earth. But how do these horrors conflict with process theology's affirmation of God's universal and impartial love? Such facts would seem more contradictory of the impartial love of the God of traditional theism—Hick's God—who has the power to prevent such horrors but fails to do so. In fact, *according to Hick, all those horrors occur only because God intentionally built their possibility into the structure of the world, without having had to do so.* Hick believes that he has provided a satisfactory answer to this problem. This is his answer that God created this world to be a vale of soul-making (not to be an intrinsically fun place), that the process of soul-making continues past this life, and that the eschaton will be so good as to justify all the horrors experienced along the way. Process theology reconciles these horrors with the impartial love of our creator in a different way. It says that the God of traditional theism does not exist, that our creator necessarily exercises persuasive rather than coercive power, and that the conditions for increased good are necessarily the conditions for increased evils. Given that hypothesis, the great inequalities in the distribution of good and evil in the world do not conflict with the "universal and impartial love" of God. And yet Hick says that they do, as if the fact that I did not give the answer required by his assumptions meant that I had given no answer at all.

Closely related is Hick's claim that the God of process theodicy is "far from being the God of contemporary liberation theology, who is the God of the poor and oppressed, the enslaved and all against whom the structures of human society discriminate."[36] One problem with Hick's treatment here is that he fails to mention my argument that process theology provides the best basis for the claim of liberation theologians that God unambiguously supports the goal of overcoming oppressive ideologies and structures (a better basis, for example, than the view that human freedom and therefore sin in relation to God were made possible by a self-limitation on God's part, which would mean that God could, if God wanted to, unilaterally overcome the historical sources of oppression, injustice, and suffering).[37]

Hick's charge also stands in some conflict with his own portrayal of my position. I quoted earlier his statement that part of the appeal of process theodicy "consists of the stirring summons to engage on God's side in the never-ending struggle against the evils of an intractable world."[38] That description is hardly compatible with Hick's portrayal of my God as a cosmic bourgeois being who is "apparently content that this great mass of human suffering has been endured and this great mass of human potentiality has been undeveloped because, as part of the same world process, the elite have fulfilled in themselves some of the finer possibilities of human existence."[39] According to process theology, God feels the suffering in the world in somewhat the same way as we feel the pains of our bodily parts, so that, as Hick said in his summary statement, "God shares ... our human as well as subhuman pains." That doctrine, which takes seriously the suffering of the crucified Jesus as a symbol of God's response to the sufferings of the world, is not faithfully reflected in Hick's portrayal of a God "apparently content" with the present balance of good and evil.

Besides being contradicted by his own portrayal of my position, Hick's charge that the God of process theodicy is the God of the elite, not the oppressed, becomes self-contradictory. On the one hand, the charge that this God is "the God of the elite" is said to mean that this God is "the God of saints rather than of sinners," of "the morally and spiritually successful."[40] And yet, on the other hand, when Hick is describing ones who "can hardly be expected to ... regard such a God as worthy of their worship and praise," he mentions "the starving and the oppressed, the victims of Auschwitz, the human wrecks who are irreparably brain-damaged or mind-damaged, and *those others who have loved and agonized over them*."[41] That last-named group, those who have loved and agonized over the victims of natural and human evils, are presumably the saints, the ones who have developed their capacity to become morally and spiritually mature beings. And my list of well-known "marvelous human beings," which Hick tendentiously labels a list of elites, did indeed include persons who either suffered great misfortune or agonized over that of others, such as Florence Nightingale, Sojourner Truth, Helen Keller, Mahatma Gandhi, Chief Joseph, and Chief Seattle, not to mention Jesus of Nazareth, who was put to a shameful death at about the age of thirty. Hick's criticism collapses into the incoherence of saying that the God of process theodicy both is and is not the God of such persons.

This incoherence seems to be due to an ambiguity in the phrase "God of the elites." It can mean either that this God is *concerned about* the elites only, or that this God could be *worshipped* by the elites only. Hick has the former meaning in mind when he defines elites as "the morally and spiritually successful in whom God rejoices." But he obviously does not have this meaning in mind when he says that this God would not be thought worthy of worship by those morally and spiritually sensitive persons who agonize over the sufferings of the oppressed, but only by those who are "fortunate" in terms of "happiness and achievements."[42] In this second usage, the "elites" are those who are successful not in terms of moral and spiritual development but in terms of worldly standards of success. In fact, by saying that these persons would worship the God of process theodicy, while those who agonize over the sufferings of the oppressed would not, he is saying that the elites are those who are not only successful by worldly standards but are also selfish and insensitive.

If Hick were able to overcome this incoherence in his criticism, I suspect he would maintain that morally and spiritually sensitive persons would not find the God of process theodicy worthy of worship. Which concept of God persons find worthy of worship, however, does not depend entirely upon their level of moral and spiritual sensitivity, but also upon their basic beliefs and the expectations to which those beliefs lead. In the context of the belief that the creator of the world possesses coercive omnipotence, persons with a developed sense of fairness will rightly expect that the creator should have produced a world in which fairness prevails, at least ultimately. If they decide that the world is not fair, they will probably conclude that there is no divine reality, no power worthy of worship. Hick feels and thinks from this point of view. For him, the idea of God, of the divine, is inextricably connected with both perfect fairness and potentially all-determining power. A putative deity without one or the other of these characteristics evokes no sense that worship is appropriate. Accordingly, unless the world is ultimately fair, there is no reality worthy of worship. Hick is further convinced, correctly, that our present world is not fair, especially for human beings. There are gross disparities in inherited capacities, available opportunities, and happenstance. Some persons seem to have every possible blessing, others not even the necessities. Hick then concludes that, unless there is a continuing life beyond this one for human beings, there cannot be a reality worthy of worship. From this point of view, he concludes that the God of a theological position that does not make life after death and universal salvation essential elements could be worshipped only by the fortunate few of this world—in fact, only by those whose good fortune is combined with a lack of compassion for the wretched of the earth. He is really saying, of course, that this God is not worthy of worship by anyone.

C. PROCESS THEODICY CONSIDERED ON ITS OWN TERMS

How would the situation look if the process position were judged in terms of its own premises, instead of Hick's? In particular, if there were a community of believers who had been molded by process theology's idea of the Holy Reality as persuasive-compassionate love, could we expect the unfortunate of the community, and those who especially identified with them, to worship and praise this God? These would be persons who had been brought up on this notion of God. All their public worship and private prayer, all their preaching and poetry, all their public images and symbols would presuppose and reinforce the idea that the divine reality is persuasive-compassionate love. Accordingly, they would not be brought up to expect the world to be fair, the good always to prosper and the wicked always to suffer. They would not expect miraculous divine interventions to prevent private tragedies or events of mass destruction due to natural or human agents. They would understand in their deepest sensibilities that the world is comprised of a plurality of powers, and could not have been otherwise, and that the world is therefore necessarily a dangerous place. They would understand from the depth of their being, from which their basic emotional stance toward life is formed, that if there was to be a world at all, it had to be such a world, in which fairness could not be guaranteed. I see no reason to believe that only the insensitive and materially fortunate in such a community would worship and praise the persuasive-empathetic power they believed to have been primarily responsible for the existence of our world.

I recently witnessed a poignant example on a television program dealing with children who had been born with terribly deformed faces. One boy, who appeared to be about ten years old, obviously had a wise and loving mother, and obviously felt loved by the universe. He told on camera, with his funny little voice (on top of everything else, he had needed a tracheotomy), that he had known from about age three that, "if God could have given me a better face, He would have." Something like process theology's view of God was evidently accepted by this boy's mother (perhaps both his parents—on the television program we were introduced only to his mother), and she had evidently had the wisdom and courage to teach him about this God from his youngest days. As a result, her son, with his pathetic little face, is one of the most cheerful, well-adjusted appearing children I have ever seen. This well-adjusted family is not, however, resigned; they are doing everything they can to see if, through surgery, the boy's face can be made more pleasing. Although this topic did not come up during the interview, my guess would be that the mother has also taught her son that this is how God works—through other persons—to overcome evil that God could not prevent unilaterally. In my view, the God of process theology is precisely the kind of God that the unfortunate of this world would worship, whether or not they expect a future life in which the inequities of this life will be overcome.

D. SUMMARY AND CONCLUSION

Hick's charge of elitism does not stick, I have suggested, mainly because he has failed to evaluate process theodicy on its own terms. He has instead judged it in terms of a requirement of his own theology, with its very different assumption about divine power. *Hick's* theology would be elitist unless it included the promise of equal fulfillment for all humans in a transearthly existence. Without this promise, God's impartial love for all persons could not credibly be asserted. Hick fails to see that process theodicy, given its rejection of the traditional notion of omnipotence, can credibly maintain God's impartial love apart from the affirmation of an eschaton in which all inequalities will be overcome and all potentialities fulfilled.

However, even if Hick did not formulate it correctly, process theology, in its usual formulations, including that in *God, Power, and Evil*, does contain an elitist element, as I suggested in chapter 1. The doctrine of "objective immortality" can surely be adequate, if at all, only for those fortunate few who have the opportunity to develop their potentialities rather fully and to make what they feel to be a significant contribution to the world. I am happy to be able to join Hick now in encouraging the belief that our present lives are part of a much longer journey, a journey that may allow all persons to satisfy their desires for more life, to realize their potentials, and to make a memorable contribution to the divine life of the universe.

Chapter 10

PROCESS THEODICY AND MONISM:
A RESPONSE TO PHILIP HEFNER

Philip Hefner's review article, "Is Theodicy a Question of Power?,"[1] begins like a rave review. After all, what higher praise could a reviewer give than to say that it is "one book that justifies its jacket blurbs"?[2] Such praise could lead the book's author to suppose that here is finally the reviewer who has found the book totally convincing. And yet, if one jumps from that first sentence to the last, one sees Hefner concluding with these words: "This book convinces me that the Christian philosopher will want to look more closely at Hegel than at Whitehead for help in some areas."[3] That not having been my book's desired effect, I need to examine what happened between those first and last sentences.

Hefner approaches the book from a fundamentally sympathetic perspective. He believes that the problem of evil "is *the* central issue for theology today." And, although he teaches at a Lutheran school of theology, he does "not take exception to . . . the quest for a philosophical expression of Christian faith" in general or to the "process methodology" in particular.[4] Furthermore, Hefner's own theological vision is deeply informed by that of Nicholas Berdyaev and others who have, like Whitehead, affirmed a primordial freedom, not created by God, at the heart of reality. Besides being sympathetic to my book's approach, Hefner also demonstrates a fundamentally accurate grasp of its main argument (including the importance of the long historical section for this argument), providing as fine a summary of the argument as could be given in two pages.[5]

Hefner nevertheless raises several serious criticisms. Although he does not so label them, I have divided his criticisms into *internal* and *external*. Under the former heading, I consider those criticisms suggesting that my position is inconsistent, unclear, or incomplete. Under the second heading, I consider Hefner's claims, reflecting his own perspective, that my theodicy is inadequate to the idea of God implied by Jewish and Christian faith and experience. My response to Hefner takes its title from this external side of his critique: he argues that only a monistic view can be adequate, even though this monism means positing evil within God. After reviewing and responding in the first two sections to Hefner's criticisms, I suggest a trinitarian monism that might reconcile Hefner's monistic concern with my own concern to affirm the perfect goodness of God.

A. GENUINE EVIL, RATIONALIZATION, AND TRAGEDY

Hefner's first internal criticism is that I have not given an answer to the basic question for theodicy, which is "why the creation is as it is." He says:

> Griffin has given an admirable description of how evil works in God's world, but he has not provided a response to the human cry, Why does it have to be this way? Or, to use Griffin's own categories, Why is the world structured according to the configuration of harmony and intensity? Why is there an evolutionary process in the first place which moves within this configuration? Why must the metaphysical principles that are beyond divine decision be *these* principles?[6]

Hefner presumes that I have not done this because process metaphysics is descriptive, not explanatory.[7]

Hefner's criticism, however, implies a misunderstanding of how metaphysical principles are defined. To call certain principles "metaphysical" is to make the hypothesis that they are necessary, meaning that they are without genuine alternative and would therefore obtain in any world that could exist. This is what is meant by saying that they are beyond decision, even God's. Within the context of this metaphysical hypothesis, it does not make sense to ask, "Why must the metaphysical principles that are beyond divine decision be *these* principles?" They *must* (by hypothesis) be these because there is no possible world in which these principles would not obtain. This is the point of my leaning toward Hartshorne, against one set of statements by Whitehead, on the relation between God and the metaphysical principles. Even some of Whitehead's statements support this view, I pointed out, in that he speaks of metaphysical principles as "necessary" and as "characteristics so general that we cannot conceive any alternatives."[8] My position, in other words, is not simply a description of the general principles that (happen to) obtain in our world. It includes the hypothesis that these principles, discoverable through experience, are not merely empirical principles, but are metaphysical, necessary principles, inherent in the very nature of things.

I therefore did give an answer to the query as to "why the creation is as it is," suggesting that it could not have been otherwise. That is, *in its most general principles* it could not have been otherwise. In its concrete details it could have been greatly different—much better or much worse. This affirmation of contingency in the concrete events of the world—in "nature" as well as "history"—is essential to the affirmation that there is genuine evil, and to the conviction that we can and ought to do what we can to prevent or overcome it. This contingency, which is rooted in the power of self-determination possessed to some degree by all individuals, is based on the most fundamental metaphysical principle: all individuals are embodiments of creativity. When someone asks "Why Lord, why?" and means "Why do these persons (or these cancerous cells) have the power to do this to me?," the answer is: "Because there could not be a world in which creatures did not have the power to do ill to each other." And with regard to the evil that human beings in particular perpetrate, the further answer is: "Because there cannot be beings such as you, with your tremendous capacity for enjoying an enormous range of values, without the comparable capacity for thwarting the value-realization of others." This answer may be wrong—it is merely a hypothesis—but it is an answer.

Hefner's second internal criticism is that my notion of "genuine evil" is ambiguous and not useful. Here I must confess to finding Hefner's argument itself somewhat ambiguous, but I will respond to what seem to be the main points.

One formulation of my formal definition of genuine evil is that it is any event "without which the universe would have been better." After quoting this definition, Hefner asks: "But how would one judge whether the universe would have been better without a certain event?" He then quotes the alternative formulation: "Some event is genuinely evil if its occurrence prevents the occurrence of some other event which would have made the universe better, all things considered, i.e., from an all-inclusive, impartial perspective." Hefner evidently finds this definition ambiguous, useless, or both, because evil is thereby defined "with reference to something that is by definition unavailable to any human experience,"[9] which makes it impossible for us to judge whether any *prima facie* evil is genuinely evil.

It appears that Hefner has here confused meaning and verification. Unless one is a positivist, the meaning of a statement and the mode of its verification are to be distinguished. My formal definition is not meant to provide a method for deciding whether some event is genuinely evil or not; it is meant only to provide a way of stating what we *mean* in speaking of genuine evil. Giving an intelligible meaning of "genuine evil" is not the same as asking whether any given event is genuinely evil, but it *is* a precondition for intelligibly asking this question. We cannot intelligibly ask whether some event is genuinely evil unless we first know what we *mean* by genuine evil. That is the usefulness of the definition.

Besides not being useless, the definition does not seem to me ambiguous, but in fact seems to make explicit what is implicit in our practical judgments about good and evil. Whenever we make a judgment that some event is *really* good, or *really* evil, we implicitly mean: "This is how it would be evaluated by an omniscient, impartially sympathetic observer." The fact that "our thoughts are not God's thoughts," so that we can never *know* what God thinks about any particular event, does not render the definition problematic (assuming that meaning is not thought to depend upon verification). The fact that we cannot *know* the total truth about anything does not negate the *existence* of a complete truth (at least about everything that has occurred thus far) to which we seek to make our ideas asymptotically approximate. To say that our perspective is partial in fact *implies* the idea of an impartial perspective.

Hefner is bothered by the fact that this view allows "God to be the sole arbiter of what is evil."[10] However, one view of the meaning of moral terms, and the one that is presupposed in what I have just said, is the "ideal observer theory." According to this theory, the only finally adequate meaning of the "right thing to do in this situation" is "what an omniscient, impartially compassionate observer would want done in that situation." This view is quite different from the (Calvinistic) view according to which the meaning of "right" and "ought" is determined by the *arbitrary* will of God. In my view, God's will cannot be arbitrary. For the meaning of moral terms to be definable in terms of an infinite being's will, it is not enough that this being have an all-inclusive (omniscient) perspective. This being's perspective must also be *impartially sympathetic;* that is, it must sympathize with the feelings and welfare of all sentient beings, and it must do so naturally, by nature. If our word "God" refers to such a reality, then God's perspective and that of an "ideal observer" necessarily coincide. This means not only that God is *necessarily* good, but also that God's will is implicitly invoked whenever we make moral judgments.[11]

A third internal criticism is that, although I *say* that my final position is fundamentally different from that of the traditional theodicies, it really is not. Hefner bases this criticism partly on the fact that I seem to answer the question "Why did God create free beings?" by saying that "freedom is worth all the evils which it can produce." This answer, Hefner suggests, would hoist me on the already too crowded petard of the "traditional theists who counseled patience in the face of evil because it works for good."[12] If this conclusion were implied by my position, it would indeed be a reversal of everything I meant to be saying. To show that this conclusion is not implied, several issues need to be sorted out.

1) Most traditional theodicies did *not* say that "freedom is worth all the evils which it can produce" for the simple reason that they did not genuinely affirm freedom—that is, what I call *theological freedom*,[13] which is creaturely freedom *vis-à-vis* God, the freedom to act contrary to the divine will. This was a central contention of my critiques of Augustine, Aquinas, Spinoza, Luther, Calvin, Leibniz, Barth, Ross, Fackenheim, and Brunner.

2) Insofar as traditional theists *have* affirmed genuine freedom *vis-à-vis* God—for example, John Hick—they have done so while asserting or at least implying that God *could* have made us just as we are—that is, capable of all the values we can enjoy—without giving us genuine freedom. We could *think* we were free, and could therefore even enjoy the values of self-congratulation and other-defamation; only God would know that we were really not free but mere playthings of the divine puppeteer. Given that assumed possibility, the affirmation that God gave us genuine freedom *vis-à-vis* God puts tremendous pressure upon freedom to be immensely valuable, either intrinsically or as an instrumental good (as a necessary condition for intrinsic good). This position must assert that it was good of God to give us theological freedom (freedom *vis-à-vis* God) even though freedom *in this sense* is not a necessary corollary of any of those values that we experience to belong to the *esse* and *bene esse* of human life. Psychological freedom and socio-political freedom are, of course, another matter. But they do not, from the perspective of traditional theism, require theological freedom. In fact, we could have much *more* freedom in these senses if there were no freedom *vis-à-vis* God, because it is precisely human sinfulness—action contrary to the will of God—that puts unnecessary limits upon our social freedoms. If this is so, how can one justify God's giving us genuine (theological) freedom in the light of all the appalling evils that have resulted from it? I have discussed this problem in chapter 5.

My own position is quite different. As a statement quoted by Hefner makes clear,[14] I do not ask, Why did God create free beings? There is (by hypothesis) no alternative: it is a metaphysical principle, beyond divine volition, that *any* beings God creates will be partly free. (This is a point with which Hefner, following Berdyaev, evidently agrees.)[15] The only question is: Why might God have encouraged beings with higher and higher degrees of freedom to evolve? Because, I suggested, God is interested in bringing forth beings with more and more capacity for value-realization, and freedom and the capacity for value-realization are correlative: the greater a being's capacity to realize values, the greater its degree of freedom. That principle is, I hypothesize, a metaphysical principle. God could not have decided instead to create beings with the value-realizing capacity of a human being but the freedom of an amoeba. Unlike traditional free-will theodicists such as John Hick, C. S. Lewis, and Alvin Plantinga, therefore, I do not see the existence of freedom in the world, or even the high degree of freedom enjoyed by human beings, as something that needs to be justified as an optional element in a world that could have otherwise been basically the same. Rather, I argue that freedom is one of several variables that necessarily rise or fall correlatively with each other. A world without a significant degree of freedom could not be remotely similar to our world, because it would not have significant degrees of experience and value-realization. If this hypothesis is correct, the choice faced by out creator was not whether to give freedom to otherwise humanlike creatures, but whether to have humanlike creatures, complete with their dangerous freedom, at all. This question makes this theodicy radically different from any traditional theodicy.

To some extent, Hefner's fear that my theodicy could lead to the traditional rationalizing of all evil as good is based on my view that good and evil are ultimately to be defined in terms of God's evaluations. Although Hefner will later criticize me for straying too far from the traditional doctrine of divine power, he believes that my closeness to the traditional doctrine with regard to the *meaning* of good and evil leads to unacceptable consequences with regard to human *judgments* about good and evil. He says:

> Any evil may be rationalized by asserting that from an all-inclusive perspective it serves a better end. . . . This larger context may render a small catastrophe a "blessing in disguise." . . . Thus the doors are opened all over again to "the classical theistic" rationalizing of evil.[16]

Those doors are not *opened*, however, by anything in my position. Those doors are permanently open, regardless of what formal definition is given to the meaning of "good" and "evil." It is always possible for persons to *assert*, with Alexander Pope, that "all partial evil [is] universal good," so that "whatever is, is right."

The question is, should we believe them? I argued that we should not. Why not? The first point is that no human being can *know* that an event that appears to be evil from our point of view is really not evil from the most inclusive perspective. I was therefore surprised to find the following assertion by Hefner: "There is no way that [Jesus'] death can be termed genuine evil by Griffin, since it manifestly turned out for the best when viewed from an all-inclusive perspective."[17] But neither Hefner nor I have viewed this event from an all-inclusive perspective, so we cannot say how "it *manifestly* turned out" from such a perspective. Any statement that we would make about it would of necessity be a *judgment*, and of course a fully fallible one. Furthermore, how would we even make the judgment that it turned out for the best? We do not know the alternatives (history being loath to reveal them). Does Hefner mean that without a crucifixion there would have been no resurrection? We do not know that. Does he mean that without Jesus' death at that time, Christianity would not have emerged? We do not know this. Gautama the Buddha developed quite a following without being crucified at a young age. If Jesus had lived another thirty years, for example, the nature of his teachings might have been clearer, and the impact more profound, and many of us think that that would have been all to the good. And even if a religion based upon Jesus had not emerged, we do not know what other religion God might have inspired as a means to the salvation of the world. After all, Christianity has not been an Unambiguously Good Thing. And so on. In other words, I have no problem supposing that the betrayal and crucifixion of Jesus of Nazareth was a genuine evil. As I have made clear, I am no advocate of the *felix culpa* theodicy. We can testify to the power and wisdom of God to bring great good out of evils without thinking those evils felicitous.

In any case, given that any assertion about some event's being ultimately evil or not is a fallible human judgment, the question is: Why should we reject the judgment that no *prima facie* evils are genuinely evil? Because, as I suggested, the fact that genuinely evil things occur "is one of those basic presumptions in terms of which we all live our lives, in spite of what we might verbally affirm." It therefore needs no justification.[18] The argument behind this too cryptic assertion, which was developed later on,[19] is that there are many notions, such as freedom and the reality of causal influence, as well as the genuineness of evil, that we all presuppose in practice, even if we deny them verbally. And I agree with Whitehead (and other "commonsense" philosophers) that these presuppositions should be accepted as the ultimate criteria for all our philosophical and theological reasoning.[20] This means that no dogma, no matter how hallowed by tradition or by claims to revelatory status, should be allowed to undermine our confidence in these presuppositions of practice. That is what happened when Leibniz said that this is "the best of all possible worlds"—which means that there is no genuine evil in it—and defended this as an *a priori* truth, deducible from the omnipotence, goodness, and wisdom of God. If those three propositions (God is omnipotent, God is perfectly good, and God is perfectly wise) together imply that genuine evil cannot occur, then we should, instead of denying the reality of evil (or the validity of logic), deny one of those propositions. The idea the genuinely evil things occur is an idea we all inevitably presuppose in practice, so that, if we deny it verbally, we are caught in a contradiction between our theory and practice. But no such contradiction results from denying Leibniz's proposition about the omnipotence of God in the traditional sense. (Implicit in my endorsement of the "ideal observer" theory of moral terms, incidentally, is the idea that God's wisdom [omniscience] and perfect goodness are, along with the reality of evil, presuppositions of human practice. Leibniz's proposition about divine omnipotence is, accordingly, the only one of the three that can be denied without running into a similar conflict between theory and practice.)

My argument is, therefore, precisely the opposite of what Hefner suggests that it could imply. I pointed out how traditional theologians have used the distinction between intrinsic and instrumental good and evil to argue that all things experienced as intrinsically evil might be judged good from an all-inclusive perspective, because it is possible that their instrumental goodness more than compensates for their intrinsic evil. The whole point of my book was, first, to argue that we should never accept this argument and, second, to provide a theodicy that allows us to hold without contradiction the genuineness of evil and the perfect goodness and power of God.

I do "rationalize" evil in two senses. First, some things that are sometimes taken to be evils by human beings should not be considered genuinely evil, because they are necessities. If biological life is not possible without eventual biological death, for example, then we should not regard the inevitability of our own death and that of our loved ones as a genuine evil. Second, even those evils that are not necessary are made rational by my theodicy in the sense of showing that their *possibility* is necessary. The existence of life does not make *premature* death or excruciating pain necessary, but it does make their *possibility* necessary. Biological life simply is not possible, according to my hypothesis, without the possibility of evils such as excruciating pain and premature death. This form of "rationalization," however, is not to be equated with the traditional form, according to which all the actual evil of the world (not merely its possibility) is said to be necessary for a greater good than could occur without it, so that its very evilness is denied. My form of rationalization says that the basic structure of the world is without fault, even though the concrete history of the universe is riddled with evil, and says that we are called upon, in the name of the good structure, to fight against the concrete evils. The traditional rationalization said that the world as a whole is without fault, down to the tiniest events, thereby conceptually leaving no evil to fight against. These two forms of "rationalization" cannot be equated.

This theodicy would not, therefore, contrary to Hefner's fear, lead to counseling patience in the face of (*prima facie*) evil on the grounds that all (*prima facie*) evil must work for good so that none of it is genuinely evil. Good does sometime come out of evil, to be sure; but evil usually produces more evil than it does good, and good is usually far more effective than evil in producing good. The importance of preventing and overcoming particular evils is, furthermore, not undermined by the thought (which is implied by all traditional theodicies) that "God must not think these evils are very bad, else God would have prevented them." In process theodicy, the fact that evils occur does not mean that God looks upon them lightly. God could not simply (unilaterally) prevent or overcome this or that evil. It is for these reasons that I have suggested that liberation theologians need this kind of theodicy to undergird their conviction that God is on the side of justice for all, and strongly so.[21]

A final criticism that can be considered internal is Hefner's comment that "Griffin makes no reference to the demonic and the tragic."[22] This charge, at least in relation to the tragic, came as a surprise to me, having been weaned philosophically and theologically on the writings of Whitehead, who refers to "the tragic issues which are essential in the nature of things," and having been greatly influenced by Hartshorne's essay "Whitehead and Berdyaev: Is there Tragedy in God?"[23] The idea that tragedy is inherent to existence, including and especially the existence of God, is so central to my vision of reality that it is usually more implicit than explicit in my writing. But Hefner's contention that there is no explicit mention of it is an exaggeration. I point out, for example, against the traditional notion that God's experience is pure bliss, that for Whitehead it is always "tragic beauty."[24] But more important is the whole structure of the argument, which is that the metaphysical principles of the world are such that God's aim for increased richness and intensity of experience *cannot* be achieved without the risk of extreme discord of all types. That is tragic in the deepest sense of the term. I entitle the final and crucial section of my book "The Furies and the Goodness of God." The question is: If it is the case that existence is necessarily tragic in this sense, can we see God as justified in having brought forth such dangerous creatures as ourselves? I point to the possibility of future horrors that will far exceed anything previously known. And, as a part of the response to this question, I stress that the risks of this dangerous state into which God (by hypothesis) has led the world are necessarily *risks for God,* and in fact *more* so for God than for any of the creatures.[25]

Hefner's observation about the absence of the demonic from my discussion in *God, Power, and Evil* is entirely correct. I seek to begin rectifying this omission below in the section entitled "Rapprochement," as I did already in chapter 1.

I turn now to Hefner's external criticisms, which are more difficult, because I need not only to clarify my meaning but also to assert that this meaning is more adequate to human experience in general and to Christian faith in particular than Hefner believes. And we have, of course, no simple and noncontroversial way to show the truth of such assertions.

B. BIBLICAL FAITH, MONISM, AND DIVINE GOODNESS

Hefner's fundamental external criticism is that my theodicy "misses the heart of . . . classical Jewish and Christian faith" and also "the heart of the problem which evil poses to [this] faith."[26] I focus, he says, on the tension between holding to the genuineness of evil, on the one hand, and belief in a God who is absolutely all-determining (and all-good, I would add), on the other. But the real problem, Hefner claims, is that "the Jew and the Christian are *monistic* in that they are convinced that all things and events are rooted ultimately in one reality; yet, in the face of the conflict of good and evil, they cannot comprehend how this common root holds."[27]

It is evidently the contrast between my way of formulating the problem faced by traditional theism and his that Hefner has in mind with the question in his title, "Is Theodicy a Question of Power?" But no real contrast exists. To say that God is omnipotent, in the sense of all-determining (actually or potentially), and that God created all things out of absolute nothingness is simply one way of stating that all things are rooted ultimately in God—that is, that monism is the ultimate truth. My solution involves the explicit denial that monotheism means monism.[28] The denial of creation out of absolute nothingness, and the distinction between God and creativity, are part and parcel of a monotheism with a real duality between God and the world: the realm of finite actualities has its own inherent power. Theodicy therefore *is* a question of power, and the issue between us is whether or not that which we call "God" is the only power in the universe. (A real distinction does exist, however, between the traditional view I am rejecting and the view Hefner intends. I shall return to this under "Rapprochement.")

Hefner believes that, in denying that God has the power unilaterally to prevent all evil, I have succumbed to the "temptation . . . to make the problem too easy to resolve."[29] I would say that I have taken the crucial step necessary to make the problem possible of being resolved at all! And, indeed, Hefner in effect admits this. After asserting that "our concept of God does not allow us" to solve the problem in my way, he says that "in its purest form" Jewish and Christian faith "has adopted Job's stance of accepting what it cannot understand."[30] In other words, he says, Brunner and Fackenhiem are right: "we must conclude that there is no adequate rational solution to the problem of evil."[31] That conclusion does follow: if one holds that both God's goodness and omnipotence (as traditionally understood) and also the reality of genuine evil are nonnegotiable, then one has in effect said that a theoretical solution to the problem is impossible.

If Hefner had stopped there, it would seem like the temptation to which *he* had succumbed was to allow one's own faith tradition to claim truth for itself while violating the law of noncontradiction. He does not, however, stop there. He in effect rejects the proposition that God is "morally perfect." The philosophico-theological tradition with which he identifies sees good and evil as coexisting within the divine.[32]

We seem here to have a standoff. We believe in the reality of genuine evil. But I believe that perfect moral goodness is essential to a Christian notion of God, and that this belief (along with other considerations) demands the rejection of monistic monotheism. Hefner believes that monism is essential, and that this belief (possibly along with other considerations) requires positing the existence of evil as well as good in God.

Is there any way for Hefner to argue for the superiority of his view? He makes a few attempts. First, he claims that my view is inadequate to the experience of those molded by the biblical tradition. "Jewish and Christian experience is *not* that of being caught in a defectively functioning cosmic machinery that not even God can put in order."[33] Aside from the fact that this is not how I would characterize my position (at the very least, no devotee of the "philosophy of organism" would talk about "cosmic machinery"), I do not believe that we can talk about such matters as simple questions of *experience*. Either to affirm or to deny process theology's idea of the God-world relation would not be a matter of reporting rather straightforwardly about one's immediate experience, but of making an *interpretation* of it—and the most far-reaching type of interpretation at that. Neither Hefner nor I can appeal to "experience" in a direct way to warrant our own theology or to rule out the other's on this issue.

A second claim by Hefner is that "our religious tradition," in particular "our concept of God," does not allow for the doctrine of creation out of chaos.[34] "Christians, Jews, and atheists [sic!] know that God was not only present at the beginning, he was the beginning."[35] Knowing that I question the biblical basis for the doctrine of creation out of absolute nothingness, Hefner says that, "regardless of how one interprets Genesis . . . our concept of God does not allow us to get him off the hook by saying that the chaos which is coexistent with him explains his inability to negate its consequences."[36] But is the question "of how one interprets Genesis" irrelevant to the question of "our concept of God"? The traditional consensus on creation *ex nihilo* was formed in part on the assumption that the doctrine had strong biblical warrant, especially from Genesis 1:1. If it is now the consensus that the biblical warrant does not exist, should this fact not influence our judgment of what "our concept of God" should be?

In any case, Hefner's appeal to "our concept of God" begs the question, which is precisely whether the dominant tradition of Christian theology can be modified on this point—especially if this modification is necessary to preserve the unqualified goodness of God, to which the dominant tradition has also held. Are such matters settled by appealing to majority vote? Is a minority view by definition unacceptable? Hefner could hardly answer these questions in the affirmative, given his allegiance to that very minority tradition that posits evil in God. He does sometimes present this viewpoint as if it had been the dominant view: "The classical Jewish or Christian believer . . . sees that good and evil coexist in a seething crucible that is itself the numinous, the divine."[37] He elsewhere shows, however, that he knows that this has been a minority tradition.[38] He therefore cannot rule out my view simply on the grounds that it has not been the majority viewpoint.

Hefner's third argument is that the God of process theism is not genuinely worshipful. Because it took me all of chapter 17 of *God, Power, and Evil* to deal with various issues involved in this complex problem and also because I devote the final chapter of this book to it, I shall here raise only one question: even if one regarded the God portrayed by process theology as "limited" in power, that is, as having less than perfect power (which I deny), should one regard this God, who is perfect in goodness, as less worthy of worship than a God who is the source of all things but who is no more good than evil? Is "being wholly good" less important for being worthy of worship than "being the origin of all things"? Hefner complains that I have ignored the tradition that holds this latter view. It is true that I did not treat those whom he mentions: Boehme, Hegel, Berdyaev, and Tillich. (I had originally intended to treat both Berdyaev and Tillich along with several others as examples of nontraditional theologies, but had to forgo this due to limitations of space.) But I did deal with E. S. Brightman, and I did register my opinion, in relation to Brightman and Calvin, that a morally imperfect reality would not be worthy of worship.[39] Hefner admits that his position "faces its own problems."[40] It seems to me that these problems are far more formidable than those he believes to exist in my position. For example: Can persons who have come to know God as the One revealed in Jesus Christ, the One whom Charles Wesley was moved to describe as "pure unbounded love," name as God a reality that is not perfectly good? Another example: Given the fact that persons tend to mold themselves in terms of what they worship, because the *imitatio dei* is an inevitable accompaniment of true worship, should we want them, especially in this nuclear world, to think of the divine as "a seething crucible" in which "good and evil coexist"?

In summary, I cannot see that Hefner has given any good reason, whether on the basis of experience, tradition, or worshipfulness, for thinking his idea of God, and hence his theodicy, to be superior. His external criticisms, therefore, seem no more successful than his internal criticisms.

C. RAPPROCHEMENT: A TRINITARIAN MONISM

But I do not want to conclude there. In this final section, I suggest three bases upon which Hefner and I could come closer together. First, I believe that our positions are already closer than would appear from our in terchange thus far. Second, one could develop a new understanding of God as trinity that would bring the Whiteheadian position closer to the more monistic tradition of Berdyaev, Hegel, and others with which Hefner feels affinity. Third, one could modify that more monistic tradition in such a way that, while those features that are most crucial to it are retained, it would be brought into harmony with the most crucial features of the Whiteheadian tradition.

Already Existing Agreements: We already agree on many central points. First, although I suggested earlier that Hefner's formulation of his monistic claim that God is the origin of all things *could* be understood as simply a rewording of the traditional doctrine of divine omnipotence (which supports and is supported by the doctrine that God created all things out of absolute nothingness), Hefner's view is in fact not the same as the traditional view. Hefner affirms Berdyaev's notion of the *Ungrund*, according to which ultimate reality is "dynamic, nonobjective, and indeterminate."[41] This notion is virtually identical to Whitehead's notion that the ultimate reality is creativity. And Hefner endorses Berdyaev's statement of the implication of this doctrine that "freedom is at the center of reality—a freedom that God cannot control, else it would not be free."[42] This is also Whitehead's position, which differs decisively from the *traditional* doctrine of creation *ex nihilo*. Whitehead and Berdyaev stand together here against the majority tradition, because both understand the "nothing" out of which God created the world to be *me on*, not *ouk on*—that is, to be nonbeing in the sense of dynamic potentiality, not nonbeing in the sense of absolute nothingness.[43] This dynamic nothingness is the *Ungrund*, or creativity.

What then, is the difference between our positions? Why does Hefner reject *my* rejection of creation *ex nihilo* in the traditional sense? Why does he insist that the problem of evil cannot be solved by appeal to a "preexisting chaos, over which God has no control," calling this doctrine a "dilution of the claim that God is the origin of all that is?"[44] For some critics, the objectionable idea would be that the chaos is "preexistent" in the sense of existing apart from and independently of God's creative and sustaining power. In reply to this objection I would only need to explain that the primordial chaos I affirm is not preexistent in this sense. Hefner's objection, however, runs deeper. His objection is to the idea that the chaos is in any sense outside of and other than God. His own view is that the eternal chaos or *Ungrund* is internal to God. Some of Hefner's statements suggest that God and the *Ungrund* are in fact identical, but that does not seem to be his meaning. Otherwise he could not speak of the *Ungrund* as "a freedom that God cannot control." Also, he cites approvingly Boehme's and Berdyaev's notion of a theogonic process, in which the *Ungrund* gives birth to God. This process is, as Berdyaev says, an *eternal* and perpetual process, "not the birth of a previously nonexistent God."[45]

This suggestion is still quite close to Whitehead's view. One of Whitehead's most controversial assertions is that creativity is the ultimate reality, and that God is its "primordial creature."[46] Although that statement is easily misunderstood, Whitehead, like Berdyaev, does not mean that this ultimate reality existed before God. This is made clear by his statements that God is creativity's "aboriginal instance," its "primordial exemplification," its "eternal primordial character," and that, just as "God" makes no sense apart from "creativity," neither does "creativity" make any sense apart from "God."[47] God is the primordial "creature" of creativity not in the sense that creativity is an agent that creates something outside itself (the ontological principle, that only actualities can act,[48] rules out this interpretation), but in the sense that the ultimate, creativity, is the eternal process by which "the many become one, and are increased by one."[49] God is the primordial actuality, as the one eternally existing exemplification of this process. The Whiteheadian view is therefore different from the Platonic view, which Hefner rejects (and perhaps sees Whitehead as exemplifying). The eternal creativity, which is the meontic nothingness out of which God creates, is not external to God. God is its primordial embodiment.

The tradition for which Hefner speaks also dislikes the Platonic view for portraying God as totally on the side of order against disorder and therefore as opposing the chaotic power out of which this world was created by subjecting it to principles of order.[50] Plato's statement about the creator—*"out of disorder he brought order, considering that this was in every way better than the other"*—is quoted and italicized by Hefner.[51] Whereas the Platonic view (at least as Hefner portrays it) does not think that chaos or disorder could be a source of possibility, Hefner wants to stress this positive side of disorder and to associate it with divine creative power.[52]

Here again the Whiteheadian view is closer to the tradition for which Hefner speaks than to the Platonic tradition.[53] It is true that Whitehead emphasizes the need for order as a necessary condition for significant intrinsic value: for example, the complex order of the human body was a necessary condition for the high-level experience we enjoy. But this emphasis does not mean that Whitehead and his God are unambiguously on the side of order against disorder. Richness of experience requires not only harmony but also variety, which includes *temporal* variety—that is, novelty. God is not only the source of order in the world, but also the goad toward novelty.[54] *God is in fact the source of order primarily by being the source of novelty:* it is through the ingression of novel possibilities into the world that new forms of order can arise. This incarnation of new forms always requires a chaotic or disorderly element in creatures, because it means that their "mental pole" must transcend their "physical pole," which represents the order achieved in the past. Mentality, which God stimulates, is always a chaotic force, from the viewpoint of the achieved order. Whitehead accordingly describes God as leading the world "along the borders of chaos." The more complete statement is:

> Thus, if there is to be progress beyond limited ideals, the course of history by way of escape must venture along the borders of chaos in its substitution of higher for lower types of order.[55]

It follows that "the pure conservative is fighting against the essence of the universe," as Whitehead says in his chapter "Adventure."[56] Henry Nelson Wieman was true to Whitehead in saying that we should worship the creative good, not the created good.[57] Whiteheadians are far removed from the vision that places being and order on the side of deity overagainst becoming and disorder, and are therefore closer to Hefner's vision than he probably supposed.

A final agreement: Hefner's tradition sees not only the world and human personhood, but also God, as emerging through *struggle*: "The true and the real are comprised of the whole struggle, not by shaking free or separation from it."[58] We are again close. The Whiteheadian view of God upon which my theodicy is based is not an impassible absolute, no Cool Hand Yahweh dispensing law and order from above it all. Rather, in the pan-en-theistic vision, we live within the Holy One who is our Father and Mother, and who is understood as groaning in travail (as well as delighting with joy) throughout our birthing process. What goes on in the world is not external to God, nor to God's own fulfillment. God is in fact the universe's "Unity of Adventure," the "Adventure in the Universe as One."[59] God is not a purely outgoing Agape without Eros. Rather, God's aim for the creatures' depth of satisfaction is "an intermediate step towards the fulfillment of his own being."[60] Our own satisfaction through the realization of truth, beauty, and goodness "provides the final contentment for the eros of the Universe."[61] The struggles of the world are thereby internal to God, and in a sense are God's own struggles.

The qualification "in a sense" in the previous sentence brings us to the fundamental issue between us: the question of monism. Having shown that Whiteheadian thought is already more closely aligned to the tradition with which Hefner identifies than he had evidently thought, I now turn to a possible way to develop Whiteheadian theology that would bring it still closer. I do not hereby commit myself to this possibility, but only put it into the public arena for discussion.

A Trinitarian Monism: Whitehead's own solution to the problem of evil depends upon a strong distinction between God and creativity. God is indeed the primordial *embodiment* of creativity, so that creativity is internal to God, as I stressed earlier. But creativity is not *wholly* embodied by God; rather, a plurality of nondivine embodiments of creativity necessarily exists as well. Creativity is therefore external to God as well as internal. The worldly actual occasions are, to be sure, always received into God's "consequent nature" as soon as their moment of subjective concrescence is completed. But during their moment of subjective becoming, in which they exercise their own creative power, they do transcend God, being outside the divine experience. A precise statement of the doctrine of pan-en-theism must accordingly say that "all things are or immediately will be in God." It is because all creatures as well as God embody their own creativity that Whitehead could hold that God is good even though the world is filled with evil.

Furthermore, Whitehead evidently never thought of creativity as divine.[62] (He did sometimes capitalize it, but he also capitalized many other words.) Many critics have claimed that, because Whitehead treated creativity as the ultimate reality, and even spoke of God as the primordial "accident" or "creature" of creativity, he had in effect made it not only divine, but more divine than God. But Whitehead's followers have shown this charge to be false.[63]

However, even if Whitehead himself did not regard creativity as divine, a Whiteheadian might be able to do so. Here is a brief sketch of one way of doing this as part of a trinitarian understanding of reality. The three *persona* or aspects of this trinitarian Godhead would be God (our Mother and Father), the World, and the Creativity they both embody. A distinction would thereby be made between God and the (trinitarian) Godhead. And there would be distinctions of divinity. Only God the Father-Mother would be unqualifiedly divine. The World would be That-Which-Is-Becoming-Divine. It would be divine only dialectically, combining the "not yet" with the "already." As long as this dialectical relationship obtains, Creativity will be divine only ambiguously. That is, while fully divine as embodied in God, its embodiment in the World remains capable of filling a spectrum that is divine at one end, neutral in the middle, and demonic at the other end.

One advantage of this view is that it would build into the Christian trinitarian discussion, which is often a quite abstract exercise with little connection to current problems, a basis for dialogue with some of the other great religious traditions. In particular, there are similarities between Whitehead's Creativity (or Boehme's and Berdyaev's *Ungrund*, or Tillich's Being Itself) and the Emptiness of Mayahana Buddhism and the Brahman of Advaita Vedanta. By coming to recognize Creativity as divine, even if only ambiguously so at present, we would be recognizing the divinity of that feature of reality that has been the primary focus of religious attention for a great part of the human family. This modification of Whiteheadian theism would, furthermore, by portraying all power as rooted in the Godhead, provide a basis for something other than an absolute no to that stream of Jewish, Christian, and Islamic thought that has treated God as the sole power.

Only a dialectical or qualified yes, however, could be given to each of these views. An unqualified, undialectical monism is what has led either to a denial of the total goodness of God or to an incredible denial of the reality of genuine evil in the world. This trinitarian monism would say that Creativity as characterized by God the Father-Mother of all things is unambiguously good, but that Creativity as characterized by Worldly actualities is (still) ambiguous. It is divine, but worthy of worship only in an anticipatory sense, only insofar as it will someday be characterized by that perfection of creative and receptive love that is possible for Worldly actualities.

This view would thereby provide a way of formulating the widespread intuition that an ambivalence exists within the Godhead itself, a tension between good and evil. This tension has been described in terms of "creator and destroyer," "right and left hands," "perfect will and irrational given," "daylight and shadow sides." The problem with such views is that they make God not totally worthy of worship and imitation. For example, Brightman counsels us to worship the perfect will of God while regretting the fact that God's total nature includes irrational and destructive impulses.[64] Other theologians urge us to call upon God to repent.[65] But a God who has worse internal problems than we, or who is morally inferior to us, can hardly be the object of unreserved adoration and worship—at least not one that we would *want* persons to worship and thereby mold themselves in relation to. This trinitarian monism would say that God is perfect both creatively and receptively, always willing and working for the best in creation, and always being perfectly sympathetic with the weal and woe of creatures. The less-than-perfect aspect of the Godhead would be Creativity as it is embodied in and characterized by Worldly actualities. Within God, this Creativity is necessarily good. But finite, Worldly actualities will never be incapable, in the strict sense, of erring. No matter how far the World fulfills its destiny of becoming fully divinized, therefore, its members will always retain the possibility of using their Creativity in destructive and unsympathetic ways.

This view would also provide the basis for a more adequate doctrine of the demonic than we have had. The official doctrine of Christianity is that the devil is a mere creature, one among a host of angels, who decided to use his powers against rather than for God. And in careful formulations this "decision" was said to have been predestined by God, so that the devil was in fact, despite all appearances, as much under God's dominion as everything else. But in the religious imagination of Christians (and others), the devil has been something more. Satan or the devil has been imagined to be a deadly enemy of God, not a mere instrument of mysterious divine purposes. Satan has been imagined to be not a mere creature, but a being of cosmic proportions, almost godlike in knowledge and power. Christian imagination and its popular theology have in fact been virtually dualistic, seeing the cosmos as a battleground between almost equal powers of good and evil. The "almost" is extremely important: no question has existed as to who would be ultimately victorious. But the contest has been imagined to be a *real* battle, which implies that Satan's power has been assumed to be in some sense autonomous, and as comparable (although not really equal) to that of God. The "demonic" power that Satan embodies has been felt to be divine or quasi-divine power turned to evil purposes.

The majority tradition of Christian theology has not been able to do justice to this sense of the autonomy and terror of the demonic. Because the line between God and world was understood to be an absolute line between divine and nondivine, the only way to do justice to the demonic seemed to be to put it *within* God, so that "Satan" symbolized one aspect of a polarity of good and evil within God. This is the approach taken by the minority tradition with which Hefner identifies. Members of this minority tradition differ among themselves about how literally to take this good-evil polarity. Hefner with Tillich considers it unjustifiably anthropomorphic to say that "God is good and evil," because this would mean "laying on God our own standards of good and evil."[66] Others, such as John Roth, Eliezer Berkovitz, and Edgar Brightman, think of God in more personal terms and therefore talk of God more directly as having an evil side.[67] In any case, the term "God" is applied to a reality that is not unambiguously good.

But the trinitarian monism suggested above can do justice to the dual conviction that God is perfectly good and that God is doing battle with a divine or quasi-divine power become demonic. The symbol of Satan or the devil stands for Creativity embodied in high-level beings insofar as it is used in ways that go strongly against God's aims with destructive consequences.

As suggested earlier, we can think of a spectrum of exercises of worldly Creativity, with high conformity to God's aims at one end, high opposition at the other, and a large more-or-less grey area in between. Some of this grey area can be thought of as more-or-less mild waywardness, some of it as fairly neutral—insofar as there are activities that are neither particularly creative nor destructive, neither particularly good nor evil. We need not and should not, therefore, trivialize the term "demonic" by using it for Creativity whenever it fails to actualize the divinely proffered possibilities to the highest degree. We can and should use it only with regard to Creativity in beings with the capacity for self-conscious reflective decisions, and only for those of their activities that are diametrically opposed to the (perfect) purposes of God.

It was with the emergence of human beings (at least on our planet) that it became possible for Creativity as embodied in the World to become demonic. Prior to this emergence, a duality of perfect and imperfect embodiments of Creativity existed within the Godhead, but there was no evil in the sense of the demonic. The evolutionary rise of conscious and then self-conscious beings, which was necessary for the world to fulfill its destiny, also allowed for a qualitative change within the Godhead from a tension between perfect and merely imperfect embodiments of Creativity to a deadly opposition between God and the demonic.

The third member of this monistic, somewhat Hegelian trinity is the World. The doctrine of the divinity of Jesus as the Christ provides a basis for including the World within the Godhead. Jesus in orthodox thought has been said to be fully human yet fully divine. Liberal christologies have tended to interpret "fully divine" as meaning that the eternal Logos, which is homoousian with the Father and therefore fully divine, was truly and fully incarnate in Jesus. The present view can also hold this. But it also accepts the stronger statement, that Jesus as a concrete human being was fully divine, as well as fully human. This affirmation cannot mean that Jesus was divine in the same sense that God his Father-Mother is—that would be nonsense. It means that Jesus was fully divine *in the sense in which it is possible for the World to be divine*. As such he was the first fruit, the proleptic appearance, of the coming Commonwealth of God, in which God will be *fully* incarnate in the World, and the World will therefore use its Creativity in harmony with and imitation of the creative and responsive love of God. That the World is *now* part of the Godhead can only be said with the meaning of "already" and "not yet." To say that Jesus is normative for understanding the World's status is to say that Jesus reveals what we essentially are, and are destined to become. To say this is to confess our belief that loving Creativity is ultimately more powerful than demonic Creativity, that the power of love will eventually, if ever so slowly, deify us, transforming us into beings who are fully divine while still fully creaturely. It is to confess that creative and responsive love is the norm for understanding the divine power of the universe, no matter how often we are tempted to take hateful or indifferent destructive power as the truly divine power that will forever dominate the world.

There would obviously be many details to work out in this sketch, many objections to answer. But I present it to Hefner as a possible way to combine his monistic conviction about a single divine origin for all things, which he shares with the majority, with the conviction that God must be perfectly good, which I share with the majority.

Needed Modifications of Hefner's Monism: If Hefner were to accept this suggestion, it would mean that his discussion of basic polarities would need to become more nuanced, especially his treatment of good and evil. He has written as if the polarity of good and evil were on the same level as the polarities of being and nonbeing, eternity and time, order and chaos, actuality and possibility.[68] But we have no good reason to assume that the polarity of good and evil has the same ultimacy as these other polarities. One could therefore assign these other polarities to God (as well as to the Godhead) while attributing the polarity of good and evil only to the Godhead.

I am speaking here of *moral* good and evil, meaning the motivation that characterizes one's intention. By moral evil I mean primarily creative, active, originating evil, which is the use of creative power to produce evil effects. This moral or originating evil is to be distinguished from aesthetic, receptive, or passive evil, which is the pain or suffering one experiences by being wounded, or by being sympathetic to the wounds suffered by others. Evil in the sense of suffering can and should be ascribed to God, especially from a Christian standpoint, which takes the suffering of Jesus on the cross as revelatory of the suffering heart of God. But to ascribe evil in this sense to God does not derogate from God's perfection. In fact, insofar as we take an absence of sympathetic love to be an imperfection, speaking of God as Perfect Love *demands* that we ascribe evil in the sense of suffering to the divine experience. One of the strengths of process theology, especially through Charles Hartshorne's influence, has been that its dipolar understanding of God shows how the presence of both moral goodness and aesthetic evil in God are not only compatible but mutually supportive. This idea can be retained in the present proposal.

This proposal may require a more personalistic notion of God than Hefner has previously entertained. His close association of God with the *Ungrund*, his apparent endorsement of Tillich's understanding of God (according to which God is Being Itself but not *a* being),[69] and his view that it would be illegitimately anthropomorphic to speak of God as good and evil, suggest that he has thought of God not as *a* being who could have personal attributes, such as feeling, consciousness, and purpose, but as Being (or Creativity) Itself. As pointed out earlier, however, he does seem to distinguish between God and the aboriginal freedom that constitutes the *Ungrund*, because he says that even God cannot control this freedom, and he speaks of it as eternally giving birth to God. I wonder if the view that God is not *simply* Creativity Itself, but the primordial *characterization* (as creative and responsive love) of the Creativity embodied in all worldly things, avoids the type of anthropomorphism Hefner rightly rejects (the idea of God as a being who is external to us and another being "alongside us" in the sense of being only different in degree), while still portraying God as an individualized embodiment of Creativity to which personal attributes can be meaningfully applied. If so, the notion that God suffers can be acceptable, and the intuition that

God embodies both good and evil can be understood as meaning good in both a moral and an aesthetic sense (God intends our good, and rejoices with our joys), but evil only in the receptive or aesthetic sense (God suffers with our sufferings).

The other polarity that Hefner most closely associates with good and evil is that of order and disorder (or chaos). It is true, as discussed earlier, that this equation is often made, and for good reasons. But Hefner's own discussion shows that no complete equation of disorder and evil should be made, because disorder is in some respects a necessary part of the goodness of the world. Only through disorder can tedious monotony be broken, and can progress be made. We can well say, therefore, that disorder is rooted partially in God without implying that evil is thereby rooted in God.

Of course, even that is too simple. My own theodicy has stressed the sense in which evil *is* rooted in God. It is because God stimulated the world to bring forth living forms that the world has pain in it. It is because God continued to encourage the world's self-creation that it has the kinds of pain and suffering that only the higher animals can undergo. And it is because God did not stop there that the unique kinds of evil that can be experienced and perpetrated by human beings exist on this planet.

God is, therefore, *responsible* for most of what we usually have in mind when we think of all the evils of the world and wonder how it can be the product of a good creator. I have also sought to show, however, that this responsibility does not make God *indictable*—that is, responsible for *unjustifiable* activity. The only alternative to a world with the possibility for these evils, I have proposed, is the one thing that would have been worse—a world that remained indefinitely in a state with no significant values at all, a purely trivial world. Showing that evil is, in an important sense, rooted in God does not therefore mean that there is an evil root in God. To account for the existence of genuine evil we need not think of God as "a seething crucible" in which "good and evil coexist." Rather, we can hold to God's perfect goodness, and explain evil in terms of the externally uncontrollable Creativity that is inherent to the World—as inherent to the world as it is to God—and in terms of those necessary conditions of existence that make every increase in the capacity for goodness also an increase in the capacity for evil.

The rapprochement with Hefner's view made possible by the trinitarian monism suggested above means that one *can* say that "good and evil coexist in a seething crucible that is itself the numinous, the divine." This Hefnerian statement would now refer not to God but to the total Godhead with its mysterious Creativity, which is experienced as numinous whether its activity be enchantingly beautiful or awesomely destructive.

Hefner's critique, especially his judgments about the heart of Jewish and Christian faith, have stimulated me to suggest a *via media* that might be affirmed equally by those whose monistic intuitions are stronger than their intuitions about divine goodness, by those in whom the opposite is the case, and by those in which the two intuitions are equal. I repeat that I do not endorse this trinitarian monism. I have, in fact, developed in chapter 1 an understanding of the demonic and the trinity in a semidualistic way, in which most of what is said above is affirmed, but in which creativity as embodied in the world is not considered divine, even ambiguously so, and in which the world is therefore not viewed as part of the Godhead. But the trinitarian monism described above, it seems to me, would be a perfectly acceptable position, and it might even have more widespread appeal, and thereby more unifying power, than the more dualistic view I have endorsed.[70]

Chapter 11

WORSHIP AND THEODICY

A. WHY THIS ISSUE IS CRUCIAL FOR PROCESS THEODICY

It might seem strange to have a separate chapter on theodicy and worship. Is this not what theodicy is all about? Has this issue, therefore, not been the topic of all the previous chapters? It is true that the basic question that motivates a theodicy is whether the evils of the world can be reconciled with a divine reality worthy of worship. There is a good reason, nevertheless, to have a separate chapter on this topic in a book on process theodicy. This reason is that the typical and fairly distinctive criticism of process theodicy is that it "solves" the problem of evil only by portraying a God who is not worthy of worship. The reason why this criticism is directed at process theodicy (and other similar approaches) in particular can be seen by reviewing the elements involved in the problem of evil. For a reality to be considered worthy of worship and thus to be called God, at least in biblically based cultures, this reality must be perfect in power and goodness. The problem of evil is generated by the fact that belief in divine goodness and power, when perfect power is understood as omnipotence in the traditional sense, seems to be rationally inconsistent with the acknowledgment of worldly evil. The reason for this apparent inconsistency is that a being of perfect goodness would presumably want to prevent all evil, and an omnipotent being would presumably be capable of preventing all evil. The various approaches to the problem of evil involve different judgments about which of the four elements—rational consistency, worldly evil, perfect divine goodness, or divine omnipotence—to reject. What the typical criticism of a theodicy is depends upon which of the four elements it rejects.

A theodicy that rejects rational consistency evokes the charge not that it portrays a God unworthy of worship, but that it is irrational. Although in *God, Power, and Evil* I discussed three theologians who rejected rational consistency in an extreme sense by rejecting *logical* consistency (Barth, Brunner, and Fackenheim), none of my critics took this extreme approach. The issue of the importance of rational consistency in a larger sense does play a role in the present book, however, especially in relation to the positions of John Knasas, Alvin Plantinga, and Stephen Davis. Davis does not programmatically deny the importance of providing plausible explanations, but he seems to assume that admitting that he does not have plausible explanations for various types of evil does not seriously undermine the credibility of his position. Knasas tries to overcome the apparent inconsistency of saying both that God fully determines all worldly events and that some worldly events are truly free. The main question Plantinga's position raises is whether the human demand for rational consistency is met as long as no outright logical consistency can be shown, or whether this demand requires an explanation that goes beyond this minimalist conception of rationality to provide a plausible explanation for the coexistence of God and evil.

A second approach to theodicy is to reject worldly evil by saying that all apparent evils are, or might be, not genuinely evil from an omniscient standpoint. The main criticism this approach evokes is that it is incredible. As I showed in *God, Power, and Evil*, this approach was finally taken by most advocates of traditional all-determining theism, such as Augustine, Thomas, Luther, and Leibniz. The fact that this approach is not of merely historical interest is illustrated by Nelson Pike in the present book, and also by Huston Smith, who, in a recent debate with me, says that "everything—the everything for which God is solely responsible—is exactly as it should be." Smith continues: "God's perfection, tied tightly to his omnipotence, precludes the possibility of any second-rate happenings—nothing that occurs would have been better had it been otherwise."[1] He thereby explicitly rejects the reality of what I mean by genuine evil: "anything, all things considered, without which the universe would have been better."[2] The main question this position provokes is: Can anyone really believe this? That is, can one consistently live in terms of the conviction that nothing that happens is really evil?

The third possibility is to reject the perfect goodness of God. This approach was illustrated in *God, Power, and Evil* by E. S. Brightman (who suggested that God has a nonrational, volatile, amoral nature, which is at odds with God's perfectly good will). This approach is illustrated in the present volume by Philip Hefner and (to be discussed below) Nancy Frankenberry.

The central criticism evoked by this theodicy is that it does not really provide a theodicy. The word "theodicy," coming from the Greek words for God and justice, means an attempt to justify the ways of God in the light of the world's (apparent) evils. This third approach provides an *explanation* for evil—by saying that the creator of the world is itself partly evil—but no *justification*. It does not defend God against the suspicion of being immoral or amoral, but simply turns this suspicion into an affirmation. In other words, this third approach, by rejecting God's perfect goodness, has not portrayed a divine being worthy of worship, and therefore in effect has not defended the existence of *God*. A book built around this approach would, like the present one, need a chapter on "theodicy and worship."

This question about worshipfulness also arises in relation to the traditional free-will theodicy (or defense). That approach provokes one or the other of the two previous criticisms. On the one hand, insofar as it acknowledges the existence of genuine evil, it evokes doubt that the God portrayed is fully good: if this God has coercive omnipotence, one wonders, why has this God allowed so many unspeakable evils? As we have seen, Davis says "I just don't know," and Plantinga denies the need to give plausible answers. On the other hand, insofar as this theodicy avoids this criticism by saying that everything will eventually work out for the best (Hick), this theodicy evokes incredulity.

The fourth possible approach is to modify the traditional doctrine of perfect power, so that it no longer implies that God can unilaterally prevent all genuine evil. This approach unambiguously retains worldly evil, divine goodness, and rational consistency (in more than a minimalist sense, insisting that a rational position must be plausible). But this approach typically provokes the response that it has reconciled God and evil only by portraying a God that is finite in power and therefore unworthy of worship. David Basinger, for example, indicates what he would say if all his other objections to process theism were overcome. Against the claim of process theists that the view that God cannot coerce is more adequate than the view that God can, he replies that many believe that "a god as 'weak' as the one affirmed by process theism is no god at all or, at least, a god not worthy of worship and thus see the coercive concept of classical theism to be more adequate."[3] Likewise, the conclusion of Reichenbach's critique is that the God of process theism is finite in the sense of having less power than some conceivable being. (Reichenbach and Basinger both make this criticism even though they both, in their effort to provide an answer to natural evils, implicitly move toward this approach themselves, insofar as they adopt the position of F. R. Tennant.) The same point is made by John Knasas and Stephen Davis, and this point was the crux of John Hick's earlier criticism of process theodicy.[4]

This criticism has already been answered in previous chapters. The answer is essentially twofold. (1) The traditional idea of God is not really a conceivable idea and therefore does not provide a standard in terms of which to call the God of process theism finite, in the sense of imperfect—namely, inferior to some conceivable being. (2) Coercive power, far from being a necessary attribute of a universal, omnipresent being, is, like a voice, a beard, and a hand, an attribute that can characterize only a finite, localized being. This twofold answer, which has been developed at length in previous chapters, need not be elaborated again here.

There are, however, three other questions revolving around the concept of worshipfulness that have been raised. One is whether worship really presupposes perfect power. A second question is whether process theism portrays God as perfectly good. A third is whether worship really requires God to be perfectly good. I have already discussed the third question while responding to Philip Hefner in chapter 10. I will here, accordingly, respond only to the first two questions.

B. DOES WORSHIP PRESUPPOSE PERFECT POWER?

Peter Hare has asked whether it is not arbitrary to insist that a reality must be perfect in power to be worthy of worship. His question was evoked by the fact that I had agreed with critics of E. S. Brightman's deity that it is not worthy of worship. I had said that this conclusion follows not only from the fact that Brightman's God is not perfectly good, but also from the fact that, according to Brightman himself, his God had imperfect—that is, less than the greatest conceivable—power.[5] Hare uses my judgment here as a test case "of how fairly process theists judge other nontraditional theists," saying that it seems "unwise and unfair to consider 'greatest conceivable' a necessary and sufficient condition of worshipability."[6] Hare believes it would be "fairer to consider the worshipability of power to be partly a matter of how far the power is from a monopoly and how far it is from the maximum in human power." Then, "instead of considering deities such as Brightman's unworthy of a theistic sort of worship" altogether, process theists should simply say that less *strength* of worship is appropriate to them than to the God of process theism, and that "the strength of worship appropriate to the process deity is the greatest strength of worship that is metaphysically and morally meaningful."[7]

The disagreement here seems to be partly semantic, and Hare's discussion points out an ambiguity in the term "worshipful." On the one hand, worship implies loving and serving the divine reality with one's *whole* heart, mind, soul, and body, and this *unreserved* devotion is not possible if the divine reality, in the worshipper's estimation, is infected with imperfection. On this basis, I said that Brightman's God was finite in a sense that makes it unworthy of worship. My main concern was to point out that, if the God of process theism be called "finite," it is not finite in the same sense as Brightman's, that of having less than the greatest power conceivable (within a given framework). That this was no idle concern I had indicated at the outset by pointing out that the only mention of the Whiteheadian position in John Hick's large book on the problem of evil was "the false suggestion that it is essentially the same as that of E. S. Brightman."[8] I had some support for connecting perfection and worshipfulness in Brightman himself, incidentally, in that he, concluding that God *as a whole* is not morally perfect, declared the object of worship to be the divine *will*, which *is* perfectly good.[9] In any case, I was here using "worthy of worship" in the sense of *unreservedly* worthy, and I agree with Anselm that nothing is thus worthy except that greater than which nothing can be (coherently) thought.

The term "worshipful," however, can also point to that which *in fact* does evoke religious devotion or commitment, and in this sense being worshipful is not an all-or-none matter but that matter of degree of which Hare speaks. I have at least implicitly used this notion by speaking of the basic religious motivation of human beings as the desire to be in harmony with the ultimate power of the universe. "To want to be in harmony with" is the basic form of worship, and this worship will be evoked by the power that is thought or imagined to be the supreme power of the universe. It need not be assumed to be the *greatest conceivable* power; it must only be thought (or felt) to be, in some sense, the *most effective* power, at least in relation to matters of ultimate importance. And it certainly need not be thought to be perfectly good. The sun, the dialectical process of history, and the evolutionary process controlled by the survival of the fittest can each be "worshipful" in this sense of the term; they have indeed evoked overriding devotion from persons. Less than fully critical devotees may, in fact, believe that the deity in question is worthy of unreserved devotion. But the fully critical spirit will protest, saying that commitment of one's *entire* heart, mind, soul, and body is not appropriate if the object of devotion is imperfect.

This distinction between the two senses of the term "worshipful" seems to be implicit in Hare's discussion. He is using it in the latter, psychological sense insofar as he speaks of worship as a matter of degree. He implies the idea of being worshipful in the former, normative sense of the term in speaking of "the greatest strength of worship that is metaphysically and morally meaningful."

The one statement of Hare's on this topic with which I would take issue is his suggestion that worshipfulness should involve the question of how far the conceived power is from having a monopoly on power. If the idea of a being with a monopoly on power is, as Hare says, metaphysically impossible and morally repugnant, we should not accept it as a standard in relation to which to judge other ways to conceive the holy power whose existence we all at some level intuit. One difficulty with Hare's suggestion is evident from my discussion above about the sense in which the God of process theology has effected a self-limitation. By evoking the existence of beings with increasingly more power of self-determination, God has become increasingly *removed* from having a monopoly on power. Hare's suggestion would imply that, by creating living beings, and finally human beings, God had become increasingly less worthy of worship. It would be appropriate for us to worship God with great strength of devotion only if we, the potential worshippers, did not exist.

C. IS THE GOD OF PROCESS THEISM PERFECTLY GOOD?

Those who deny God's perfect goodness will, naturally, be critical of the notion that worship presupposes perfect goodness. Nancy Frankenberry, who wants to "collapse the ontological distinction Whitehead made between God and creativity"[10] and thereby, like Hefner, move toward a more monistic worldview,[11] also, like Hefner, cannot regard God as unambiguously good. She accordingly wants to challenge the "theological habit of connecting worshipfulness with moral goodness."[12] Because I have already addressed this question in the response to Hefner in chapter 10, I will not treat it here, but will instead move directly to a related question raised by Frankenberry— whether the God of process theism (without her proposed collapse of the ontological distinction between God and creativity) portrays God as perfectly good. While her critique of the distinction between persuasion and coercion, discussed in chapter 6, was meant to apply to process theology somewhat broadly, her claim about my theodicy in particular is that it does not salvage "a valid meaning of the goodness of God."[13]

Frankenberry begins her argument for this point by citing "Griffin's own admission that God is responsible for 'all of the evil of discord in the world.'" She comments: "This in itself is a major admission,"[14] seeming to imply thereby that my statement has already partly made her case against the unambiguous goodness of the process God. Why it does not do so was explained in the final section of the previous chapter, in the discussion of the sense in which God can be responsible for discord or suffering without being indictable for it. Process theodicy asks: If the choice was either humanlike beings who might treat each other very inhumanely, even engage in genocide, pollute the globe, and even build nuclear weapons with which to threaten all forms of life, or no humanlike creatures at all, could we honestly say that God should have forgone higher-than-ape creatures altogether? Frankenberry seems to think my question was purely rhetorical, as she says: "But there are clearly two answers to this question." But that is what I had already said.[15] Although I do not think that God chose wrongly (assuming the truth of this picture of the options), I realize that others, especially those less fortunately situated, might well think otherwise. Certainly some persons with strong ecological sensitivities have become misanthropic, deciding it would have been better if human beings had never been evolved.

Frankenberry, however, does not merely want the possibility of that answer recognized; she thinks it should, at least to an extent, be affirmed. She holds it against me that I do "not wrestle with those voices in our century who have been disposed to take Job's side of the case against God, and who, like Elie Wiesel, have been able to articulate a much more complex and agonized affirmation of the reality of God than has yet appeared in process theodicy."[16] But "to take Job's side against God" is to assume, with Job, the existence of a God who is more strongly responsible for the events of the world than the God of process theology. Frankenberry's comment thereby begs the question.

Likewise, the "more complex" affirmation of God that Frankenberry prefers is necessary only because she is suggesting a *simplification* of the Whiteheadian doctrine of God by advocating that the ontological distinction Whitehead made between God and creativity be collapsed. Whitehead's famous statement, "All simplifications of religious dogma are shipwrecked upon the rock of the problem of evil," which Frankenberry cites,[17] is directly relevant here. In introducing this topic, Whitehead had pointed to "three main simple renderings" of the concept of God: the Eastern Asiatic concept of an impersonal order, which is the self-ordering of the world; the Semitic concept of a "personal individual entity, whose existence is the one ultimate metaphysical fact"; and the pantheistic concept, which is the Semitic concept with the world as a phase within God. Whitehead suggests that we should not think of these "extremes of simplicity" as "mutually exclusive concepts, from among which we are to choose one and reject the others."[18] We should instead engage in that "complexity of thought" required to find some "mediation" between these concepts. Whitehead clearly meant his own doctrine of God to be a more complex doctrine in which that mediation is achieved, and which, among other things, would therefore not be shipwrecked upon the rock of the problem of evil. Frankenberry's proposal to collapse the distinction between God and creativity seems to lead back toward the type of simplification Whitehead wanted to overcome. One of the theses of *God, Power, and Evil* is that the complexity of traditional theology, with its notorious "scholastic distinctions," was due to the fact that it had not made distinctions soon enough, especially a distinction between the creativity of God and that

of the world. If Frankenberry wants to collapse that distinction, it is not surprising that she should feel the need for a "more complex and agonizing
affirmation of the reality of God" than those of us who believe Whitehead's
distinction to be one of the greatest breakthroughs ever made in the history
of philosophical theology. In any case, the proposal to modify process theism
to make God more responsible for evil says nothing about the goodness of
God in a process theism that has not been thus modified.

Frankenberry's main argument for the conclusion that the God of process theology cannot be considered morally perfect seems to be based on the
principle that the God of process theology first of all promotes aesthetic
value, meaning complexity and intensity as well as harmony of experience.
She believes that looking at "aesthetic considerations would seem to lead to a
more ambiguous and mixed estimate" about divine goodness. "Upon close
examination," she says, "this aesthetic order at concrete moments of history
can appear to be at best utterly indifferent and at worst implacably malevo-
lent towards human good."[19]

How does Frankenberry's argument fare "upon close examination"? One
problem with her statement is that it is about how the aesthetic order "can
appear." No one doubts that it can appear as she describes it; but the task of
philosophical theology, like that of natural science, is to try to discern the
reality *beneath* the appearances.

If what she means, however, is that the aesthetic order *really is* as she
describes it, then two responses are in order. First, process theology, being
evolutionary, nondualistic, and nonanthropocentric, specifically rejects the
idea that the world was designed for human beings in particular. To regard
the world as reflecting a divine teleology is not to say that everything is
supposed to work together for *human* good. The divine purpose promotes
harmonious intensity of experience in general. We humans generally benefit
from this promotion, both directly and indirectly; but this promotion has
necessarily had the possibility of resulting in forms of order and types of
events, such as viruses, cancerous growths, earthquakes, and meteorites, that
sometimes conflict with our welfare. To point out that the aesthetic order is
not unambiguously favorable to human good is therefore to affirm, not to
refute, one of process theology's basic points. Second, Frankenberry's statement is relevant only if we have already accepted her modification of Whitehead, collapsing the distinction between God's creativity and the creative
energy of worldly beings (through which they can partially determine themselves and inflict themselves on each other in ways that run strongly counter
to the divine suasion). As long as we *hold* to this distinction, the indifference
and malevolence that characterize creaturely creativity cast no shadow upon
the divine creativity. We can believe that Divine Creativity is always perfectly characterized by Creative and Responsive Love, with no admixture of

malevolence or indifference. Frankenberry's counter-suggestion, that we must read indifference or malevolence into the divine nature, is to beg the question, which is whether we *should* collapse the distinction between God and creativity.

One of the reasons that I, as well as other process theologians, have given for regarding God as unambiguously good is based on the doctrine of God's "consequent nature," according to which God necessarily feels the sufferings as well as the joys of creatures along with us. I suggested that this doctrine is relevant to God's goodness in the light of the idea that God has lured the creation forward to heights where extreme suffering is possible. The idea that, because of the metaphysical correlations involving value and power, great values are not possible without the risk of great suffering surely provides the most important justification for God in this framework. But it is also helpful, I suggested, to reflect on the fact that God, in this theology, is no impassive spectator, goading the creation on to risk sufferings that will be the creatures' alone. Rather, "God does not promote any new level of intensity without being willing to suffer the possible consequences."[20]

Frankenberry seeks to turn this argument against the goodness of process theology's God. She constructs a damned-if-you-do, damned-if-you-don't argument around the question whether the "evil which lacerates the life of creatures . . . cuts deeply into the life of the creator." On the one hand, if it does not, then God as the "fellow sufferer" does not really "understand" the sufferings of creatures. I agree. On the other hand, she says, "if the lacerations are suffered more immediately by God . . . then the 'complexity' of the concrete nature of God may just as well spell the viper's tangle, and its 'intensity' reflect the full force of evil's perversity." In other words, "Whitehead's 'fellow sufferer' may be too deeply riddled with antagonistic impulses to be unambiguously 'good.' "[21]

Frankenberry has again confused two quite different things. This time the confusion is between aesthetic evil, or suffering, and moral evil, or perversity. This distinction, which was mentioned in the previous chapter, has been emphasized countless times by Charles Hartshorne, among others. When a woman suffers during childbirth because, being naturally sympathetic to her bodily members, she feels the trauma experienced by her cells, we do not call her evil. When a father suffers in sympathy with the sufferings of his child, we do not call him evil; in fact, we would doubt his complete goodness if he did not suffer. We do say that suffering is evil, and that evil is thereby present in the sufferer. But this is evil *undergone*, not evil *intended*; it is *aesthetic* evil, not *moral* evil. To say that God suffers deeply is no basis for saying that God has "antagonistic impulses" unless one has already decided, with E. S. Brightman or Nancy Frankenberry, that God is the only natural locus of creative energy in the universe. Again, Frankenberry's criticism of process theology presupposes that the revision she would propose has already been made.

For a final point in her argument that I have not convincingly portrayed God as perfectly good, Frankenberry quotes the following statement from Robert Neville:

If God's primordial decision regarding values and limitation in general is at root arbitrary, as Whitehead says it is, then it is only coincidence if God is metaphysically good, this being an arbitrary decision God makes in determining the metaphysical principles to which divinity must conform.[22]

Although this statement is used by Frankenberry to buttress her rejection of God's goodness, it is not at all relevant to her critique of *my* position. In a section entitled "The Notion of Metaphysical Principles Beyond Divine Decision," I argued directly against the view that Neville's statement enunciates. I not only presented Hartshorne's argument that the notion of a "primordial decision" is self-contradictory, because the eternal or primordial is necessary and therefore beyond all decision; I also argued that this position was implicit in Whitehead's own thought, so that the revision is not *ad hoc* but makes Whitehead's position more self-consistent.[23] More recently, I have argued that, if one accepts the Whiteheadian view that all direct perception is sympathetic prehension, then the necessary goodness of God follows from God's omniscience.[24] This argument, it should be noted, proceeded from the side of Whitehead that Frankenberry most appreciates, his radical empiricism; it says that all our *direct* perception is sympathetic. God's perception of the world, by analogy, could not be indifferent or antagonistic. That argument is found explicitly in Hartshorne, and *may* be implied in Whitehead's enigmatic statement that God's "necessary goodness expresses the determination of his consequent nature."[25] This statement in any case shows that Whitehead himself, contrary to Neville, did not see his position as implying that God's goodness is at best a contingent truth.

I do not find, in conclusion, that Frankenberry has provided any good reasons to contend that the God of process theism, at least as portrayed in my theodicy, is morally not unambiguously good.[26] That contention would follow only insofar as Frankenberry's proposed collapse of the distinction between God and creativity is read into process theism; it therefore has no relevance to my position, which emphasizes that distinction. But the question of the perfect goodness of the God of process theism, as portrayed in my theodicy, has been raised from a different direction by Peter Hare.

The topic raised in earlier writings by Hare (and Edward Madden) to which I responded most fully was that of God's values. Having omitted harmony of experience from the criteria of beauty or aesthetic value, and having thereby assumed that aesthetic value could be achieved at the expense of moral and physical evil, Hare (and Madden) had declared the God of process theology, being concerned to promote primarily aesthetic value, to be not morally approvable. Hare (and Madden) had also interpreted some of Whitehead's statements about the transmutation of evil into good in God's experience to mean that the reality of genuine evil was ultimately denied.[27] My response on this topic in God, Power, and Evil was graciously called by Hare "an especially impressive achievement."[28] His point is that it takes careful interpretation and judicious emphasis to produce a tenable position out of the writings of Whitehead and Hartshorne, which contain some "seriously misleading things about God's values" that had dismayed and even outraged him. He says: "Griffin's careful account of the divine values of 'intensity' and 'harmony' seems to me such a tenable position."

A critical point, however, lurks behind this praise. Hare continues:

> It needs to be pointed out, however, that other tenable positions are possible even for those who accept a Whiteheadian-Hartshornean metaphysics as sound. Someone could consistently accept such a metaphysics and accept also a being of perfect power who has the values Griffin describes, yet legitimately refuse to worship that being. Such a person could grant that intensity and harmony are real values, but feel, for example, that the relative weight given by this deity to harmony in both the short and the long run is not sufficient to justify his worship. In other words, process theists should recognize that process theism can be legitimately regarded as good metaphysics but bad religion. We should be suspicious of any attempt to show that one and only one system of moral priorities is legitimate. The fact . . . that a being of perfect power happens to have a certain set of moral priorities does not establish those priorities as worthy of worship by everyone. Worshipability is always an open question.[29]

I can agree with all these statements, but only by making some distinctions. I do not know if any real disagreement between us would exist once these distinctions are made.

The fact that "a being of perfect power happens to have a certain set of moral priorities" would not, I agree, make that set of priorities worthy of universal allegiance. No necessary connection exists between "being right" and "having perfect power." This is true at least if by power here we mean outgoing, creative, efficient power, as distinct from receptive power.

If a being, however, had perfect receptive power, meaning the power to feel sympathetically all the experiences of the universe, and this perfect receptive power were understood to be a necessary characteristic of the being, then a necessary connection with being right *would* exist. As pointed out earlier, this position involves the "ideal participant theory" that the very meaning of *right* and *good* is to be understood in terms of what an omniscient participant in the universe who is impartially and perfectly sympathetic to all other participants would prefer in particular situations. Although the basis for this account of the right and the good is present in the description of God as "the universal recipient of the totality of good and evil that is actualized," in contrast to "an impassive spectator deity,"[30] and in the endorsement of Hartshorne's position that the ideal of good belongs to God's necessary essence,[31] I did not develop this account in the book, so Hare cannot be faulted for not seeing it. According to this account, however, which I articulated only several years later,[32] the God of process theism *is* the ideal participant, so that God's values are worthy of universal allegiance, because they constitute the very meaning of *right* and *good*. It is not that God *happens* to have a certain set of valuational priorities, as Hare suggests; rather, because God is *necessarily* impartially and perfectly sympathetic to the entire creation, God's own values are part and parcel of God's eternal and necessary essence. God's preferences coincide with the very essence of goodness not because of coercive omnipotence, or even perfect persuasive power (this is no process version of "might makes right"), but because of God's perfect receptive power.

Even on the basis of this understanding, I would agree with Hare's statement that "worshipability is always an open question," *if* it means that what persons in fact find worthy of worship is a contingent matter. Persons differ in this respect because of cultural, biographical, and temperamental differences. I had pointed out, for example, that many persons, because of cultural conditioning, cannot consider a being without coercive omnipotence worthy of worship.[33] But we can distinguish, as I did in that context, between this psychological question and the normative question of what persons *ought* to find worthy of worship. Likewise, a distinction exists between the values to which persons in fact give allegiance and the values to which they ought to give allegiance. This is Dewey's distinction between the preferred and the preferable. Although many give allegiance to the values of a tribal deity, all persons *ought* to give allegiance to the values that would be preferred by an impartially and perfectly sympathetic, omniscient being, because for such a being no distinction between the preferred and the preferable is meaningful.

All this is compatible, finally, with Hare's statement that process theism in general, and my formulation of it in particular, may be "bad religion"— that is, that persons might rightly refuse to worship the deity as described. It is one thing to state, in a purely formal way, that God's values are worthy of allegiance by definition (assuming that God is characterized by impartially and perfectly sympathetic omniscience). It is something else to state what God's values are, and therefore how, for example, the concerns for harmony and intensity are related. Every attempt to do this is extremely fallible, and should be formulated as a tentative hypothesis. Bias from one's religious up-bringing, one's wider culture, one's race, one's social position, one's sex, one's temperament, and one's age, among other factors, will inevitably color one's attempt, so that no one's estimation of the divine moral priorities will be found universally acceptable. It may be, for example, that the Whiteheadian emphasis on the necessity of novelty for sustained intensity reflects a Western and especially modern bias. Also, I would now speak less of (momentary) "enjoyment" and more of (enduring) "character" in human life. We should therefore, as Hare says, be "suspicious of any attempt to show that one and only one system of moral priorities is legitimate." This is especially true if one is speaking very concretely about particular moral values, but it is even true to an extent with regard to very abstract issues, such as the proper balance between harmony and intensity. We should never confuse the idea that axiological truth *exists* with the idea that *we*, with the help perhaps of our hero (be it St. Thomas or St. Alfred), have discovered and adequately expressed it.

The distinction Hare draws between process metaphysics and the religious vision advocated by process theologians is an important one. Process theology, to be sure, cannot be separated from process metaphysics and still be process theology. But the metaphysical position that is largely shared by Whitehead and Hartshorne does not imply any particular version of process theology; even less does it imply some particular form of religious practice. One who accepts the metaphysical position could be a Catholic, an Eastern Orthodox, an Anglican, a Unitarian, a Quaker, a Pentecostal, a Jew, a Buddhist, a Theosophist, or a devotee of Satya Sai Baba (although there would probably be some tension between process metaphysics and some of the historical doctrinal formulations of most of those movements). Even within the writings of Whitehead and Hartshorne themselves, one can distinguish between the strictly metaphysical vision and the cosmological vision, and between the cosmology and the even more contingent, culturally and biographically influenced, religious sentiments (both men were, for example, sons of Anglican clergymen). If the metaphysics could be consistent with different cosmological speculations, all the more could it be consistent with a wide variety of religious sentiments, emphases, and practices. One could well, then, look at the writings of any process theologian and conclude, "good metaphysics, bad (at least for me) religion."

I agree, therefore, with Hare's formal point, that a form of process theodicy that is superior to mine, either in general or at least for some persons, could be produced.

D. CONCLUSION: LIVING BETWEEN GODS

Thus far I have discussed the relation between theodicy and worship in primarily philosophical terms. The central question, that about divine power, has been about the kind of power we (intellectually) find *worthy of* worship. This becomes the philosophical question of the kind and extent of power that is the greatest conceivable.

But we are not only, or even primarily, intellectual beings; intellectual operations comprise only a fraction of the processes occurring in the human psyche. Emotional feelings and images are more fundamental, and more controlling. A more basic and generally more decisive question than the philosophical one is the psychological question of the kind of power that in fact *evokes* our religious worship. Our religious drive is to be in harmony with that power that we believe—or better, *imagine* and *feel*—to be the supreme power in the universe. If a theodicy solves the problem of evil intellectually, but does so in terms of a conception of divine power that does not fit our feelings and images about what real power is, about the kind of power that is in fact supreme in the nature of things, this theodicy will not fully satisfy. This theodicy, we will feel, will not have really portrayed *God*, the supreme power of the universe. A theodicy may fail psychologically, then, even if we find it impeccable philosophically.

Because we are social beings, psychological questions of this nature are largely sociological questions. The question of what idea or image of God in fact evokes a religious response from us is largely a question of the image or concept of God we have been conditioned by our social upbringing to associate with religious feelings. Because the dominant religion of Western culture has been Christianity, the crucial question for most of those in this culture is what notion of deity has been portrayed by Christianity. For the issue at hand in particular, the crucial question is what notion of divine power has been conveyed.

The central theological tragedy of Christianity is that, having originated with events that radically challenged the prevailing notion of divine power as controlling, unilateral, overwhelming force, it soon returned to and even intensified this notion.

Christianity takes as the supreme incarnation and revelation of God a man who taught love of enemies, forgiveness, and nonretaliation, and who died on a cross as the victim of the powers of this world. Christianity even adopted the cross of Jesus as its chief symbol, thereby suggesting that salvation comes through God's suffering love. The idea that God's agent of deliverance from evil would be one who was the victim, rather than the conqueror, of the coercive powers of this world stood in strong tension with the idea of God as the one whose "mighty hand" controls all earthly forces, including the coercive power of an imperialistic state. There is good reason to believe that many persons in the early centuries of Christianity had their religious sensibilities shaped by this new notion of divine power, so that it, not coercive omnipotence, evoked their religious worship. And this side of Christian teaching and imagery has continued through the centuries to work its influence upon the sensibilities and imaginations of Christians and others within its orbit of influence.

But from the outset this radically different understanding of divine power (which had roots within the Hebrew Bible and analogues in other traditions, such as Platonism) had to contend with tendencies to dilute it, and even to absorb it within the prevailing view of divine omnipotence. Already within the New Testament we see the attempt to say that Jesus' death was the fulfillment of the divine plan, which means that God was in complete control all along. The fact that Jesus did not fit the preconception of a messianic warrior-king was handled by distinguishing between the first and the second comings. As Burton Cooper critically summarizes this rationalization: "in the first coming, Christ comes as the vulnerable one, the one who suffers for us; but in the second coming, Christ will show himself as the monarchial Christ, the one who comes with coercive power."[34] The result of this rationalization is that the revolutionary implication of taking a "suffering servant" as the chief incarnation and revelation of God is muted. In Cooper's words: "In principle, then, the life, death, and resurrection of Christ reshape our understanding of God's redemptive power. But instead, the redemptive action of Christ has been interpreted through the monarchial image of God's controlling unilateral power."[35]

This tendency was reinforced by several theological developments. The Greek idea that God is completely impassible, incapable of suffering, was accepted. The human and divine natures of Jesus were radically distinguished, with only the human nature being allowed to suffer; the divinity of Jesus was associated with his miracles and his resurrection, in which he was said to have demonstrated omnipotent power over the forces of nature. God's omniscience was said to be immutable, which implied that God knew the future down to the last detail, which led easily to the notion that God caused it. This latter notion was, in fact, explicitly proclaimed at least as early as the fifth century by St. Augustine. His doctrine of God's predestinating omnipotence, which exerted a very strong influence on Western Christianity, did not even have room for human cooperation with divine grace, as the Pelagians discovered. Although this Augustinian vision of the all-determining power of God was muted in the Middle Ages, at least verbally (as in Thomas Aquinas), it was reasserted in all its purity in the nominalist-voluntarist movement beginning in the fourteenth century, which was foundational for both the Protestant Reformation and (through thinkers such as Descartes, Pascal, Boyle, and Newton) the movement we call the "rise of modern science."

Although the two ideas of divine power have coexisted side by side, the idea of coercive omnipotence has been dominant. Persons in our culture have thereby been taught, in countless ways, to equate divine power, and therefore real power, with the power to control, the power to coerce, the power to destroy. The dominant image of the end of the world is that of an apocalyptic event of overwhelming violence brought about unilaterally by divine power. It is no aberration, then, that the test site for the atomic bomb would be dubbed "Trinity" and that a nuclear missile would be called "Peacekeeper." Given these images and feelings embedded deep in our psyches, it is very difficult to feel that some other kind of power—in particular, the power of suffering, persuasive love—is real power, divine power, power worthy of worship.

Some philosophers of religion and theologians believe that this psychological problem is not their problem. The problem for philosophy of religion and theology, they believe, is the conceptual problem; the psychological problem is for others—parents, churches, psychotherapists—to handle. But that is, I believe, to take a too narrow, a too professionalized, view of the task of theodicy. As I suggested in chapter 2, the task is to produce a *plausible* account of how God and evil are compatible. And plausibility cannot be limited to philosophical, intellectual plausibility isolated from the deeper currents of the human psyche. The theodicy is not plausible in the deep sense to persons unless they believe that the "God" thus reconciled with evil is really God, really the supreme power of the universe—unless, in other words, they find that this image or concept of God evokes their religious devotion. The psychological-sociological dimension of the problem cannot be ignored.

The essence of this dimension of the problem can be spelled out as follows. On the one hand, the image of God that still evokes widespread religious response in our culture is one that prevents an adequate theodicy and has many other deleterious effects as well. On the other hand, the idea of God suggested by process theism can solve the problem of evil, is intellectually satisfying in many other respects, and would have many beneficial psychological and social effects—in particular, I have suggested (in chapter 8), it would induce a pacific spirituality. And yet it is widely perceived to be religiously inadequate, because it does not portray God as having the kind of power with which religious awe has been associated from childhood on.

To suggest a solution to this problem, with all its dimensions, would require a book in itself. In this conclusion I can suggest only the central idea of a possible solution. We need a generation willing to "live between Gods." By this I mean that persons would give up the idea of God that has hitherto evoked religious devotion, while committing themselves to a new idea of God that does not yet evoke this response, and perhaps never will, at least not as powerfully as did the old idea. This is likely because which idea of God evokes religious worship in us is heavily determined by early childhood influences. But it is just this fact that requires the willingness to live between

Gods. We need a generation—a generation of religious leaders, artists, and parents—who will work in terms of an idea of God that they themselves do not fully, except intellectually, feel to be *God*. They would teach this image—through symbols, stories, doctrines, and example—to the young people under their influence, with the goal that they, in adulthood, would have an understanding of God that is not only intellectually satisfying but religiously satisfying in the deepest sense of the word.

This program calls for tremendous psychic discipline. While recognizing that human feelings, images, and attitudes ingrained from childhood, and constantly reinforced by culture, are more powerful than recently acquired intellectual convictions, it nevertheless calls on persons to try to live, feel, think, teach, and worship in terms of a recently acquired idea of God that is found to be philosophically and theologically superior to the older idea, even though the new idea does not yet naturally evoke strong religious feelings.

The goal is to bring about a transformation such that the idea of God that intellectually seems *worthy* of worship will actually *evoke* worship. To some extent, this goal can be realized within the lifetime of a single person, and thus of a single generation. By a deliberate plan of reading, thinking, meditating, praying, teaching, sermonizing, worshipping, and acting, we can transform our sensibilities so that that which at first seemed intellectually correct, but only that, can come also to carry emotional clout. But to some extent such a generation will always remain between Gods. It will have lost the old God, and the new God will not be fully born. The full transformation can probably occur only in the next generation. We can portray the new image of God to our young in such a way that it will evoke stronger religious feelings in them than it ever will in us. At this time, our discipline, our sacrifice, will reap its reward. In this new generation, the gap between theodicy and worship, between intellect and emotion, which makes a fully satisfactory solution virtually impossible in our time, will be overcome.

Some may believe these psychological, even religious, reflections to be out of place in an academic book published by a university press. But the dualisms implicit in such a belief between the academy and life, between intellect and emotion, between theory and practice, and between reason and religion are some of the central dualisms of modernity that need to be overcome. The university will begin to realize its full potential for overcoming the existential, social, and global crises of our times when it overcomes these dualisms.

In any case, I have argued that process theism can provide us with a satisfactory solution to the problem of evil. I have suggested that the gap between such a solution and the position I presented in *God, Power, and Evil* can be bridged by reformulating some of the ideas more carefully, by filling in some omitted presuppositions, and by making some revisions, especially with regard to ultimate meaning and hope. In saying that such a solution can be satisfactory, I mean philosophically and theologically satisfactory: it can be seen to be self-consistent, adequate to and even illuminating of the facts of experience, adequate to the generic idea of God in our tradition, and expressive of the distinctively Christian suggestions about divine power in particular. Whether this theodicy is found to be *fully* satisfactory, in terms of other dimensions of the psyche, is, I have suggested in conclusion, finally dependent upon us—upon the kind of power we find divine, and therefore upon the kind of persons we are, or become. If we do find this idea of God theologically satisfactory, it is up to us to (help God) bring about the kind of persons who will find it religiously satisfying.

Appendix

EVIL AND THE TWO TYPES OF EFFICIENT CAUSATION: A RESPONSE TO MADDEN AND HARE

[Foreword: An explanation for including this response, which was written in 1973, is found at the end of the Introduction.]

In "Evil and Persuasive Power,"[1] Edward Madden and Peter Hare examine the role played by the idea of divine persuasive power in process theism's treatment of the problem of evil. They raise five questions, which will be discussed here in order. I will then make a few comments about their earlier criticisms of process theism expressed in *Evil and the Concept of God*.[2]

A. CAN DIVINE POWER BE A MIXTURE OF COERCION AND PERSUASION?

Madden and Hare are willing to grant the moral repugnance and conceptual incoherence of the idea of God's power as totally coercive. But they ask why coerciveness and persuasiveness need be mutually exclusive. Why should God's power not be an "appropriate mixture of coercion and persuasion"? Their question reflects a misunderstanding of the notion of persuasive power in process thought. For example, they say that "process theists excuse God of evil of saying that he quite properly respects the freedom of his creatures."[3] But this statement falsely implies that God's use of persuasion rather than coercion is thought to be a self-imposed restraint, so that God

could occasionally fail to "respect" our freedom if this was necessary to produce a compensating good. It is probably due to this misunderstanding that
these authors could elsewhere imply that their rebuttals to the "free-will defense" were applicable to process theism's theodicy.[4] I would agree, for example, that if God could have stopped Hitler, some earthquakes, and the
internal combustion engine, God probably should have done so.

That Madden and Hare only partially understand the process position
is revealed by the following comment: "We recognize that in a metaphysics
of social process 'coercive power' is considered a self-contradictory term and
existence of any kind, sentient or non-sentient, entails freedom"; but because
degrees of freedom are admitted, "something equivalent to degrees of coercion are recognized."[5] Three misunderstandings are revealed in these statements. For process thinkers, (1) the idea of coercive power is not considered
self-contradictory, (2) insentient existents do not have freedom, and (3) recognizing degrees of freedom in sentient beings does not imply recognizing
degrees of coercion (in the strict or metaphysical sense, which is at issue).[6]
These misunderstandings represent, in part, careless study. But they are surely
also in part due to the failure of process thinkers to explain clearly the difference in principle between persuasive and coercive power, and the metaphysical (not simply moral) reasons for assigning only the former to God.

In Whiteheadian-Hartshornean cosmology, there is no *ontological dualism*
between sentient (prehending) and insentient individuals. Every genuine individual prehends other actualities and decides how to appropriate data from
them into its own experience. But there *is* an *organizational duality* between
genuine individuals and mere aggregates. The criterion of genuine individuality is unity of experience. Actual occasions (occasions of experience) and
serially ordered societies (in which only one actual occasion is present at a
time) are genuine individuals. Electrons, atoms, molecules, cells, animal psyches, and God can be conceived as true individuals. A mere aggregate may
be a quite cohesive society, but it has no unity of experience and is therefore
not a genuine individual.

This organizational duality is correlated with a causal duality. The efficient causation between genuine individuals is necessarily persuasive,
whereas that between aggregates is coercive. In persuasive efficient causation,
the antecedent cause(s) can never completely determine the effect. This type
of causal relation necessarily obtains when the *effect* is a genuine individual,
because such an individual is defined as a partially self-determining effect.[7]
But persuasive efficient causation is also necessarily involved when the *cause* is
a genuine individual. The reason for this can be made clear only after discussing coercion.

An aggregate such as a billiard ball is simply the sum product of the
activities, including the causal relations, of its individual entities. It is comprised of molecules, each of which is a true individual; each molecular occa-

sion is sentient, and makes a decision as to how to respond to its environment. But the billiard ball *as such* is not sentient, and makes no decisions, because there is no one individual in the ball that exercises a more or less controlling influence over the rest to enable the ball to react to its environment in a more or less unified way. The ball's individual molecules are instead all equal with regard to the power they influence on the ball as a whole. In Whitehead's terms, the ball is a "corpuscular" society with no "regnant" or "dominant" member. In such a society, the spontaneous movements of the individual members, not being coordinated by a "monarch," are chaotic and cancel each other out. The aggregate as such is thus largely what it appears to be—a mere object, with no sentience or experience, no purpose, and no self-movement. It waits upon some external force for movement. It is inert, and accordingly obeys the law of inertia.

It is important to stress that this type of aggregate does form a "society." That is, it is not simply a group of individuals, in which case all transactions would have to be carried out with the individual members. Rather, more or less strong bonds of cohesion exist among the individual members, such that they can be acted upon as a group, as one object. Such an object can be coerced. The billiard ball, when struck at the correct angle with sufficient force, will go into the pocket every time (presupposing no tilt or grooves to coerce the ball out of a straight path, or any other unusual external forces). There is no decision involved on the part of the ball that could render the law merely statistical. If all the relevant antecedent conditions are calculated correctly, the ball's behavior can be predicted almost exactly (the qualifier "almost" is added to allow for slight deviations due to quantum indeterminacies). The cause in a coercive relation must be another aggregative society. A genuine individual exerts efficient causation merely be constituting itself (exercising final causation or self-determination) in a particular way, thus providing efficient data that succeeding individuals must prehend. But aggregates do not prehend, and therefore they as such cannot be affected by individuals. An aggregate as such can be moved only by another aggregate, which can exert coercive influence due to the bonds of cohesion among *its* individual members. The mass average effect of one aggregate meets the mass average effect of the other, and the result is almost totally predictable, at least in principle (again assuming no other extraordinary influences, such as magnetism). The classical, deterministic laws of mechanics apply.

Madden and Hare are therefore mistaken in thinking that process thinkers attribute freedom even to insentient existents, so that the idea of coercive power would be self-contradictory. Where both terms of the causal relation are aggregates, the efficient causation is necessarily coercive.

The causal relation is *not* coercive where at least one of the terms is a true individual, meaning an occasion of experience or a serially ordered society of occasions. Here are four examples. (1) One moment of my experience cannot coerce another; it can only hope that its aim for that later occasion will prove sufficiently attractive to be freely actualized when the time comes. For example, I can begin a program of abstinence as a New Year's resolution, but I cannot thereby guarantee that I will still be abstaining three months later. (2) One psyche cannot coerce another. I cannot force Peter Hare to accept Whitehead's metaphysics—even for his own good! (3) My body cannot coerce my psyche. The influences coming from my empty stomach can be very persuasive; but I can refuse to obey their promptings to eat, even to the point of voluntarily starving to death. (4) Nor can my psyche coerce my body; otherwise I would not miss so many shots in pocket billiards.

The second, third, and fourth of these types of relationships require discussion of "monarchical societies," to which category human beings belong. In such a society, the psyche (a serially ordered society) is the monarch, insofar as it synthesizes the various experiences of the cells into a unity of experience. The monarchical society as a whole—that is, the human being as psychophysical organism—is to be regarded as a genuine individual, *insofar* as in each moment a single actual occasion unifies the experiences of all the members into a single experience and then exercises dominating control over the members in the next moment, so that the society makes a unified response to its environment.

However, the control exercised by these dominant occasions is not complete. Their power over the rest of the society is persuasive, not coercive. The control in normal circumstances is so great that one might suppose it to be complete, and thereby to be an example of coercion. But we testify to the awareness that it is only a matter of degree (that is, less than 100 percent) by saying that some persons are more "coordinated" than others. Also, when the body is tired, drugged, or otherwise impaired, the psyche's degree of control is generally lessened.

The monarchical society combines features of both aggregates and genuine individuals. Whether or not a monarchical society can be coerced depends upon how it is being regarded. Consider the relations between two persons. Regarded as two aggregates of cells, the causation of the one on the other is purely coercive. In an arm-wrestling match between two men, the stronger one does not have to wait upon the consent of the weaker one's arm; he simply forces it to the mat. But where one is trying to elicit an effect in the other person's psyche, coercion is not possible. If you are stronger than I, you can force me out of the room. But you cannot force me to *walk* out of the room; you can only try to persuade me. This persuasion may involve the *threat* of coercion; for example, you may say that if I do not leave voluntarily, you will force me out. But this threat is itself an example of persuasion, not coercion. If I walk out, it is because I choose to do so.

Nor can one coerce another person's psyche even by actually inflicting pain on this person's body. The inflicted pain usually results in the body's exerting very powerful causal influence on the subject's psyche, but the body can never, in the strict sense, coerce the psyche. Prisoners of war are not, strictly speaking, coerced into giving information or signing confessions. They choose to act in these ways, rather than to suffer any more pain. This is not to say that they should be condemned—the persuasion exerted on the mind by means of coercion on the body can be *very* persuasive; it is only to point out that true individuals cannot be coerced in the strict, absolute sense of the term being employed here. That the influence is not coercive is evidenced by the widely varying reactions among prisoners to similar physical tortures.

When one says that the White House "twisted several arms" in the senate to get some crucial votes, one does not thereby mean to absolve the senators in question from responsibility. In literal arm-twisting, you may persuade me to say "uncle" by making it more attractive than the alternative. In metaphorical arm-twisting, the president may promise a senator support in a coming election, or promise not to reveal some past indiscretions. The president thereby may make the prospect of voting against conscience seem less unattractive to the senator than the probable consequences of opposing the president's bill. In real or metaphorical arm-twisting, the victim still makes a free decision, even though the decision is between unattractive alternatives.

The correlation between aggregates and coercion, on the one hand, and true individuals and persuasion, on the other, can be illustrated by a shot in billiards: the eight ball is coerced by the cue ball, which is coerced by the cue stick, which is coerced by the hand. But the hand was persuaded by the mind. Even if the player knows well enough what the cue stick must do if the shot is to be made, the shot may therefore still be missed. The correlation is also illustrated by the damsel's cry in a Gothic novel: "You might take my body, but you will never possess my soul."

To summarize the major points and implications of the above analysis: (1) Efficient causation between two aggregates is coercive. (2) Where at least one of the terms is a genuine individual, the efficient causation must be persuasive. (3) The two types of efficient causation are different in kind, because persuasion involves at least some iota of self-determination on the part of the effect, while coercion involves none at all. (4) Recognizing degrees of freedom therefore does not involve recognizing degrees of coercion: coercion totally excludes freedom, so that "degrees of coercion" is self-contradictory.[8]

In a Whiteheadian system, God is not to be conceived as an exception to the general metaphysical principles. Because God is an individual, divine causation on the world can never be coercive. This is true whether it be God's causation on actual occasions or on aggregates that is at issue, for an individual cannot act directly on an aggregate as such, but only upon its individual members. Each worldly occasion must respond to all the other efficient causes on it besides God, and must decide how to synthesize all these influences into a new experience. The divine causation on each individual cannot be coercive, because God is one efficient cause among many (although there are senses of this phrase that would not apply), and because the worldly individual has the power (final causation or self-determination) to decide how to respond to the innumerable influences upon it.

The idea that the power of God is persuasive, not coercive, is therefore not an *ad hoc* idea; nor is it based upon some supposed self-restraint on God's part. It is an implication of the metaphysical position as a whole. It is also not a demeaning idea, because God is thereby said to have the kind of power exhibited by true individuals. *And this kind of efficient power is primary*, whereas coercive power is derivative. To revert to the example from billiards: the movements of the eight ball, the cue ball, and the cue stick must all be traced back to the persuasive power of the psyche on its hand (*via* the central nervous system). In other words, while it is true that genuine individuals only have persuasive power and therefore cannot guarantee anything, it is equally true that all change is finally rooted in this persuasive power, for only genuine individuals initiate activity.[9]

One can reply, of course, that *we* are true individuals, and yet have coercive power. This is true in a sense: insofar as the psyche is successful in persuading its body to do its wishes, it can work through the body to coerce aggregates in the outer world. The psyche can, by means of its intimate relationship to its body, exert coercion indirectly. But in this indirect sense, God also can exert coercive power. Most process theists follow Hartshorne in conceiving the God-world relation by analogy with the psyche-body relation. Reality as a whole is a monarchy. Just as a human psyche cannot coerce its body, the all-persuasive soul cannot coerce its world. But the psyche can persuade one part of its body to act coercively on another part—for example, to cut off an infected finger. Likewise, insofar as the divine soul can persuade us to do its will, it could work through one part of its "body" to coerce another part. It would be metaphysically allowed, for example, to believe that the attempt to assassinate Hitler was carried out partly in response to divine persuasion. (Whether process theists would actually believe this would depend on a number of other judgments—theological, ethical, historical, political, pragmatic.)

This indirect sense in which some cases of coercion might be regarded as divine activity does not imply, however, the kind of "mixture of coercion and persuasion" that Madden and Hare seem to think the process theist should consider intelligible. The coercive causation can never flow directly from God's decision, but must depend upon intervening persuasive relations.

The poetic statement "God has no hands but our hands" is true in a quite literal sense, taking "hands" to stand for all coercive instrumentalities. The indirect sense in which God can exert coercion is therefore *not* a sense that would warrant an indictment of God for not preventing gratuitous evil, such as Hitler's atrocities.

B. IS THE WORLD'S EVIL COMPATIBLE WITH GREAT PERSUASIVE POWER?

Madden and Hare believe that the extent and distribution of evil in the world are not compatible with the exercise of great persuasive power for good. More specifically, although process theists can readily show how the existence of *some* who are unpersuaded is compatible with great persuasive power on the part of God, they are said not to have shown the compatibility of "the very high proportion remaining unpersuaded."[10]

The controversy here may hinge partly on differing evaluations of the world's possible consistency with an overarching purpose. When I reflect on the Whiteheadian sketch of the evolutionary process, in which serially ordered societies are evoked out of random occasions, compound individuals out of simple ones, life out of nonlife, centered life out of noncentered life, consciousness out of mere awareness, and symbolizing self-consciousness out of mere consciousness, I am quite impressed. Each of these steps represents a jump in complexity that made possible an increase in the intrinsic value of the creatures, which is (by hypothesis) God's chief purpose. The difference in evaluation may be due to the tendency of Madden and Hare to focus primarily on *human* life, and to assume that a worshipful being's purpose must be to produce *morally* good beings, rather than seeing with Whitehead the production of moral goodness as a derivative aspect of the production of intrinsically valuable beings, with the aesthetic criteria of harmony and richness providing the measure of intrinsic value.[11] But even if the focus is on moral goodness alone, I am quite impressed with the extent to which the natural egoism and tribalism (which is largely a collective form of egoism) of individuals have been increasingly challenged in the past 3,000 years by the ideals of objective truth and universal justice and love.

More importantly, if the existence of *some* unpersuaded creatures is compatible with great persuasive power, then so is the existence of *many*. To hold otherwise is not to understand the logic of persuasion. In persuasive relations, the effect is a partially self-determining effect of many persuasive causes, and as such *it* decides how the persuasive influences will be appropriated. The result can therefore never be the basis for determining precisely how "powerful" a given persuasive agent was. For example, say that two prisoners, Smith and Jones, are to be tortured in the same way by the same guard. Smith breaks in a few minutes, while Jones refuses to talk even after several months of torture. Was the guard more persuasive in relation to Smith? If one replies in the affirmative, then one must also admit that the persuasiveness was partly a function of the prisoner's predisposition. If a negative answer is given, then a distinction is being made between persuasive power and success, and the latter is not being regarded as an adequate indicator of the former.

The critic might reply that the persuasive power of an agent could be determined by success where large numbers of effects are involved. But even this is problematic. Guard A may simply happen to get prisoners who are easily persuaded to agree to demands, whereas guard B happens to receive ones who are very resistant to persuasion through torture. Guard B may be promoted, whereas guard A, had he received other prisoners, might have had even a higher percentage of converts.

Consider a more positive analogy. Peabody serves as the chairman of the board of directors for two firms. In firm X he has always been very effective in persuading the majority of the board to accept his proposals. But in firm Y he is not nearly as effective, even though he is equally informed, personable, hardworking, and cogent in his arguments. An observer of Peabody's dealing with firm X would probably conclude that he was very persuasive, whereas an observer of his dealings with firm Y would probably deem him ineffectual. The most persuasive chairman in the world cannot guarantee any particular percentage of success, for he cannot persuade those who, for one reason or another, refuse to be persuaded by him.

God has perhaps been more successful on other planets, and perhaps less successful on others, even with regard to producing rational creatures that are morally good. Also, the present world (in Whitehead's view) represents one of many cosmic epochs. God has possibly been more successful in some of these, and less successful in others. Once the logic of creation through persuasion has been grasped, a very great range between the ideal limits of the best and the worst of possible created worlds can be recognized, while still maintaining the perfect power of the universal creator, where "perfect power" means "the most power that one individual could possibly have."

Finally, we must remember that the story of the response of the human species to the divine persuasion is not yet completed. We should not judge the effectiveness of parents by the antics of their pubescent children. It would have been misleading if a visitor from another galaxy had judged the creator's persuasive power in relation to life on our planet by the results a billion years ago, when several billion years of evolution had produced nothing more remarkable than mats of blue-green algae. In the same way, it may be terribly premature to assess the creator's persuasive power in relation to human beings.

C. ARE THE LIMITATIONS ON FREEDOM COMPATIBLE
WITH GREAT PERSUASIVE POWER?

Madden and Hare next provide a countermove to process theists who might answer the previous question by claiming that God is interested in maximizing only the intrinsic values of freedom and creativity, not good acts and experiences. For their rebuttal, Madden and Hare say that process theists have not shown the limitations on freedom and creativity in this world to be compatible with great persuasive power.

Process theists should not, however, give that rebutted answer. Increased freedom is good, in general, but not in abstraction from experiences that are qualified by beauty (harmony and intensity) and/or that contribute beauty to other experiences. We would never say that God promotes freedom and creativity *instead of* good acts and experiences. The promotion of freedom in its various forms is part and parcel of the promotion of beauty, or richness of experience.

On the basis of this response, which indicates that increased freedom is generally correlated with increased capacity for beautiful and beautifying experiences, the critic could still ask whether perfect persuasive power could not have inspired more of it. Madden and Hare presuppose that an adequate theodicy would have to show that it could not have inspired more. But this is again to misunderstand the logic of persuasion. Surely more creative freedom could have been inspired on this earth—*if* the partially free creatures had responded to the Universal Inspirer in such a way as to become more free or to provide the necessary conditions for greater creative freedom in the future. And, again, perhaps this has been the case on other planets, or in other cosmic epochs; but if so, this difference is rooted in differences in the partially self-creating creatures' responses to God's lures, not in a difference in the power of God in relation to the various contexts.

D. IS A GREAT EVIL PERSUASIVE POWER EQUALLY PLAUSIBLE?

Madden and Hare's fourth point is that, if the above questions are not answered, one could equally well believe that a great evil persuasive power exists, and that good acts are acts of resistance to it. Insofar as the previous questions have been answered, this one could be passed over. However, one point might be worth making. Madden and Hare would presumably agree that morally evil acts are ones in which selfishness or egoism prevails over unselfishness in agents who have the capacity for acting unselfishly. Now it is a widespread observation that almost complete egoism is "natural," in the sense that it is exemplified by animals and human babies. Belief in a devil is therefore superfluous, because self-centeredness does not need explanation but is given with sentience. What does require explanation is the development of a neglible concern for other beings into a significant degree of altruism. Whitehead accordingly speaks of God as "that element in virtue of which our purposes extend beyond values for ourselves to values for others."[12]

One *could*, of course, maintain that human beings are born with the tendency to develop into perfectly altruistic beings, who would always act in accordance with an impartial evaluation of the interests of all humanity, or even all life, and that it is a devil that inspires them to act as if their own exclusive desires were more important than those of others. But this would either require making human beings completely the reverse of all other sentient beings with regard to natural tendencies, or else require positing a satanically thwarted innate morality in *all* sentient beings. But I suspect that Madden and Hare would withdraw their suggestion before reaching this stage of trying to make it consistent with some possible world.

E. Is Persuasive Power a Coherent Concept?

Finally, noting the importance that conceptual coherence has among process theists, our critics ask whether persuasive power is itself a coherent concept, given the fact that it is "a sort of power whose nature and extent is in principle impossible to estimate experientially." Insofar as their question is whether the *nature* of persuasive power is experientially rooted, it reflects their failure to see that, for process thinkers, persuasive causation is the primary form of efficient causation that is experienced.[13] (For example, they have suggested that God's giving of initial aims involves affecting the world only indirectly,[14] as if there were some more direct type of efficient causation than persuasion.) I experience the persuasive power of my past decisions on my present experience; the same for the persuasive power of my bodily parts and the entreaties of another person. In each of these cases, I experience an urge to actualize a certain possibility—to conform to a past resolution, to satisfy bodily appetites, to avoid bodily pain, or to help a person in need. In Whiteheadian language, what is derived from the other actualities are certain possibilities with the subjective form of appetition that they be realized.

Our experience of God is similar in kind. We are confronted with certain ideals relevant to our situation with an urge toward their realization. The explanation here is that, if these ideals are derived from God, what we prehend is God as envisaging certain possibilities with the subjective form of appetition that they be actualized. In the initial or conformal phase of our experience, we share that subjective form with regard to the felt ideal. But in the succeeding phases of concrescence, the "initial aim" is transformed into the occasion's "subjective aim," during which the possibility serving as the occasion's final cause may or may not be modified. This possibility of modifying what is received efficiently from God means the divine causation is persuasive rather than coercive, and that it is similar in nature to all the other types of efficient causation on our experience.[15]

The other half of this fifth question concerns the *measurability* of persuasive power. Madden and Hare are not positivistically requiring a laboratory experiment, complete with pointer readings. They only say that "in ordinary contexts power is always something that can be, at least indirectly and roughly, measured experientially."[16] Their query here again seems to be based on misunderstanding. The fact that they could ask whether the *nature* of persuasive power is rooted in experience, and that they contrast it with power in "ordinary contexts," suggests that they think "persuasive power" is an *ad hoc* notion applied only to deity to solve the problem of evil. If persuasive power is the primary type of efficient power that is experienced, however, it is the primary form of power experienced in "ordinary contexts"—the power of bodily appetites and pains, the power of social custom and prejudice, the power of ideals, including the ideal of achieving truth. It is these forms of power, which *can* be, "at least indirectly and roughly, measured experientially," that are forms of persuasive power. In saying that God's power is persuasive, therefore, process theists are only attributing to God the primary type of efficient causality that is immediately experienced, and the only type that is attributed to genuine individuals.

F. EARLIER CRITICISMS

The article discussed above represents the second criticism of process theism by Madden and Hare. Their first criticism contained several misunderstandings and distortions, as well as a few criticisms valid against Whitehead's formulations.[17] That article evoked replies from Charles Hartshorne[18] and Lewis Ford,[19] in which most of the major errors were pointed out, as well as the fact that the valid points scored against Whitehead's formulations do not undermine the essential position.[20] Regrettably, in the revised version of the article printed in their book, the corrections derivable from Ford's essay are incorporated only minimally,[21] and those from Hartshorne's response (which gives a more point-by-point rebuttal) not at all. While the criticisms and clarifications made by Ford and Hartshorne need not be repeated, a few points remain that do require comment.

The basic thesis of their book is that "neither theism nor quasi-theism [under which they classify process theism] is able both to make sense of the facts of evil and to have an acceptable concept of God."[22] While they agree that process theism can make sense of evil, they claim that it does so by means of an unacceptable concept of God—a God not worthy of worship.[23] The "worst deficiencies of all" in Whitehead's position are said to be in his ideas of the nature of evil and value.[24] I will only note in passing Madden and Hare's transformation of Whitehead's statement that perpetual perishing is the "ultimate evil" into the assertion that loss of immediacy is the "only genuine evil," their interpretation of "all order is aesthetic order" as "what appears as gratuitous evil is really just the makings of aesthetic value in the Consequent Nature," and their suggestion that Whitehead's theory of value can be boiled down to the idea that "good is the preservation of immediacy."[25] Whitehead is difficult to understand, but surely not that difficult.

More potentially serious is their charge that Whitehead's God is "not all good as a theistic God should be," because this God is concerned only for aesthetic value.[26] There are two problems with their charge. First, in the passage they quote,[27] Whitehead does not say that God is interested only in aesthetic value to the exclusion of moral value, but only that moral order is an aspect of aesthetic order. Second, for the criteria of aesthetic value they refer only to "massiveness" and "intensity" of experience, omitting "harmony" (a lack of which is involved in all pain), and then proceed to demolish their straw man by pointing out that "surely many earthquakes, for example, could be eliminated without a sacrifice of aesthetic value."[28] Their self-induced outrage continues: "Certainly a God who is willing to pay any amount in moral and physical evil to gain aesthetic value is unlovable."[29] The false antitheses in this statement were probably allowed by their omission of harmony from the criteria of aesthetic harmony. The same omission is probably behind their self-contradictory statement that Whitehead's God "sacrifices human feelings to aesthetic ends."[30]

Some of the criticism, however, is evidently not based on misunderstanding, but on a different evaluation of good and evil in the world, as suggested earlier. For example, they criticize Whitehead's God for being either unable or unwilling to "jam the mechanism of creation" and thereby to "call the whole thing off."[31] To indict the Whiteheadian God for not having done this presupposes that it would be preferable if this world did not exist. Their assumption that Whitehead would reply that "something is better than nothing" is not quite accurate, because Whitehead believed that *some* finite realm exists necessarily (Hartshorne even more explicitly affirms this). But one could well raise the related question as to whether God should have urged the world on to its present level of complexity and freedom, which provides simultaneously the necessary conditions for both tremendous evil and tremendous good. Were the potential positive values sufficient to justify the risks? And have the actual positive values been such as to compensate for the actual evils? On these questions, good and honest persons can differ. At one place, Madden and Hare imply that "even if there is more good than evil in the world," God should not have chosen to create a world if God could not prevent the occurrence of gratuitous evil.[32] This is a possible, if difficult, position to hold. It may be that the debate finally hinges upon this type of value judgment, so that the remainder of the criticisms, and my response to them, are finally irrelevant.

It may also be, however, that their concepts and attitudes have been shaped primarily by their battles against traditional theism, and that they carry these concepts and attitudes over into discussions in which they are not appropriate. Specifically, their key concept, "gratuitous evil," refers to all the evil that is not logically necessary for the production of compensating goods. This notion of gratuitous evil was worked out in discussions of traditional theism, and is pertinent in such discussions, because the slightest amount of gratuitous evil in this sense would be inconsistent with a God who is perfectly good and wise, and coercively omnipotent. But in the context of process theism, the notion of "gratuity," to perform a similar function, would have to be redefined. It can no longer have any bite if it refers simply to actual evils that could not be reasonably supposed to contribute to a total greater good. It would have to refer to general cosmological *conditions* that (1) allow for the *possibility* of certain types of evil and (2) are not simultaneously necessary for the possibility of certain types of compensating goods.[33] In this sense of the term, the process theists can deny the existence of gratuitous evil.

Likewise, Madden and Hare's discussion of all theistic theodicies is tinged with a sense of outrage (as is most discussion of traditional theodicies by nontraditional theists, such as myself). But in the context of their own naturalistic position, presumably, reflections on the evils of the world do not produce the same kind of outrage. In that context, no one is suggesting the (outrageous) position that all these evils were caused or allowed by some cosmic being in view of a "compensating" good. And in that naturalistic context, many of the evils of the world, the so-called natural or nonmoral evils, are not intended by anyone—they just happen. In that context, one still wishes to prevent as much evil as possible, and this is very important, because the outcome of the struggle between good and evil is not guaranteed by anyone. But there is also an acceptance of evil as part of the givenness of things. On this issue, the position of the process theist is closer to that of the ethical naturalist than to that of the traditional theist. To transfer the sense of outrage that is appropriate when directed toward traditional theism to process theism is therefore a case of unjust guilt by association.

[Afterword: The book and the article by Madden and Hare to which this essay responded were published in 1968 and 1972, respectively. As they pointed out in their article,[34] their book was exceptional among books of the time in giving serious attention to the unique theodicy made possible by process theism. No philosophical or theological position can either demonstrate its strengths or correct its weaknesses apart from serious criticism from persons with other points of view. Any inadequacies in their critiques of process theodicy (which are, in any case, the type to be expected in the earlier stages of a discussion) are far outweighed by their contribution to breaking the conspiracy of silence. As the remainder of this book demonstrates, process theodicy is now being widely and seriously discussed. Madden and Hare are to be commended for their role in getting this discussion started. Their critiques were, in fact, an important stimulus for my own book, *God, Power, and Evil*. I hereby thank Edward Madden and Peter Hare for that stimulus.]

NOTES

INTRODUCTION

1. David Ray Griffin, *God, Power, and Evil: A Process Theodicy* (Philadelphia: Westminster Press, 1976; Lanham, Md.: University Press of America, 1990). This book will be cited in the notes hereafter as GPE. (The University Press of America edition has a new preface but otherwise the same pagination.)

2. Whereas the present book deals only with responses from within academic circles, the general public has also been exposed much more extensively than in previous decades to the type of approach taken to the problem of evil by process theology. The chief source of exposure at this level has been Rabbi Harold Kushner's book *When Bad Things Happen to Good People* (New York: Summit Press, 1981), which was one of the publishing phenomena of the decade, selling over three million copies and being translated into ten languages. Although Kushner had not intended the book as an example of process theology, it did (for the most part) give the same type of answer: God does not cause and cannot (unilaterally) prevent tragedies (although in the final chapter Kushner does suggest, somewhat inconsistently with the remainder of the book, the voluntary divine self-limitation spoken of by traditional free-will theists). On the basis of Kushner's book, plus the volume edited by Stephen T. Davis, *Encountering Evil: Live Options in Theodicy*, which also appeared in 1981 and in which John Cobb and I were included, John Dart, a religion writer for the *Los Angeles Times*, wrote a front-page story (October 19, 1982) with the provocative heading: "Process Theology; God's Power over Evil Questioned," complete with a photograph of Cobb and me. The story did provoke: the entire section for letters the following Saturday was give over to responses, followed by the remark: "The Times received 99 additional letters on this subject." Cobb and I wrote a lengthy response, which was followed by still more letters. Seeing the intense interest evoked by this issue, CBS television prepared a special segment on process theology and the problem of evil, in which Rabbi Kushner and I were featured (although Kushner had not previously considered himself a process theologian). It was aired on the *CBS Evening News with Dan Rather* on January 4, 1983.

3. John Hick, *Evil and the God of Love* (New York: Harper & Row, 1966), 36.

4. John Hick, *Philosophy of Religion*, 3rd ed. (Englewood Cliffs, N.J.: Prentice-Hall, 1983), 41.

5. Some other treatments of process theodicy have also appeared. Barry L. Whitney's *Evil and the Process God* (New York: Edwin Mellen, 1985) is an excellent and exhaustive study of Charles Hartshorne's theodicy. (Hartshorne himself has provided a semi-popular treatment of the problem of evil, alongside other topics, in *Omnipotence and Other Theological Mistakes* [Albany: State University of New York Press, 1984].) Also, Whitney, who is fast becoming the world's authority on the problem of evil, has a chapter entitled "Process Theodicy" in his *What Are They Saying about God and Evil?* (New York/Mahwah: Paulist Press, 1989). Marjorie Hewitt Suchocki's *The End of Evil: Process Eschatology in Historical Context* (Albany: State University of New York Press, 1988) deals, as the title indicates, with the overcoming of evil. She believes, as I now do, that being "the overcomer of evil" belongs to the very meaning of "God," and that the standard Whiteheadian doctrine of objective immortality is not sufficient. But her own approach, built around the idea of the subjective immortality of each occasion of experience, is quite different from mine. (My review of her book and her response are in *Process Studies* 18/1 [Spring 1989]). Burton Z. Cooper's *Why, God?* (Atlanta: John Knox, 1988), which is written for the church and is biblically well grounded, is to my knowledge the best book of its kind on the problem of evil yet to appear.

6. Critiques of my theodicy by Stephen T. Davis, John Hick, John Roth, and Frederick Sontag, and my responses to them as well as my critiques of their positions, are contained in *Encountering Evil: Live Options in Theodicy*, ed. Stephen T. Davis (Atlanta: John Knox, 1981). My exchange with Davis is continued in *Concepts of the Ultimate*, ed. Linda J. Tessier (London: Macmillan, 1989). Because those interchanges are readily available, I have not repeated the points unique to them in the present book. There have been, of course, numerous other criticisms of process theology in general that, if valid, would bear upon the question of the cogency of process theodicy. But to keep this book within reasonable limits without arbitrary decisions of what to include, I have limited my responses to substantial critiques of *God, Power, and Evil*.

7. Because in the present book I affirm belief in life after death, it may seem as if I have departed from the position of Charles Hartshorne, to whom the book is dedicated, on one of his essential points. This is true only in part. It is true that Hartshorne does not believe in life after death, in the sense of our continuing subjective experiencing, and he often writes as if this idea were philosophically and theologically objectionable. For example, in *Omnipotence and Other Theological Mistakes*, he lists as one of the "mistakes" the affirmation of "Immortality as a Career after Death," according to which "we survive death in some form" (4). But in private conversation and correspondence, as well as in more careful formulations, he makes clear that all that he means to rule out philosophically and theologically is the idea that we would continue "forever" (ibid., 35), and that idea is not implied by my position. I do affirm a "career after death," but not "(subjective) immortality."

8. See my *God and Religion in the Postmodern World* (Albany: State University of New York Press, 1989); *Varieties of Postmodern Theology* (Albany: State University

of New York Press, 1989), co-authored with William A. Beardslee and Joe Holland; *Primordial Truth and Postmodern Theology* (Albany: State University of New York Press, 1990), co-authored with Huston Smith; and my introduction to *Archetypal Process: Self and Divine in Whitehead, Jung and Hillman* (Evanston: Northwestern University Press, 1989).

9. The argument that everyone believes in genuine evil as defined here is often misunderstood. For example, Stephen Davis cites the definition in GPE 22 ("anything, all things considered, without which the universe would have been better. Put otherwise, some event is genuinely evil if its occurrence prevents the occurrence of some other event which would have made the world better, all things considered") and also several passages in which I indicate that the existence of evil in this sense cannot be plausibly denied (GPE 71, 222, 230, 250, 254, 256). But, says Davis: "As *Griffin* defines the term 'genuine evil', we do *not* in fact know that genuine evil exists. It may well be—as Christians often claim—that in the end God ensures that all *prima facie* evil leads to a greater good" ("God the Mad Scientist: Process Theology on God and Evil," *Themelios* 5/1 (September 1979), 18–23, esp. 20). But, had I been making the absurd claim that no one had ever verbally denied the reality of genuine evil, most of my own book would have constituted a refutation of that claim, because I showed that the most common solution to the problem of evil among traditional theologians was to deny the reality of genuine evil. This fact should have led Davis to suspect that I was making a different claim. The claim is that, just as Humeans presuppose the reality of causation as real influence (rather than simply "constant conjunction") *in practice*, even though they may deny it *verbally*, all persons in practice presuppose that some things are genuinely evil, even though some of them may deny this verbally. This issue is central to my debate with Huston Smith in *Primordial Truth and Postmodern Theology*.

10. For example, John Hick's later grappling with the question of how to understand the variety of the religious traditions theologically has led him to a doctrine of God quite different from the one employed in his theodicy. In Hick's later thinking, the personal God who effects a voluntary self-limitation to allow freedom for human beings can be only one of the many phenomenal faces of the unknowable Real behind all the appearances. See *God Has Many Names* (London: Macmillan, 1980) and *The Interpretation of Religion: Human Responses to the Transcendent* (London: Macmillan, 1989).

11. I have discussed this point in "Creation *ex nihilo*, the Divine *Modus Operandi*, and the *Imitatio Dei*," in *Faith and Creativity: Essays in Honor of Eugene Peters*, ed. George Nordgulen and George W. Shields (St. Louis: CPB Press, 1988), 95–123.

12. J. E. Barnhart, "Persuasive and Coercive Power in Process Metaphysics," *Process Studies* 3/3 (Fall 1973), 153–57; Dalton D. Baldwin, "Evil and Persuasive Power: A Response to Hare and Madden," *Process Studies* 3/4 (Winter 1973), 259–72.

CHAPTER 1. THE DIVINE AND THE DEMONIC

1. As in John Dewey, *A Common Faith* (New Haven: Yale University Press, 1934), and Donald Cupitt, *Taking Leave of God* (New York: Crossroad, 1981).

2. For God as being itself, see Paul Tillich, *Systematic Theology*, 3 vols. (Chicago: University of Chicago Press, 1951, 1957, 1963) and *The Courage to Be* (New Haven: Yale University Press, 1952), and John Macquarrie, *Principles of Christian Theology* (New York: Charles Scribner's Sons, 1977). For God as creative interchange, see Henry Nelson Wieman, *The Source of Human Good* (Chicago: University of Chicago Press, 1946).

3. E. S. Brightman distinguished between God's "will," which is perfect, and God's "nature," part of which is not. For a summary and discussion, see GPE 242–50. John Roth and Fred Sontag both say that God must not be wholly good, at least in terms of any criteria we can affirm. See their contributions, and my criticisms, in *Encountering Evil: Live Options in Theodicy*, ed. Stephen T. Davis (Atlanta: John Knox, 1981); see also Sontag's *God, Why Did You Do That?* (Philadelphia: Westminster, 1970) and *The God of Evil: An Argument from the Existence of the Devil* (New York: Harper & Row, 1970), and Roth's *A Consuming Fire: Encounters with Elie Wiesel and the Holocaust* (Atlanta: John Knox, 1979). Henry L. Mansel in *The Limits of Religious Thought* (London: John Maurray, 1859) maintains that the term "good" is used equivocally when applied to God, having no analogy to its use when applied to human beings, so that we can deduce from God's perfect goodness nothing about what God would or would not do. This position does not affirm that God is partly evil, but it also does not affirm that God is perfectly good in any intelligible sense.

4. Martin Heidegger has argued that the deeper meaning of the "death of God" is that we can no longer affirm any transcendent norms or values in terms of which to criticize the world process ("The Word of Nietzsche: God is Dead," *The Question Concerning Technology: Heidegger's Critique of the Modern Age*, William Lovitt, trans. [New York: Harper & Row, 1977]). Hans Jonas connects this aspect of Heidegger's philosophy with Heidegger's infamous endorsement of Hitler (Hans Jonas, *The Phenomenon of Life: Toward a Philosophical Biology* [New York: Harper & Row, 1966], 247).

5. According to Paul Tillich, faith in God does not negate the meaninglessness of life but gives us courage to affirm life in spite of its objective meaninglessness (*The Courage to Be*, 143, 147, 175–76).

6. Richard Rubenstein, *After Auschwitz: Radical Theology and Contemporary Judaism* (Indianapolis: Bobbs-Merrill, 1966), esp. 46, 48, 64–65, 153. I have a brief summary in GPE 220–21.

7. Richard L. Rubenstein, *The Cunning of History: The Holocaust and the American Future* (New York: Harper & Row, 1978), 88–92, cf. 63–65, 67.

8. See Jonathan Schell, *The Fate of the Earth* (New York: Avon, 1982), 118–29, 154–55, 163–66; and Robert Jay Lifton, *The Broken Connection: On Death and the Continuity of Life* (New York: Simon & Schuster, 1979), esp. part 3, and *Indefensible Weapons: The Political and Psychological Case against Nuclearism*, co-authored with Richard Falk (New York: Basic Books, 1982), Section I.

9. Emil Fackenheim has adopted this approach. See his *Quest for Past and Future: Essays in Jewish Theology* (Bloomington: Indiana University Press, 1968) and *God's Pres-*

ence in History: Jewish Affirmations and Philosophical Reflections (New York: Harper & Row, 1972), and my critique in GPE 220–23. Two recent Christian theologians taking this approach, at least in part, were Karl Barth and Emil Brunner; for summaries and critiques, see GPE, chap. 12 and 15.

10. I am referring primarily to John Hick's position as developed in *Evil and the God of Love* (New York: Harper & Row, 1966) and summarized in *Encountering Evil*, ed. Stephen Davis. I provided a summary in chapter 13 of GPE.

11. John Hick, *Evil and the God of Love*, 138.

12. Thomas Aquinas, who employed Aristotelian categories, held that angels were pure form, embodying no matter.

13. For a more complete statement, see "The Holy, Necessary Goodness, and Morality," *Journal of Religious Ethics* 8/2 (Fall 1980), 330–49, or "Imperialism, Nuclearism, and Postmodern Theism," which is chapter 8 of *God and Religion in the Postmodern World* (Albany: State University of New York Press, 1989).

14. In Whitehead's own account, in which God is a single, everlasting actual entity (rather than a personally ordered society of divine occasions of experience), it usually seems as if God influences the world only in terms of an unchanging, even abstract, "primordial nature." Whitehead did indicate in places that he believed that God's response to the world (God's consequent nature) also influenced the world. But within the terms of his doctrine it was hard to see how this could be the case. I hold the more Hartshornean doctrine of God as a series of divine occasions of experience, although without following Hartshorne's rejection of Whitehead's notion of a primordial, appetitive envisagement of pure potentials. The content of the aims reflecting God's Creative Love for the world at any moment is based on that appetitive envisagement in the light of God's Responsive Love in the previous moment.

15. See "Postmodern Animism and Life after Death," which is chapter 6 of my *God and Religion in the Postmodern World*.

16. An earlier version of this chapter was written in 1985 for the Faculty Colloquia Series of the Jameson Center for the Study of Religion and Ethics at the University of Redlands (California). The final section has been almost entirely rewritten for inclusion here.

CHAPTER 2. THE TASK OF PHILOSOPHICAL THEOLOGY

1. David and Randall Basinger, "Divine Omnipotence: Plantinga vs. Griffin," *Process Studies* 11/1 (Spring 1981), 11–24. Much of that article is contained in "Evil: Does Process Theism Have a Better Explanation?," which is chapter 3 of David Basinger's *Divine Power in Process Theism: A Philosophical Critique* (Albany: State University of New York Press, 1988), henceforth DPPT. The chapter in DPPT adds nothing new, and in fact omits some of the issues, so I respond primarily to the article. But because some

readers may have access only to the book, I cite the page numbers in DPPT parenthetically for those passages that are repeated in the book.

2. Alvin Plantinga, "Reply to the Basingers on Divine Omnipotence," *Process
Studies* 11/1 (Spring 1981), 25–29.

3. Plantinga, "Reply," 26.

4. Ibid., 26–27.

5. GPE 272.

6. Plantinga, "Reply," 26.

7. The Basingers, "Divine Omnipotence," 22.

8. GPE 136–39.

9. Ibid., 254.

10. Ibid.

11. Ibid., 256.

12. I make no claim that my summary of Plantinga's views on the basis of this
1981 essay represents his complete or more recent thinking on this issue. I am concerned here with the *issue*, not with Plantinga's position as such.

13. Plantinga, "Reply," 27–28.

14. Ibid., 28.

15. Ibid.

16. Ibid.

17. Ibid.

18. This way of understanding the intellectual's cultural responsibilities is, to be
sure, out of fashion in much of the university community today, insofar as deconstructive postmodernist attitudes have taken hold. I cannot address this enormous issue
here, however, beyond referring to my brief comments about it in the Introduction
and to other writings, expecially *Varieties of Postmodern Theology*.

19. Bruce Reichenbach, *Evil and a Good God* (New York: Fordham University
Press, 1982), 20.

20. Ibid., 190–92.

21. See my introduction to *Archetypal Process*, 34–36.

22. Stephen Davis, *Encountering Evil*, 81, 95, 97.

23. John Roth, in Davis, ibid., 90.

24. Nelson Pike, "Hume on Evil," in Pike, ed., *God and Evil*, 102, cited in GPE 255.

CHAPTER 3. THE TRADITIONAL DOCTRINE OF OMNIPOTENCE

1. See the discussion of Pike's so-called standard view of omnipotence in section B of this chapter.

2. Bruce Reichenbach, *Evil and a Good God* (New York: Fordham University Press, 1982), 176–87.

3. See note 1 of chapter 2 for the article referred to here as The Basingers, "Divine Omnipotence," and the chapter cited as DPPT.

4. GPE 269.

5. Ibid.

6. Ibid., 269–70.

7. The Basingers, "Divine Omnipotence," 13 (DPPT 58).

8. GPE 270.

9. Reichenbach illustrates this point with the proposition, "George freely performed the action of yelling at his dog." Being (rightly) an incompatibilist, Reichenbach says that although the proposition about George specifies "a state of affairs that it is logically possible for a being unilaterally to bring about," it is not a state of affairs that God as an omnipotent being could unilaterally bring about. It would be self-contradictory to say that God unilaterally brought it about that George yelled freely at his dog. (One quibble I have with Reichenbach's illustration is that, strictly speaking, even yelling is not a unilateral action, but a cooperative one, because the psyche requires the cooperation of billions of bodily cells. That distinction will be shown to be important in chapter 6.)

10. GPE 271.

11. Ibid., 263.

12. Reichenbach believes that I have wrongly formulated the four-term fallacy involved. The fallacious argument that I called the *omnipotence fallacy* was formulated thus:

P. An omnipotent being can unilaterally bring about any state of affairs that it is logically possible for a being unilaterally to bring about.

R. An actual world (i.e., one with a multiplicity of actual beings) devoid of genuine evil is a logically possible state of affairs.

   S. Therefore, an omnipotent being could unilaterally bring about an actual
   world devoid of genuine evil (GPE 264).

Reichenbach says that I am right to claim that this argument commits the fallacy of
four terms, but that I incorrectly locate the fallacy in an "oscillation between a logically possible action (P, S) and a logically possible state of affairs (R)" (*Evil and a Good
God*, 177). He suggests rewording the argument thus:

   P*. All states of affairs that it is logically possible for a being unilaterally to
   bring about are states of affairs an omnipotent being can unilaterally
   bring about.

   R. As above.

   S*. An actual world devoid of genuine evil is a state of affairs that an omnipotent being can unilaterally bring about.

Reichenbach then says:

   So presented, it is readily apparent that the formal fallacy does not rest
   where envisioned by Griffin. The fallacy of four-terms is committed in
   that whereas P [*sic*] speaks about states of affairs that it is logically possible for a being unilaterally to bring about, R [*sic*] speaks of logically
   possible states of affairs [P and R should be P* and R*].

However, no significant change has been introduced. P* and S*, in speaking about
"states of affairs that it is logically possible *for a being unilaterally to bring about*," still
refer to a *logically possible action*, while R refers to a logically possible state of affairs.

   13. GPE 264.

   14. Ibid.

   15. Ibid., 16.

   16. Ibid., 12.

   17. Ibid., 264.

   18. The Basingers, "Divine Omnipotence," 16. This statement is not quoted in
the version in David Basinger's DPPT, but the same effect is created by a parenthetical
insert. After citing my definition of I omnipotence, Basinger (DPPT 57) inserts this
statement: "(Such power, it must be understood, is not simply the power to control
what humans do. It is the power to control what humans freely do, since any actual
human option is an intrinsically possible state of affairs. It is the power, for example,
to control unilaterally what a Hitler *freely* does.)" Basinger thereby portrays I omnipotence so that it could apply only to those traditional theologians who held that God
fully determines all worldly events. His parenthetical "clarification" of my meaning
rules out the possibility of the qualification that I quickly introduce, which makes
clear that one accepts I omnipotence if one believes that God *could* unilaterally control

all events in an actual world, while perhaps believing that God does not actually do so but has relinquished total control in order to allow for the existence of genuinely self-determining beings. Having ruled out this qualification, Basinger takes the acknowledgment that some traditional theists posit genuine self-determination *vis-à-vis* God to be an acknowledgment that some traditional theists affirm C omnipotence (DPPT 60).

19. GPE 270.

20. Quoted at ibid., 264, 270.

21. Quoted at ibid., 271.

22. Quoted at ibid.

23. Ibid.

24. The Basingers, "Divine Omnipotence," 15.

25. GPE 264. Reichenbach (177, 178) has misunderstood my statement to mean that what was "accepted by all traditional theists" was the argument PRS (see note 12, above). That would, of course, be false, in the light of the existence of traditional free-will theists, such as Reichenbach himself.

26. GPE 264.

27. The qualification "at least generally" is important, because Plantinga's position allows for the possibility that God occasionally intervenes to bring about effects unilaterally, thereby momentarily canceling out human freedom. This possibility constitutes a crucial difference between Plantinga's view and that of genuine C omnipotence, as will be elaborated in chapter 5.

28. The Basingers, "Divine Omnipotence," 15. I have taken these statements verbatim from their formulations except for changing (the nonrestrictive) *which* to (the restrictive) *that* in each statement, because each clause must be read as a restrictive clause if the meaning is to be clear. (Many of my own statements in GPE, unfortunately, did not honor this distinction.)

29. Alvin Plantinga, "Reply to the Basingers on Divine Omnipotence," *Process Studies* 11/1 (Spring 1981), 25–29, esp. 25.

30. Ibid.

31. The Basingers, "Divine Omnipotence," 15.

32. Ibid.

33. Ibid., 16.

34. Plantinga, "Reply," 29.

35. See GPE 55, 59, 66–67.

36. Plantinga, "Reply," 29.

37. GPE 117.

38. GPE 17.

39. Plantinga, "Reply," 29.

40. Nelson Pike, "Process Theodicy and the Concept of Power," *Process Studies* 12/3 (Fall 1982), 148–67, esp. 154.

41. Ibid., 151, 153–54.

42. GPE 17.

43. Ibid.

44. Ibid., 18.

45. Ibid.

46. GPE 268, italics added.

47. Charles Hartshorne, *The Divine Relativity: A Social Conception of God* (New Haven: Yale University Press, 1948), 116; quoted by Pike, "Process Theodicy," 153.

48. GPE 103–05.

49. Ibid., 221.

50. Ibid., 117.

51. Ibid., 151.

52. Ibid., 151, 153.

53. Ibid., 154.

54. Ibid.

55. Ibid., 116.

56. Ibid., 116–17.

57. Ibid., 74, 76.

58. Pike, "Process Theodicy," 154.

59. GPE 257.

60. Ibid., 259.

61. Ibid., 260.

62. Stephen T. Davis, "God the Mad Scientist: Process Theology on God and Evil," *Themelios* 5/1 (September 1979), 18–23, esp. 18.

63. Ibid., 19.

64. E.g., GPE 218.

65. GPE 237, 211.

66. Davis, "God the Mad Scientist," 19.

67. GPE 251.

CHAPTER 4. TRADITIONAL ALL-DETERMINING THEISM

1. GPE 272.

2. John F. X. Knasas, "Super-God: Divine Infinity and Human Self-Determination," *American Catholic Philosophical Association Proceedings* 55 (1981), 197–209.

3. Ibid., 197.

4. Ibid., 206, referring to GPE 272.

5. GPE 270.

6. GPE 266. The argument for this point is stated thus: "Power to influence others presupposes the power of self-determination. If an entity contributes nothing to itself, but is a mere product of other powers, it cannot meaningfully be said to have any power to influence others" (quoted by Knasas, "Super-God," 197).

7. Knasas, "Super-God," 206.

8. Ibid., 198.

9. Ibid., 197, 206.

10. Ibid., 198.

11. Many years ago, I gave a public lecture on the problem of evil in which I, among other things, suggested that the distinction between causing and permitting was illegitimate, if the traditional notion of divine power is accepted, and that we need a different doctrine of divine power. The Roman Catholic priest who had been asked to give the closing prayer began by invoking "God, who does not cause but permits evil. . . ." This is the only time I recall being rebutted in a prayer.

12. St. Thomas Aquinas, *Summa Theologiae* I-II, 79, 2, sed contra.

13. Knasas, "Super God," 208, n. 36, citing *Summa Theologiae* I, 19, 9, ad 3.

14. Ibid., 199.

15. Ibid., 200.

16. Ibid., 201.

17. Ibid.

18. Ibid., 198.

19. Ibid., quoting *De Potentia* 3, 7.

20. Ibid., quoting *De Potentia* 3, 7, ad 13 (Knasas translation).

21. Ibid., 199.

22. Ibid.

23. Ibid., quoting GPE 79.

24. Ibid.

25. Ibid., quoting *De Veritate* 23, 5, ad 3 (Schmidt translation).

26. Ibid., 200, quoting *De Veritate* 23, 5c (Schmidt translation).

27. Ibid.

28. Ibid.; Knasas here cites *Summa Contra Gentiles* I, 43.

29. Ibid., 200–01.

30. Ibid., 201.

31. Ibid.

32. Ibid., quoting Joseph Owens, *An Interpretation of Existence* (Milwaukee: Bruce, 1968), 118–19.

33. Ibid., 201–02.

34. Ibid., 203, quoting Joseph Owens, *An Elementary Christian Metaphysics* (Milwaukee: Bruce, 1963), 362–63. For the epistemological background to Owens' position, Knasas refers to Owens, "Aquinas—'Darkness of Ignorance' in the Most Refined Notion of God," *Southwestern Journal of Philosophy* 5 (1974), 99.

35. Ibid., 202.

36. Ibid., 198.

CHAPTER 5. TRADITIONAL FREE-WILL THEODICY

1. Nelson Pike, "Process Theodicy and the Concept of Power," *Process Studies* 12/3 (Fall 1982), 148–67, esp. 149.

2. Ibid., 166.

3. Ibid.

4. GPE 21–23.

5. Ibid., 69–71.

6. Ibid., 84–87, 90, 94, 111, 129, 135, 170, 199–201, 217, 242.

7. Ibid., 252–53.

8. Ibid., 253, 255.

9. Ibid., 29, 71.

10. Ibid., 125.

11. Robert Mesle, "The Problem of Genuine Evil: A Critique of John Hick's Theodicy," *Journal of Religion* 66/4 (October 1986), 412–30.

12. GPE 252.

13. The Basingers, "Divine Omnipotence," 14.

14. Alvin Plantinga, "Reply to the Basingers on Divine Omnipotence," *Process Studies* 11/1 (Spring 1981), 25–29, esp. 26.

15. GPE 94.

16. The Basingers, "Divine Omnipotence," 17 (DPPT 60–61), citing John B. Cobb, Jr., and David Ray Griffin, *Process Theology: An Introductory Exposition* (Philadelphia: Westminster, 1976), 71–72. Although *Process Theology* is jointly authored, the Basingers are correct to attribute this part to me.

17. The Basingers, "Divine Omnipotence," 17 (DPPT 61).

18. Ibid., citing *Process Theology*, 71.

19. GPE 294.

20. Ibid., 293.

21. The Basingers, "Divine Omnipotence," 18.

22. Ibid. (DPPT 61), citing *Process Theology*, 75.

23. GPE 182–83, 188.

24. The Basingers, "Divine Omnipotence," 18 (DPPT 62), quoting GPE 271.

25. Ibid., 18–19 (DPPT 63).

26. Ibid., 19 (DPPT 63).

27. Bruce Reichenbach, *Evil and a Good God* (New York: Fordham University Press, 1982), 83.

28. Ibid., 84.

29. The Basingers, "Divine Omnipotence," 19 (DPPT 63).

30. GPE 272.

31. The Basingers, "Divine Omnipotence," 19. (In DPPT 64, David Basinger deletes the discussion of Plantinga and Satan, while adding the judgment that process theism's claim that it can present a much more plausible theodicy in relation to *natural* evil is its "strongest challenge.")

32. Reichenbach, *Evil and a Good God*, 87.

33. Ibid., 101–02, 106–07, 110–11.

34. Ibid., 113–17.

35. The Basingers, "Divine Omnipotence," 20 (paraphrased at DPPT 64).

36. Ibid. (paraphrased at DPPT 66), citing F. R. Tennant, *Philosophical Theology*, vol 2: *The World, the Soul, and God* (1930; Cambridge University Press, 1956), 201.

37. Ibid., 21 (DPPT 65).

38. GPE 206–07, quoting James F. Ross, *Philosophical Theology* (Indianapolis: Bobbs-Merrill, 1969), 237.

39. Tennant, *Philosophical Theology*, 200.

40. Ibid., 129, 143, 168, 183, 184.

41. Ibid., 129, 183. I believe that Tennant's position on this issue is essentially the same as my Whiteheadian-Hartshornean position: our particular world, with its particular forms of order, is one among many possible worlds; but all these possible worlds share some basic, eternal, metaphysical principles, which could not be otherwise. Tennant's talk of "God's one world" would therefore not mean our particular world with its particular forms of order, which has existed perhaps for only fifteen to twenty billion years.

42. Ibid., 184.

43. Ibid., 218, 210.

44. Ibid., 210, 214.

45. Ibid., 218.

46. Ibid., 173, 175, 176.

47. Ibid., 173, 184, 188.

48. Ibid., 176, 185.

49. Ibid., 188.

50. The Basingers, "Divine Omnipotence," 23.

51. Ibid., 22, 23.

52. Ibid., 22.

53. Ibid., 23, cf. 11.

54. Reichenbach, *Evil and a Good God*, 113.

55. Ibid., 101, 103.

56. GPE 190–92.

CHAPTER 6. THE COHERENCE OF PROCESS THEISM'S CLAIM

1. Bruce R. Reichenbach, *Evil and a Good God* (New York: Fordham University Press, 1982).

2. Reichenbach seems unclear whether worship requires belief in omnipotence. He appears to say that it does on page 176 and that it does not on page 190.

3. Ibid., 165, 182, 187.

4. Proposition k is not worded precisely enough. Reichenbach's phrase "there being self-determining beings" would allow for the existence of some actual beings that are not partially self-determining, which, with some doctrines of God, would allow God to employ a mixture of persuasive and coercive causation. Reichenbach's wording does not allow for the distinction between the self-determining and the efficient powers of God. A better wording for k would be: "The only efficient (transuent) causal power an omnipotent being can have consistent with an actual world comprised entirely of partially self-determining beings is persuasive power." I did not correct the wording in the text because it seemed to play no role in Reichenbach's analysis and critique.

5. I do not know that I have spoken of "unlimited persuasive power," although I can accept this expression as long as it is specified that "unlimited" means "not less than some possible persuasive power" (and not, for example, "unimpeded"). I would more naturally speak of "perfect persuasive power."

6. Reichenbach, *Evil and a Good God*, 184.

7. Ibid., quoting from GPE 277.

8. Although I did not point out this distinction in GPE, I think of God, with Charles Hartshorne, as a "living person," and therefore as an everlasting serial society

of actual entities, rather than, with Whitehead, as a single, everlasting actual entity. But this change does not affect Reichenbach's point, that God should have both creative powers: final causation and efficient causation. In fact, this revised doctrine makes it clearer that God can exert efficient causation on the world without violating any general principle—namely, the principle that an actual entity cannot exert efficient causation until its final causation is completed.

9. Reichenbach, *Evil and a Good God*, 185.

10. Ibid., 181, 186.

11. GPE 265.

12. Reichenbach, *Evil and a Good God*, 185. A confusing feature of his discussion is that he oscillates between interpreting my position and that of process theology in general. This creates a problem in that, although I am the only process theologian mentioned in the text, the writings of other process theologians are cited and even quoted in the text without warning. This causes problems in the case of the article by Dalton D. Baldwin, "Evil and Persuasive Power: A Response to Hare and Madden," *Process Studies* 3/4 (Winter 1973), which is quoted three times in the text. Although these quotations would appear to any reader not checking the backnotes to be from my writings, they all express ideas foreign to me. (I should add that this article was written while Baldwin was still a graduate student and before he had completed his dissertation, in which prior inaccuracies in his portrayal of Whitehead's philosophy were overcome.)

13. Ibid.

14. Ibid.; the passage he quotes is from Alfred North Whitehead, *Process and Reality*, corrected edition (New York: Free Press, 1978), 47, which I had quoted at GPE 278 (page 75 in the 1929 Macmillan edition of *Process and Reality*, which was used in GPE).

15. Ibid., 186.

16. Ibid., 187.

17. Ibid.

18. Ibid., 183–85. This point occurs in Reichenbach's discussion of a distinction, which he derived from Alvin Plantinga, between a strong and a weak sense of God's "bringing about" a state of affairs in the world. The strong sense, he says, is the sense that I have in mind in denying that God can unilaterally bring about any logically possible state of affairs in the world (because that would be inconsistent with the existence of actual entities that are partially self-determining). But in the weak sense of "bring about," he says, I should be able to affirm that God brings about worldly states of affairs. In this weak sense, God does not directly bring about a state of affairs, such as Y. But God knows that, if X is actual, then a particular person will do Y. God can therefore bring about X (in the strong sense) and thereby bring about

Y in the weak sense. Reichenbach explains: "God does not directly cause all states of affairs; however, he does bring about some states of affairs which if actual" entail that other states of affairs will be actual. Reichenbach believes that this idea of how God brings about things in the weak sense "would be consistent with Griffin's appeal to God's persuasive power." He suggests that "much of the confusion" surrounding process theology would be cleared up if I would only recognize this (183).

One problem with this suggestion is that for God to bring about something in the weak sense presupposes that God brings about *some* things in the strong sense— that is, unilaterally—which would only be possible if Reichenbach were correct in saying that process theology should attribute coercive as well as persuasive causal power to God. A second problem is Reichenbach's assumption that God, for process theology, can have infallible knowledge of future contingent events. He says: "God brings about the state of affairs 'X is being persuaded by God to do S,' God knowing that if this state of affairs is actual, X will do S (though he is not caused by God to do S, but freely responds to the persuasion)" (183). In other words, God knows, before seeking to persuade us to do something, just how we will respond. But that is one of the traditional ideas denied by process theology. The idea that the world is comprised of partially self-determining events means that the future is not yet determinate. Omniscience, or perfect knowledge, meaning knowledge of everything that is knowable, cannot include the future, because the future is not determinate, therefore not knowable. Reichenbach himself believes that future contingents *can* be known, so that to deny that God knows them would be to attribute ignorance to God (173–76). He evidently failed to see that I explicitly reject the compatibility of creaturely freedom with foreknowledge or immutable omniscience (GPE 60–61). In any case, what we process theologians mean by divine persuasion is not the same as what Reichenbach means by God's bringing things about "in the weak sense." That sense is still too strong for us. The affirmation that the divine power is persuasive, not coercive or controlling, means that God cannot *infallibly* bring about any state of affairs in the world, whether directly or indirectly.

19. Nancy Frankenberry, "Some Problems in Process Theodicy," *Religious Studies* 17/2 (June 1981), 179–97. Her article reflects the revisionary form of Whiteheadianism advanced by her teacher, Bernard Loomer, in which God is equated with creativity or the "totality of inseparably interrelated events" (182, 183, 196).

20. Ibid., 179.

21. Ibid., 182.

22. GPE 265, 276–81; *Process Theology*, 23–36.

23. Frankenberry, "Some Problems," 182.

24. GPE 277; *Process Theology*, 23–25.

25. Frankenberry, "Some Problems," 179.

26. See note 12, above.

27. I see that I myself said this (GPE 43, 51). In doing so, I was thinking of "efficient causation" in the older sense of an agent that actively does something to produce an effect, while Aristotle's God influences the world passively, simply by existing. But if efficient causation is defined as the effect of one actuality on another, then Aristotle's God is an efficient cause.

28. Whitehead, *Process and Reality*, 344.

29. Ibid., 343.

30. Ibid., 32, 87.

31. Frankenberry, "Some Problems," 182, 180.

32. The phrase *unilateral determination* taken strictly is not, however, completely interchangeable with *coercive efficient causation*, but refers only to one (sometimes imagined but impossible) form of it. Unilateral determination in the strict sense would occur if an agent (such as God) were to be the sole cause of a state of affairs involving others. There would be no causal contribution either by the affected things *or by other efficient causes*. Such causation cannot occur because, even in coercive efficient causation, in which no self-causation is exercised by the effects, these effects are causally influenced by all prior events. However, I have in some places used *unilateral determination* to refer to coercive efficient causation among finite things, which does occur. In such places the force of the term *unilateral* is that the determination comes entirely from the side of the efficient causation, not partly from the side of the effect. The term does *not* mean, in this usage, that some finite agent or aggregate of such has brought about an effect apart from the combined influence of the rest of the past universe. A human being or a billiard ball can do this no more than God can.

33. In his well-known contrast between "persuasive agencies" and "senseless agencies" in *Adventures of Ideas* (New York: Macmillan, 1933), Whitehead uses persuasion to refer to the effects of formulated ideals or aspirations (6–7), while compulsion refers to both the "iron compulsion of nature," meaning the necessity for food, heat, and shelter, and the "compulsory domination of men over men" in war, slavery, governmental laws, or any other restrictions of liberty (71, 87, 198). I am proposing that "compulsion" be used to refer primarily to what Whitehead calls the "iron compulsion of nature," which is based on the fact that our bodies have various needs combined with the fact that, because of the intimate relation between psyche and body, our psychic state tends to be heavily dependent upon our body's welfare. The "compulsory domination of men over men," which I have referred to as coercion in the psychological sense (which depends upon the capacity to employ coercion in the metaphysical sense—for example, to break someone's legs), depends upon the strong sympathy we have with our bodies. Threatening to break a man's legs only works because of his natural concern for legs that function and are not a source of intense pain. Accordingly, coercion in the psychological sense depends upon both the compulsion of nature and the perceived capacity to exercise coercion in the metaphysical sense.

34. Whitehead's distinction between persuasion and compulsion would seem to correlate fairly well with his technical distinction between hybrid physical feelings and pure physical feelings (especially if compulsion is limited, as I propose in the previous note, to the "iron compulsion of nature," which is due to our heavy dependence upon our bodies). This correlation might seem to suggest that persuasive and compulsive causes would fit into two quite distinct classes, rather than constituting a continuous spectrum, as I propose. But it should be stressed that, for Whitehead, hybrid physical feelings are, like pure physical feelings, *causal* feelings in which creativity, not simply a set of abstract ideals, is transmitted (*Process and Reality*, 236, 246). And from our own experience we know that ideals received from our own past moments of experience, or from others (e.g., the Freudian "superego"), can sometimes be stronger than bodily urges.

35. Daniel Day Williams, in "Deity, Monarchy, and Metaphysics: Whitehead's Critique of the Theological Tradition" (*The Relevance of Whitehead*, ed. Ivor Leclerc [London: Allen & Unwin, 1961], 353–72), complained that "Whitehead's doctrine leads him to ignore wide ranges of types of force, of coercion . . . [that] would seem to . . . find their place in God's being," and that "Whitehead has underestimated the disclosure of the divine initiative in religious experience" (370). But in that essay Williams thought that "Whitehead's doctrine" that God acts only persuasively entailed that God does not act "as one efficient cause among others" (368). In a later essay, "How Does God Act? An Essay in Whitehead's Metaphysics" (in *Process and Divinity: The Hartshorne Festschrift*, ed. William L. Reese and Eugene Freeman [Lasalle, Ill.: Open Court, 1964], 161–80), he says that Whitehead does in some sense "add God as efficient cause to the other efficient causes in the world" (175). In this essay he sees process thought as doing more justice to "the coercive aspects of our religious experience" and to the "large coercive aspects in the divine governance of the world" (177). However, I would use the term compulsive, as I explain in the text and the two preceding notes, for what Williams here calls coercive.

36. Frankenberry, "Some Problems," 183.

37. Ibid., 182. Her view would be correct of *Science and the Modern World*, in which God was a mere principle. But in subsequent writings, God is an actual entity and therefore by definition an instance of creativity. In Whitehead's language, "God is the aboriginal instance of . . . creativity" (*Process and Reality*, 225; see also 88, 222). To distinguish between God and creativity, as Whitehead did, is not to separate them. All actual entities are embodiments of creativity, and God is the primordial embodiment (7).

38. Frankenberry, "Some Problems," 182, 183, 185, 196.

39. Whitehead, *Process and Reality*, 32, 87–88.

40. Ibid., 344.

41. Ibid., 246–47, 250.

42. Ibid., 246.

43. Ibid., 350–51. This passage shows that Whitehead did not stipulate, contrary to Frankenberry's suggestion ("Some Problems," 185), that "God's own physical feelings are simply not available as a datum for feeling." (I learned from Frankenberry that she was here referring to the view expressed by Lewis Ford in *The Lure of God* [Philadelphia: Fortress, 1978], 121 n. 8.)

44. David Basinger, "Divine Persuasion: Could the Process God Do More?," *Journal of Religion* 64/3 (July 1984), 332–47. A revised, abbreviated version of this article is reprinted as "Divine Persuasion: Could the God of Process Theism Do More?" in Basinger's DPPT (see note 1 of chapter 2, above). When passages cited from the article are repeated (more or less exactly) in DPPT, the page references are given parenthetically.

45. Ibid., 332.

46. Ibid. (DPPT 27).

47. Ibid. (DPPT 28); this formulation comes from Barry Whitney ("Process Theism: Does a Persuasive God Coerce?," *Southern Journal of Philosophy* 17 [1979], 133–41), but it reflects wording that I use.

48. Basinger refers to the initial aim provided by God to each occasion of experience as a "cognitive/affective lure," and says that each occasion "automatically becomes aware of God's initial aim at each moment and feels some compulsion to actualize it" (ibid., 333 [DPPT 28]). This is misleading. Most occasions of experience do not become aware of the divine aim, if "awareness" is taken to connote anything approaching conscious awareness. Most occasions of experience are devoid of consciousness altogether, and even those that are conscious very seldom become consciously aware of the initial aim as such. It is even more misleading to say that God unilaterally produces "cognitive" experiences, insofar as that term connotes conscious knowledge, which is a very rare thing and occurs, if at all, only in the final phase of a concrescence, which God emphatically cannot unilaterally determine. Finally, by "state of affairs" I meant either any concrete experience of an individual—that is, its completed concrescence (or satisfaction)—or any configuration among a multiplicity of individuals, resulting from those concrete experiences. I precisely did not mean the first phase of a concrescence, which is what Basinger is here calling a "state of affairs." Within process metaphysics, nothing is determinate within a process of concrescence until that process has reached satisfaction. For Basinger to say that God "unilaterally lures each entity" is to empty the word "unilaterally" of any meaning, because it is simply to say that an actual entity can influence another actual entity. In that trivial sense, every actual entity acts unilaterally. The word has a point with regard to the problem of evil only in raising the issue of whether any actual entity can ever completely determine the condition of one or more other actual entities.

49. Ibid., 333, 334 (DPPT 28, 29).

50. Ibid., 335 (DPPT 29), quoting GPE 281.

51. Ibid. (DPPT 29), quoting GPE 266.

52. GPE 266 is here quoted.

53. GPE 267 is here quoted.

54. Basinger, "Divine Persuasion," 335 (DPPT 29, but see note 56, below).

55. Ibid. (DPPT 30).

56. At DPPT 29, Basinger correctly has "powerless actualities"; but the remainder of the argument proceeds as if this correction had not been made.

57. GPE 267.

58. Ibid., 232–33.

59. Ibid., 268.

60. Ibid., 277. The term "aggregate" is not wholly satisfactory for corpuscular societies such as sticks and stones, because it suggests a *mere* aggregate, such as a pile of stones, which is not a cohesive society. My use of "aggregate" in such cases should be taken as shorthand for "aggregational society."

61. For a Whiteheadian, the crucial distinction between an *actual* entity and the other forms of existence is that "an actual entity functions in respect to its own determination" (Whitehead, *Process and Reality*, 25).

62. Basinger, "Divine Persuasion," 335 (DPPT 30).

63. Ibid., 336 (DPPT 30).

64. Ibid. (DPPT 30).

65. Ibid., 336–37 (DPPT 30–31).

66. Ibid., 337 (DPPT 31–32).

67. Ibid., 338 (DPPT 32).

68. Ibid. (DPPT 32).

69. Ibid. (DPPT 32).

70. Ibid. (DPPT 32).

71. Ibid. (DPPT 32–33).

72. Ibid., 339 (DPPT 33).

73. Ibid., 340.

74. Ibid., 339 (DPPT 33).

75. Ibid., 341 (DPPT 37), quoting *Process Theology*, 71.

76. Ibid., 342 (DPPT 37).

77. I had quoted with approval Hartshorne's statement that "God is not 'subject' to the categories, as though they were something antecedent to his own individuality" (GPE 298, quoting Charles Hartshorne, *The Divine Relativity* [New Haven: Yale University Press, 1948], 41).

78. Basinger, "Divine Persuasion," 342, supposedly quoting *Process Theology*, 73. (In DPPT [38] Basinger correctly has the quotation begin with "to disregard . . . ," so that *his* words are no longer included within the quotation marks. But otherwise everything is left the same [except the spelling of "proffered"], so the statement still distorts my position.)

79. Ibid., 342–43 (DPPT 38).

80. See GPE 189, 271.

81. *Process Theology*, 73 (see note 78, above).

82. Ibid.

83. GPE 293.

84. Basinger, "Divine Persuasion," 343 (DPPT 38).

85. GPE 264.

86. More accurately, one attempts to show the truth of the basic metaphysical hypothesis by producing a complete worldview that is more coherent, adequate, and illuminating than others; the specifically theodical aspect of this worldview is only one feature of it, although one of the most important with regard to the principle in question.

87. Basinger, "Divine Persuasion," 343.

88. Ibid. (DPPT 38). Basinger develops this strange point to conclude his chapter in a bizarre way. He grants that, "within the process system, the possibility of coercion is not an open question" (39). But he then says that "it does not follow from the fact that the God of process theism *can* (in the sense of *will*) *never* exercise coercive power that such a being does not possess the capacity to coerce." I wonder from which dictionary Basinger learned that *will* is a possible synonym for *can*. In any case, on the basis of this unique ratiocination he concludes that process theism is little different from traditional free-will theism, because the reason for the divine noncoercion is moral, not metaphysical.

89. GPE 276–81.

90. Basinger had anticipated this second argument to an extent, seeing that the process theist claims to have a "more adequate perspective than that held by the classical theist" (344)—namely, a perspective adequate to the reality of genuine evil, the perfect goodness of God, and the reality of (human) freedom. He raises two problems against this claim. The first is that, while process theists find the view that God cannot coerce more adequate, "this is by no means a universally shared sentiment" (344). Many persons, he tells us, believe that "a god as 'weak' as the one affirmed by process theism is no god at all or, at least, a god not worthy of worship and thus see the coercive concept of classical theism to be more adequate" (345). It is not clear what Basinger's point is here. If what he means is that that to which a concept of God must be "adequate" is the traditional concept of God, then obviously only the traditional concept of God can be adequate. But if Basinger is referring to demands the human psyche allegedly places on a potential object of worship, I had devoted chapter 17 of *God, Power, and Evil* to that topic, and will return to it in chapter 11 of the present book.

Basinger's second rebuttal of the claim that process theism is more adequate is to argue that traditional free-will theists can be consistent with genuine evil, human freedom, and divine goodness, while admitting that process theists may find these responses "ad hoc and unsatisfying" (345). The question, however, is not whether traditional theists, by means of the free-will defense, can manage to show that belief in divine goodness is not absolutely ruled out by the world's evil; the question, Basinger had agreed in the article with his brother, is whether that position can develop an account that is *as* self-consistent, *as* adequate to all the relevant facts, and *as* illuminating of those facts as can a process theodicy. This, I have argued in chapter 5, has not been shown.

91. GPE 267.

CHAPTER 7. THE TRUTH OF PROCESS THEISM'S CLAIM

1. I had published an earlier response, "Actuality, Possibility, and Theodicy: A Response to Nelson Pike," in *Process Studies* 12/3 (Fall 1982), 168–79, which followed immediately upon Pike's critique. The response in the present chapter, which could not presuppose familiarity with Pike's critique, is an almost completely new response, with only a few passages taken over from the earlier one.

2. Nelson Pike, "Process Theodicy and the Concept of Power," *Process Studies* 12/3 (Fall 1982), 148–67, esp. 148.

3. Ibid., 151.

4. Ibid.

5. Ibid., 152.

6. Ibid.

7. Ibid., 151, citing GPE 279.

8. Ibid., citing GPE 267–68.

9. Part of the difference of opinion here is based on Pike's misunderstanding of what I call the monopolistic view. As I pointed out in chapter 3, Pike thinks I define it as the view that God actually controls everything, thereby exercising a monopoly on power. In contrast with this view, he rightly points out that many theologians (even if fewer than he thinks) have distinguished between God's *possession* of power and God's *exercise* of it. My definition of the monopolistic view, however, allows for this distinction, because it says that God is the actual *or potential* controller of all events. Pike's "standard view" is therefore an example of the monopolistic view.

10. Pike, "Process Theodicy," 149.

11. In a note to this sentence, Pike says that at this point "the already obvious parallel between Griffin's argument for process theodicy and Alvin Plantinga's most recent effort to defend the free will theodicy becomes most apparent" (167 n. 5). This comment reflects Pike's erroneous assumption that I am defending the traditional doctrine of omnipotence (see the next note).

12. Ibid., 153. The final ellipsis replaces the word "traditional." Pike's conclusion that I am defending traditional theism, because I affirm that God's power is the greatest conceivable, is not deterred even by the fact that the final part of *God, Power, and Evil* is entitled "A Nontraditional Theodicy."

13. Ibid., 151, quoting GPE 264.

14. Ibid., 151–52, 154.

15. Ibid., 154.

16. Ibid., 155, 156–57, 158, 161.

17. Ibid., 155.

18. Ibid.

19. Ibid., quoting GPE 267.

20. GPE 266; cited and quoted by Pike, "Process Theodicy," 155.

21. GPE 266; quoted by Pike, ibid., 155.

22. Pike says that he has two arguments (155, 158), which are what I list as the first and third; but the argument about inconsistency seems to be a distinct argument.

23. Pike, ibid., 155.

24. Ibid., 156. Stephen Davis ("God the Mad Scientist: Process Theology on God and Evil," *Themelios* 5/1 [September 1979], 18–23) writes similarly of a "surprisingly unsophisticated version of the empiricist criterion of meaning," which he be-

lieves that not even I could consistently hold: "For he [Griffin] obviously believes that talk of God is meaningful, and yet no one directly perceives God" (21). On the basis of the distinction made in the text between a superficial (sensationist) and a radical empiricism, I would say that we *do* directly perceive God. "Perceive" is used here in Whitehead's sense of a (nonsensory) "prehension."

25. Whitehead, *Process and Reality*, 166.

26. Pike seems to share this view about Hartshorne in comparison with Whitehead (148, 160).

27. Hartshorne, *Beyond Humanism: Essays in the Philosophy of Nature* (1937; Lincoln: University of Nebraska Press, 1968), 231. Although Hartshorne is famous (or notorious) for insisting that the method of metaphysics is *a priori* or nonempirical, he means thereby not that it is unrelated to experience altogether, but only that it is based on the general or universal, as distinct from the merely contingent, features of experience (ibid., 268–69; *Man's Vision of God and the Logic of Theism* [1941; Hamden, Conn.: Archon Books, 1964], 29, 53 n. 5, 63; *Creative Synthesis and Philosophic Method* [Lasalle, Ill.: Open Court, 1970], 31).

28. Pike, "Process Theodicy," 156.

29. Pike is referring to Whitehead's "method of extensive abstraction" as developed in *The Principles of Natural Knowledge*. Whitehead in *Process and Reality*, incidentally, indicates that his earlier approach was deficient in being "unable to define a 'point' without the intervention of the theory of 'duration'" (287).

30. Pike, "Process Theodicy," 156–57.

31. Ibid., 157.

32. Hartshorne, *Beyond Humanism*, 157; *Man's Vision of God*, 12.

33. *Man's Vision of God*, 69.

34. Pike, "Process Theodicy," 157.

35. GPE 266.

36. Pike, "Process Theodicy," 157.

37. Ibid.

38. GPE 268, 277. See note 60 of chap. 6, above, for a comment on the term "aggregate."

39. GPE 106, 118.

40. Ibid., 64–65.

41. Ibid., 157. Stephen Davis makes a similar point, saying: "'X is totally causally determined by Y' does indeed entail 'X is causally impotent,' but 'X is totally

causally determin*able* by Y' does not. It may be that Y can fully control X if Y wants to but Y has chosen not to do so, thus leaving X with some self-determining power" ("God the Mad Scientist," 21).

42. GPE 268.

43. Pike, "Process Theodicy," 158.

44. Ibid.

45. Ibid.

46. Ibid., 160.

47. Ibid., 159.

48. GPE 269; Pike on 158 refers back to his quotation of this passage on 153.

49. Pike, "Process Theodicy," 158.

50. Ibid., 160, referring to Whitehead, *Adventures of Ideas*, chap. 15, and *Process and Reality*, part I, chap. 1.

51. Ibid.

52. Ibid., referring to GPE 269.

53. Ibid.

54. GPE 27.

55. Another reason that no simple semantic error is involved is that the semantic issue involves primarily the *formal* meaning of an actual being (*res vera*) as a finally real thing, not primarily the substantive definitions given by various philosophers.

56. Pike, "Process Theodicy," 160.

57. Whitehead, *Process and Reality*, 145.

58. Ibid., 158.

59. Ibid., 159.

60. Whitehead, *Process and Reality*, 5, 288.

61. GPE 265.

62. Ibid.

63. Ibid., 265–66.

64. Ibid., 266. After having claimed that I had not earlier made clear what the "metaphysical issue par excellence" is, Pike says, with reference to the present statement, that I finally identified this issue to be "determining whether Premise X is true."

But this passage says that my answer to the metaphysical issue will indicate *my reason for* rejecting premise X. The metaphysical issue itself is as I stated: deciding what distinguishes actual beings as such (or actuality *qua* actuality) from other forms of existence.

65. Ibid.

66. Ibid., 267–68.

67. Pike, "Process Theodicy," 161.

68. Ibid.

69. Ibid., 162.

70. Ibid.

71. Ibid., 163.

72. Ibid.

73. Ibid.

74. Ibid.

75. Ibid., 148, 163.

76. Ibid., 148.

77. Ibid.

78. Reichenbach, *Evil and a Good God*, 180.

79. Ibid., 194–95 n. 33.

80. GPE 266. This endorsement of the empirical criterion of meaning depends upon the rejection of sensationist empiricism; see note 24, above.

81. Ibid.

82. Ibid., 267.

83. Ibid.

84. Reichenbach, *Evil and a Good God*, 194 n. 33, citing GPE 267.

85. Ibid., 194–95.

86. GPE 267.

87. Ibid.

88. See note 24, above, and the discussion in the related text.

CHAPTER 8. FURTHER QUESTIONS ABOUT DIVINE PERSUASION

1. See Edward H. Madden and Peter H. Hare, *Evil and the Concept of God* (Springfield, Ill.: Charles C. Thomas, 1968), and "Evil and Persuasive Power," *Process Studies* 2/1 (Spring 1972), 44–48.

2. Peter H. Hare, "Review of David Ray Griffin, *God, Power, and Evil: A Process Theodicy*," *Process Studies* 7/1 (Spring 1977), 44–51. Hare calls the book "a revolutionary challenge to traditional ways of thinking about the problem," and says that it supersedes the hitherto definitive work—that of John Hick—as "the most challenging, thorough, lucid, and useful book concerned with the problem" (44).

3. Ibid., 44, 48, 51.

4. Ibid., 50.

5. Ibid., 48.

6. Hare points out that I acknowledged the existence of several nontraditional theodicies, and that I was under no obligation to present possible alternatives to my position (48). I had, in fact, originally planned a section dealing with a number of nontraditional theodices besides E. S. Brightman's, but the book had already grown too large. That whole section, which would have dealt with thinkers such as J. S. Mill, Nicholas Berdyaev, William James, D. C. MacIntosh, W. P. Montague, C. S. Peirce, and Edwin Lewis, was reduced to one brief sentence (GPE 275).

7. Hare, "Review," 51.

8. Ibid., 50.

9. Ibid., 51.

10. Ibid.

11. Charles Hartshorne, *Creative Synthesis and Philosophic Method* (London: SCM Press, 1970; Lanham, Md.: University Press of America, 1983), 19–22, 57–58, 292; *The Logic of Perfection and Other Essays in Neoclassical Metaphysics* (Lasalle, Ill.: Open Court, 1962), 157; *Man's Vision of God and the Logic of Theism* (1941; Hamden, Conn.: Archon Books, 1964), 62.

12. Hare, "Review," 51.

13. Hartshorne, *Beyond Humanism: Essays in the Philosophy of Nature* (1937; Lincoln: University of Nebraska Press, 1968), 147, 292, 293.

14. Ibid., 260.

15. Ibid., 143, 144; *The Logic of Perfection*, 224; *Creative Synthesis and Philosophic Method*, 203.

16. *Creative Synthesis and Philosophic Method*, 187, 189; *The Logic of Perfection*, 218.

17. *Beyond Humanism*, 257.

18. Charles Hartshorne, "Physics and Psychics: The Place of Mind in Nature," in John B. Cobb, Jr., and David Ray Griffin, ed., *Mind in Nature: Essays on the Interface of Science and Philosophy* (Washington, D.C.: University Press of America, 1977), 92.

19. Hare, "Review," 51.

20. Ibid.

21. David Basinger, "Human Coercion: A Fly in the Process Ointment?," *Process Studies* 15/3 (Fall 1986), 161–71. A slightly revised version of this article, with the same title, constitutes chapter 2 of DPPT; pages for it are given parenthetically.

22. Basinger says that process theists "uniformly agree that every entity [instead of every *actual* entity] always possesses some degree of self-determination" (ibid., 161 [DPPT 41]). And he says that process theists therefore "deny that any entity, divine or human, can coerce" (ibid. [DPPT 41]). But every process theist knows that human beings, by virtue of their hands, can coerce a rock or another human body. He also misquotes me again, turning "there are degrees of (relative) coercion" into "some activity can be called coercive in a relative sense" (ibid. [DPPT 42], citing GPE 326). Thanks to this misquotation, Basinger evidently takes this passage to be support for his notion of "coercion in the weaker sense," which is absolute coercion (as explained above in the text), whereas my statement refers to relative coercion. This distortion, unlike the others, is harmless, however, because I fully agree that absolute coercion occurs.

23. Ibid., 161–62 (DPPT 42).

24. Ibid., 163 (DPPT 43).

25. Charles Hartshorne believes that determinism is implicitly atheistic; see *The Logic of Perfection*, 122–24, 143, and *Omnipotence and Other Theological Mistakes* (Albany: State University of New York Press, 1984), 62–63.

26. Basinger, "Human Coercion," 165 (DPPT 46).

27. Ibid., 162 (DPPT 42).

28. Ibid., 162, 163, 165–66 (DPPT 42, 43, 46).

29. Ibid., 163–65 (DPPT 43–46).

30. Ibid., 162–70 (DPPT 42, 52).

31. Ibid., 165, 170 (DPPT 45).

32. I allude here to GPE 276; Basinger ("Human Coercion," 163) appropriately cites GPE 271 and *Process Theology*, 71 (although cited as 72).

33. Basinger, "Human Coercion," 164 (DPPT 44), quoting *Process Theology*, 118, 119. These statements were written by John Cobb.

34. Ibid., quoting my "Values, Evil, and Liberation Theology," John B. Cobb, Jr., and W. Widick Schroeder, ed., *Process Philosophy and Social Thought* (Chicago: Center for the Scientific Study of Religion, 1981), 183–96, esp. 195, 196 (although cited as 190).

35. Ibid., 164 and 169, quoting Schubert M. Ogden, *Faith and Freedom* (Nashville: Abingdon Press, 1979), 77.

36. Ibid., 169.

37. Ibid. (DPPT 52).

38. Ibid., 165 (DPPT 46).

39. Ibid., 165–66, 168 (DPPT 46–47, 50).

40. This phrase, often attributed to Heschel himself, was actually coined to describe Heschel's God by Fritz A. Rothschild in his editor's introduction to *Between God and Man: An Interpretation of Judaism from the Writings of Abraham J. Heschel* (New York: Free Press, 1959), 25. This is pointed out by John C. Merkle, *The Genesis of Faith: The Depth Theology of Abraham Joshua Heschel* (New York: Macmillan, 1985), 9, 253.

41. Basinger, "Human Coercion," 168 (DPPT 49).

42. I have a manuscript in process tentatively entitled "Postnuclear Theology." Some of the relevant ideas are contained in "Creation *Ex Nihilo*, the Divine *Modus Operandi*, and the *Imitatio Dei*," George Nordgulen and George W. Shields, ed., *Faith and Creativity: Essays in Honor of Eugene H. Peters* (St. Louis: CPB Press, 1987), and "Imperialism, Nuclearism, and Postmodern Theism," chap. 8 of my *God and Religion in the Postmodern World* (Albany: State University of New York Press, 1988).

43. I presented the evidence for this point in "Whitehead and Niebuhr on God, Man and the World," *Journal of Religion* 52 (April 1973), 149–75. I no longer believe, however, that Niebuhr provides the ethic needed by process theology, as my chapter on Niebuhr in "Postnuclear Theology" (see previous note) will show.

CHAPTER 9. JOHN HICK'S CHARGE OF ELITISM

1. John H. Hick, *Philosophy of Religion*, 3rd edition (Englewood Cliffs, N.J.: Prentice-Hall, 1983).

2. Ibid., 49–56.

3. Ibid., 41.

4. He did not know of its existence when, still in England, he wrote the Preface for the second edition of his *Evil and the God of Love* (London: Macmillan; New York: Harper & Row, 1978), in which he responded to various critiques.

5. Stephen T. Davis, *Encountering Evil: Live Options in Theodicy* (Atlanta: John Knox, 1981).

6. In an earlier version of his critique, which he sent for my comments, Hick said: "One can criticise the basic conception of a finite God, and/or one can accept it as the premise of the process theodicy and criticise the theodicy itself on its own terms. The latter will be more to the point here." Although this statement was deleted from the published version, that version was surely meant to embody this approach.

7. Hick, *Philosophy of Religion*, 50.

8. Ibid., 51.

9. Ibid.

10. Ibid., 52.

11. Ibid.

12. Ibid., 53.

13. Ibid.

14. Ibid.

15. Ibid., 54.

16. Ibid., 55.

17. Ibid., 56.

18. Thomas Aquinas, for example, said that the reason some creatures have more goodness than others is because God loves them more; see my discussion at GPE 83.

19. William R. Jones, *Is God a White Racist? A Preamble to Black Theology* (Garden City, N.Y.: Anchor Press, 1973). I cited Jones's book in relation to this point in "Values, Evil, and Liberation Theology" (see note 37, below).

20. *Process Theology*, 9 (this part of this co-authored book was written mainly by me).

21. I connected the denial of this image of God with the political issue at ibid., 57–58.

22. GPE 309; quoted by Hick, *Philosophy of Religion*, 52–53.

23. Hick, *Philosophy of Religion*, 54–55.

24. One problem is that Hick's discussion, by characterizing the "marvelous human beings" of whom I spoke as the "elite" and the "cream" of humanity, leaves the impression that I was speaking only of well-known public figures. But after giving the illustrative list of such figures, from Jesus to Margaret Mead, to make my point somewhat concrete (and the list obviously had to be comprised of well-known figures if readers were to recognize the names), I added: "and millions of other marvelous human beings, well known and not well known alike." If by "elite" one means what I meant by "marvelous," that is, living a life that is highly valuable both intrinsically and instrumentally, then I was indeed speaking of an elite group (although one consisting of millions or billions of persons). But the term "elite" generally, and as used by Hick, has quite other connotations.

25. Hick, *Philosophy of Religion*, 56.

26. GPE 311–12.

27. GPE 312–13.

28. Hick, *Philosophy of Religion*, 56.

29. Ibid.

30. Ibid.

31. See GPE 201–08, and note 2 for chapter 8 of the present book.

32. GPE 70, 86.

33. Ibid., 199–201. C. Robert Mesle, in "The Problem of Genuine Evil: A Critique of John Hick's Theodicy" (*Journal of Religion* 66/4 [October 1986], 412–30), has concluded that Hick does, in many passages, deny the reality of genuine evil, even though he elsewhere affirms it. Mesle believes that Hick has misunderstood my criticism because Hick equates "genuine evil" with "intrinsic evil." Hick takes his affirmation of intrinsic evil therefore to be an affirmation of genuine evil, even though he often says that the evil of the intrinsically evil events will be canceled out by their instrumental goodness—which is precisely what I mean by the view that all *prima facie* evil is only apparently evil. Mesle's analysis seems correct.

34. Hick, *Philosophy of Religion*, 55.

35. Ibid.

36. Ibid.

37. In a letter I sent to Hick dated May 15, 1981, in response to an earlier version of his critique, I pointed out that several process theologians had written supportively of liberation theology, mentioning several writings including two of my own articles ("Values, Evil, and Liberation Theology," and "North Atlantic and Latin American Liberation Theologians," which were first published in *Encounter* 40/1 [Winter 1979], 1–30, then reprinted in *Process Philosophy and Social Thought*, ed. John B.

Cobb, Jr., and W. Widick Schroeder [Chicago: Center for the Scientific Study of Religion, 1981], 183–209). I concluded: "for those of us inside, it seems there is a pre-established harmony between the two. This need not be decisive of course, as we may be deluded. But it at least should give you a minute's pause." It did give Hick a minute's pause, but evidently only that. He added a footnote, which reads:

> This charge seems to me to hold despite the fact that some of the process theologians have aligned themselves with the contemporary liberation theology movement. (See Schubert Ogden, *Faith and Freedom: Toward a Theology of Liberation* . . . and John B. Cobb, Jr., *Process Theology as Political Theology.* . . .) For the question remains whether this move is compatible with the process theodicy as formulated by Griffin [55].

Besides the selective reporting involved in Hick's failure to mention my own writings on liberation theology, his point also seems to depend upon the assumption of some important tension between Cobb's theology and my theodicy. That assumption would be *prima facie* implausible, given the fact that I wrote the section on theodicy in our co-authored *Process Theology.*

38. Hick, *Philosophy of Religion*, 53.

39. Ibid., 54.

40. Ibid., 55.

41. Ibid., 56.

42. Ibid.

CHAPTER 10. PROCESS THEODICY AND MONISM

1. Philip Hefner, "Is Theodicy a Question of Power?," *Journal of Religion* 59/1 (January 1979), 87–93.

2. Ibid., 87.

3. Ibid., 93.

4. Ibid., 87–88.

5. Ibid., 87–89.

6. Ibid., 90.

7. Ibid., 90, 93.

8. Whitehead, *Process and Reality*, 5, 288.

9. Hefner, "Theodicy," 92.

10. Ibid.

11. I have developed this idea in "The Holy, Necessary Goodness, and Moral-ity," *Journal of Religious Ethics* 8/2 (Fall 1980), 330–49, and in chap. 8 of *God and Religion in the Postmodern World* (Albany: State University of New York Press, 1989).

12. Hefner, "Theodicy," 93.

13. I have distinguished theological freedom from both cosmological freedom and axiological freedom in chapter 7 of *God and Religion in the Postmodern World*.

14. Hefner, "Theodicy," 93.

15. Hefner, "God and Chaos: The Demiurge Versus the *Ungrund*," *Zygon* 19/4 (December 1984), 469–86.

16. Hefner, "God and Chaos," 92.

17. Ibid.

18. GPE 29.

19. Ibid., 125–29.

20. See Whitehead, *Process and Reality*, 13, 151.

21. David Ray Griffin, "Values, Evil, and Liberation Theology," *Encounter* 40/1 (Winter 1979), 1–15; reprinted in *Process Philosophy and Social Thought*, ed. John B. Cobb, Jr., and W. Widick Schroeder (Chicago: Center for the Scientific Study of Religion, 1981), 183–96.

22. Hefner, "Theodicy," 89.

23. Whitehead, *Adventures of Ideas* (New York: Macmillan, 1933), 368; Hart-shorne, "Whitehead and Berdyaev: Is There Tragedy in God?," *Journal of Religion* 37/2 (April 1957), 71–84.

24. GPE 303, 309.

25. GPE 309–10, 313.

26. Hefner, "Theodicy," 89.

27. Ibid.

28. GPE 270; see also 153 and chaps. 8 and 14.

29. Hefner, "Theodicy," 91.

30. Ibid., 89.

31. Ibid., 93.

32. Ibid., 90, 91.

33. Ibid., 91.

34. Ibid., 90, 91.

35. Ibid., 90.

36. Ibid., 91.

37. Ibid., 90.

38. Hefner, "God and Chaos," 484.

39. GPE 246, 129–30. I have also subsequently dealt with the positions of John Roth and Frederick Sontag in Stephen T. Davis, ed., *Encountering Evil: Live Options in Theodicy*, 26–29, 152–54.

40. Hefner, "Theodicy," 91.

41. Hefner, "God and Chaos," 479.

42. Ibid.

43. Ibid.

44. Hefner, "Theodicy," 91.

45. Quoted by Hefner, "God and Chaos," 479.

46. Whitehead, *Process and Reality*, 7, 31.

47. Ibid., 225, 344.

48. Ibid., 19, 24.

49. Ibid., 21.

50. Hefner, "God and Chaos," 482–83.

51. Ibid., 476.

52. Ibid., 477, 481, 483.

53. Whitehead has, to be sure, been misinterpreted by many as essentially Platonic on this point. Reinhold Niebuhr, for example, portrayed Whitehead as associating good with form and evil with vitality (*The Nature and Destiny of Man* [New York: Charles Scribner's Sons, 1941], vol. 1: 30–31, 112–13.

54. *Process and Reality*, 88, 164, 247.

55. Ibid., 111.

56. *Adventures of Ideas*, 354.

57. See Henry Nelson Wieman, *The Source of Human Good* (Chicago: University of Chicago Press, 1946).

58. Hefner, "God and Chaos," 478.

59. Whitehead, *Adventures of Ideas*, 389, 381.

60. *Process and Reality*, 105.

61. *Adventures of Ideas*, 13.

62. Whitehead can be read as referring to the creative process as divine in *Dialogues of Alfred North Whitehead*, as recorded by Lucian Price (Boston: Little, Brown, 1954), 370–71. But the statement is ambiguous, and in any case the alleged quotations in this book are to be read with much skepticism, especially doctrinal points that are not supported by Whitehead's writings.

63. For example, Lawrence F. Wilmot's book *Whitehead and God: Prolegomena to Theological Reconstruction* (Waterloo, Ontario: Wilfrid Laurier University Press, 1979) is built around this charge. I provided a rebuttal in "Whitehead, God, and the Untroubled Mind: A Review Article," *Encounter* 42/2 (Spring 1981), 169–88.

64. See my discussion of Brightman in GPE 242–50.

65. See John Roth in Stephen Davis, ed., *Encountering Evil*, and Eliezer Berkovitz, *Faith after the Holocaust* (New York: OKTAV, 1973).

66. Hefner, "God and Chaos," 483.

67. See notes 64 and 65, above.

68. Hefner, "God and Chaos," 476, 484.

69. Ibid., 483.

70. It might be that this trinitarian monism would provide a basis for Nancy Frankenberry's desire to move toward a more monistic position, in which the distinction between God and creativity is overcome, and yet to retain the partial self-creation of finite creatures in relation to God (see chapter 11, esp. n. 11).

CHAPTER 11. WORSHIP AND THEODICY

1. David Ray Griffin and Huston Smith, *Primordial Truth and Postmodern Theology* (Albany: State University of New York Press, 1990), 162, 163.

2. GPE 27.

3. David Basinger, "Divine Persuasion: Could the Process God Do More?," *Journal of Religion* 64/3 (July 1984), 332–47, esp. 345.

4. For Knasas, see chapter 4, above; for Davis, see "God the Mad Scientist: Process Theology on God and Evil," *Themelios* 5/1 (September 1979), 18–23, esp. 22; and see Hick's criticism of my theodicy in Stephen Davis, ed., *Encountering Evil: Live Options in Theodicy* (Atlanta: John Knox, 1981).

5. GPE 246.

6. Peter H. Hare, "Review of *God, Power, and Evil: A Process Theodicy,*" *Process Studies* 7/1 (Spring 1977), 44–51, esp. 47.

7. Ibid., 47–48.

8. Quoted in GPE 11.

9. See GPE 246.

10. Nancy Frankenberry, "Some Problems in Process Theodicy," *Religious Studies* 17/2 (June 1981), 179–97, esp. 183.

11. Frankenberry does not, however, mean to return to an all-determining, monistic theism. Her idea is that the creative energy provided by God to finite occasions is "not entirely determinative" ("Some Problems," 183); she wants to avoid the conclusion that "our free acts are only apparently ours." She believes that this can be avoided "by a conception of creativity as that which becomes the creature's own in God's very giving of it moment-to-moment," so that it is not "so determinative that one can only conform slavishly to it" (183). It seems to me that this idea makes sense only if the distinction between God and creativity is *not* totally collapsed. In any case, Frankenberry's attempts to work out this idea can be found in "The Power of the Past," *Process Studies* 13/2 (Summer 1983), 132–42; "The Emergent Paradigm and Divine Causation," *Process Studies* 13/3 (Fall 1983), 202–17; "The Logic of Whitehead's Intuition of Everlastingness," *The Southern Journal of Philosophy* 22/1 (Spring 1983), 31–46; and "Language about the Totality," *Encounter* 44/1 (Winter 1983), 41–58.

12. Frankenberry, "Some Problems," 187.

13. Ibid., 186.

14. Ibid., 186–87. Frankenberry adds that my statement "ought to suggest, if anything could, that the doctrine of divine goodness is not the conclusion of an *a posteriori* mode of reasoning." Her position here is doubly problematic. In the first place, she makes this statement as if she were thereby making a point against my formal position. But I had said that my enterprise is not a "natural theology" in the allegedly neutral sense, calling it instead a *Christian* philosophical theology (GPE 25–27). In particular, I pointed out that the idea that the divine reality, to be worthy of worship, must be morally good is a historically conditioned valuation that I share (GPE 20–21, 23, 25–27, 275–76). The question is not whether one would, without that prior idea, be led by a survey of the world to the idea of a morally perfect creator. The question is: Given the idea of such a divine being, can we develop an account of reality that is more consistent, more adequate to the facts of experience,

and more illuminating of those facts, than accounts starting from some other "*a priori*" preconception? My claim is that every worldview in fact begins with some "vision of reality" that functions in this *a priori* way, analogous to Christian faith. This point leads to the second problem implicit in her statement. She seems to think that the view she advocates, which does not distinguish between God and creativity, and therefore does not regard God as unambiguously good, is somehow more empirical, more *a posteriori*, than the Whiteheadian view. She suggests that the divine reality is "revealed in concrete events for both good and for ill," so that we can look to see how good the world in its entirety is and say that "to that extent and no more, God is good" (189). But this view is no less an *a priori* idea than the view she rejects. In any case, her point here, even it were deemed valid, would provide no argument against the goodness of God as portrayed in my theodicy.

15. GPE 309; *Process Theology*, 75.

16. Frankenberry, "Some Problems," 187.

17. Alfred North Whitehead, *Religion in the Making* (Cleveland: World Publishing, 1960), 74; quoted by Frankenberry, "Some Problems," 197.

18. *Religion in the Making*, 66–67, 74–75.

19. Frankenberry, "Some Problems," 188. Frankenberry seems to think that the use of the aesthetic criteria of harmony and intensity will somehow diminish the user's or reader's sense of the genuineness of evil. She says: "Surely one of the few conclusions to emerge with overwhelming clarity from the persistent theoretical and existential challenges to traditional theodicies is that 'explanations' of evil either by way of looking backward to a causal genesis, or forward to a teleological outcome, have the effect of negating or diminishing perception of the genuineness of the present evil with which we have to struggle. I suggest this applies also to the aesthetic criteria which Whiteheadians would have us recognize" (193). This statement confuses explanations with criteria. To settle upon criteria to define or describe evil, and to distinguish its forms, so that you can know and communicate what you are talking about, is not to give an explanation for why evil occurs.

Furthermore, insofar as my theodicy, which employs these criteria, does show some *prima facie* evils not to be genuine evils, the purpose is to help us distinguish clearly between those *prima facie* evils that are genuinely evil and those that are not. This distinction is important in itself for practical purposes, and also serves to block in advance the inference that, because some *prima facie* evils turn out to be only apparently evil, this is likely true of all of them. Frankenberry's own discussion provides a nice example. Many people believe that it is evil that we all must die sometime. Frankenberry rightly points out that this eventuality is not an evil, because it could not be otherwise (191). People who see that death is a natural, necessary feature of biological life will not waste emotion railing against the universe because they must eventually die, or waste time, energy, and resources trying to find a way to prevent eventual death. They will therefore have a more appropriate emotional relation to the universe, and will be more likely to devote their energies to trying to overcome *genuine* evils, such as the fact that millions of people each year die *prematurely*, often without even having had the possibility of a good life beforehand. Another example: my theodicy suggests that the possibility of intense pain is necessary if organisms are to have the possibility of realizing great values. Once this is accepted, people will not bemoan the fact that we are subject to intense pain. But this realization that the possibility of pain is not genuinely evil does not mean that the actual suffering people undergo is not genuinely evil, insofar as it has arisen from contingent factors. Through this type of distinction, we can hold that the world in its *basic structure* is *one of the best* of all possible worlds, while avoiding the enervating conviction that the world in its *concrete details* is *the* best of all possible worlds.

20. GPE 310; quoted by Frankenberry, "Some Problems," 188.

21. Frankenberry, "Some Problems," 188–89.

22. Ibid., 190, citing Robert Neville, *Creativity and God: A Challenge to Process Theology* (New York: Seabury Press, 1980), 11–12.

23. GPE 297–300.

24. In "The Holy, Necessary Goodness, and Morality," *Journal of Religious Ethics* 8/2 (Fall 1980), 330–49, and in "Nuclearism, Imperialism, and Postmodern Theism," chap. 8 of *God and Religion in the Postmodern World* (Albany: State University of New York Press, 1989).

25. *Process and Reality*, 345.

26. I have not discussed Frankenberry's third criticism of process theodicy, which she evidently takes to be the decisive one. She says that "the real issue in this theodicy concerns the grounds for realistic hope" ("Some Problems," 194). My reason for not discussing this criticism is that, as I indicated in the first chapter, I agree with it. Process theology as generally presented, including the way it was presented in *God, Power, and Evil*, does not provide sufficient grounds for hope. This general agreement with Frankenberry does not mean, however, that I concur with all her related criticisms of process theism or with her proposals about how to reformulate it. For example, one of the dimensions of her criticism is that process theology does not provide grounds for hope that the future of humanity on earth will be better than the past, or for "any final or ultimate transformation as such of history or the cosmos or even of individual lives" (194). Although Frankenberry regards Whitehead's discussion of the way worldly events are "transmuted" in God as referring primarily to a redemption occurring in God alone ("beyond history," to use Reinhold Niebuhr's expression), she does recognize the fact, to which I had devoted considerable attention, that this transmutation in God becomes the basis for the next set of ideal aims directed to overcoming evil in the temporal world (193; cf. GPE 302–07). Frankenberry's discussion of this point, however, is colored by her assumption, discussed in chapter 6, that God for process theology is not a "physical" agent and therefore only opens up new possibilities but does not provide any creative energy to support some particular direction (194). Not much historical transformation can therefore be expected. What we need,

she says, are "redemptive concrete social energies, not just the assurance of unlimited future possibilities" (195). Frankenberry's own proposal provides no help here, of course, even though her revision attributes "concrete social energies" to God, because the price she pays for this more robust view of divine power is the loss of God's unambiguous moral character. A divine eros that favors good no more than evil cannot provide a basis for hope for moral and aesthetic progress. A better basis for hope is provided by the God of process theology, who wills betterment unambiguously, who exerts more power than Frankenberry's portrayal suggests, and who can be thought to be even more effective, especially in the long run, than most portrayals of process theism heretofore have suggested.

27. For my discussion of their criticisms, see GPE 301–08.

28. Hare, "Review," 50.

29. Ibid.

30. GPE 309–10.

31. Ibid., 297–98.

32. See note 24, above.

33. GPE 258.

34. Burton Z. Cooper, Why, God? (Atlanta: John Knox, 1988), 100.

35. Ibid., 103.

APPENDIX

1. Peter H. Hare and Edward H. Madden, "Evil and Persuasive Power," Process Studies 2/1 (Spring 1972), 44–48.

2. Edward H. Madden and Peter H. Hare, Evil and the Concept of God (Springfield, Ill.: Charles C. Thomas, 1968); henceforth ECG.

3. "Evil and Persuasive Power," 45.

4. ECG 49, 122.

5. "Evil and Persuasive Power," 46.

6. This topic is subject to considerable confusion because the terms persuasion and coercion are, in most contexts, used in a psychological sense, in which the distinction between persuasion and coercion is a matter of degree, while process philosophy uses them in a metaphysical sense, in which the distinction is one of a kind. In this metaphysical sense, efficient causation is persuasive if the being upon whom the causation is exerted makes a self-determining response to this causation. It is coercive if there is no room for such a response, so that the result is determined solely by the

efficient causation. Coercion and persuasion in the psychological sense are both forms of persuasion in the metaphysical sense. There is in fact a spectrum ranging from purely persuasive persuasion to extremely coercive persuasion. For example, to threaten to shoot someone if he or she does not do as you wish is generally (and rightly) considered coercive behavior. But this type of action is an example of persuasion in the strict or metaphysical sense, because the threatened person must decide just how to respond to the threat. When coercion in the metaphysical sense occurs, as when the cue stick strikes the cue ball, there is no room for a decision: the cue ball does not decide how to respond to the impact. In the discussions of divine causality by process philosophers and theologians, the distinction between coercion and persuasion is intended in the metaphysical sense. The contrast is between divine causation as portrayed by traditional theism, in which this causation unilaterally brought about its intended effect, and divine causation in process thought, according to which it is an influence on partially self-determining actual entities, who must decide just how to respond to it. The divine efficient causation provides an "initial aim," but the finite occasion of experience transforms this initial aim into its own "subjective aim," during which the initial aim may be modified more or less radically.

7. The term "efficient causation" has become so widely equated with mechanistic models that many writers understandably contrast persuasion with efficient causation. For example, A. Seth Pringle-Pattison endorsingly summarizes the view of G. H. Howison: "A self-conscious being is, by his very nature, raised above the sphere of efficient causality as that operates in a world of things. Such a being is inaccessible to force or action from without: nothing can be effected in a self except through the personal will of the agent himself. A person cannot be coerced, he can only be persuaded. . . . In such a sphere, then, the causation is final causation, the causation of the ideal" (*The Idea of God in the Light of Recent Philosophy* [Oxford: Clarendon Press, 1917], 319). But if "efficient" causation is defined broadly as that which occurs when one actual entity affects another, then persuasion is a form of efficient causation. While it is true that nothing can be simply *effected* in a self by an alien power, it is not true that a self cannot be *affected* by action from without. While it is true that a self exercises self-determination in terms of an ideal that serves as a final cause, it is also true that the presently deciding self forms that ideal on the basis of ideals received from one or more other agents (even if the most important of these other agents are past moments of experience belonging to the same enduring person).

8. "Degrees of coercion" is not self-contradictory when the term is being used in the psychological sense, as opposed to the metaphysical sense, which is at issue here; see note 6.

9. Hartshorne comments in *Philosophers Speak of God*, by Charles Hartshorne and William L. Reese (Chicago: University of Chicago Press, 1953), 274–75: "There is no 'power' anywhere, on earth or in heaven, except the direct and indirect workings of attractiveness ('persuasion'). We have power over other men's minds through the value they find in our thoughts and feelings; we have power over our bodies because the sentient unities composing them derive such inspiration as their lowly natures can receive from these same thoughts and feelings; and through controlling our own bod-

ies we can indirectly influence other men's bodies and minds. But the direct influence of God is analogous only to the direct power of inspiration or suggestion. It could not possibly suppress all freedom in the recipient, since a minimum of response on his part is presupposed."

10. "Evil and Persuasive Power," 46.

11. Cf. ECG 121–25.

12. A. N. Whitehead, *Religion in the Making* (1926; Cleveland: World Publishing, 1960), 152.

13. The process thinker might be inclined to say that persuasion is the only type of efficient causation that is immediately experienced, and that coercion or complete determination is merely inferred. In this way one could agree with Hume that necessity is never experienced, while still maintaining the perception of real influence. Due to the summing-up nature of the psyche's experience of its body, however, it can rather directly experience the coercion involved, for example, when one's arm is being twisted. This does not involve coercion *on* the psyche; but the psyche does experience the fact that its arm is being coerced. Hence, although persuasion is the primary type of efficient causation experienced, talk about coercive efficient causation is also rooted in our direct experience.

14. ECG 121.

15. I am therefore uncomfortable with Lewis Ford's contrast between God's initial aim for an occasion and the "efficient causal influences" on it ("Divine Persuasion and the Triumph of the Good," *The Christian Scholar* L [Fall 1967], 235–50, reprinted, with a few additions in notes, in Delwin Brown, Ralph E. James, and Gene Reeves, eds., *Process Philosophy and Christian Thought* [Indianapolis: Bobbs-Merrill, 1971], 287–304). This contrast reflects the antithesis between persuasion and efficient causation discussed in note 7. That Ford recognizes God as an efficient cause in the broad sense of the term is shown by his statement in the same paragraph that "Aristotle's insight that God influences the world by final causation . . . must be reformulated so that God can *act* to provide each actuality with its own final cause" (238–91).

16. "Evil and Persuasive Power," 48.

17. "Evil and Unlimited Power," *Review of Metaphysics* 20 (December 1966), 278–79.

18. "The Dipolar Conception of Deity," *Review of Metaphysics* 21 (December 1967), 273–89.

19. See note 15.

20. The major valid points revolve around Whitehead's separation of the primordial nature of God (which replaced the earlier "principle of limitation") from the consequent nature, and his assigning efficient causality almost exclusively to the former and consciousness exclusively to the latter (see ECG 118–21). This criticism

of Whitehead's view had been made long ago by Hartshorne, and had been formulated in detail by John B. Cobb, Jr., *A Christian Natural Theology: Based on the Thought of Alfred North Whitehead* (Philadelphia: Westminster, 1965), chap. 5.

21. A major point of their original article was that Whitehead did not provide an acceptable view of God, because a theistic God must guarantee the "triumph of good." In the revision, this phrase is softened to "growth of value."

22. ECG 16.

23. The criticism that "the process theist will have difficulty in making the *amount* of evil in the world compatible with great persuasive power" (ECG 122) was added in response to Ford's essay.

24. ECG 122.

25. Ibid.

26. Ibid., 123.

27. Whitehead, *Religion in the Making*, 105.

28. ECG 123.

29. Ibid., 123–24.

30. Ibid., 124.

31. Ibid., 125.

32. Ibid., 111.

33. Accordingly, when Madden and Hare criticize Hartshorne for not seeing that the "crucial problem of evil" is not evil as such but *prima facie* gratuitous evil (ECG 49), the failure is really theirs for not seeing that this distinction does not have the same relevance in a system in which finite beings have inherent (not merely loaned) and therefore inviolable freedom. They show a similar misunderstanding in saying that Whitehead "must show that *all* the evil in the world is genuinely necessary to the achievement of [God's] end" (ECG 136). Where there is multiple freedom, much evil beyond that which is absolutely inevitable will probably occur.

34. "Evil and Persuasive Power," 44.

INDEX